The Managerial Grid III

Gulf Publishing Company
Book Division
Houston, London, Paris, Tokyo

The Managerial Grid III

A new look at the classic that has boosted productivity and profits for thousands of corporations world-wide.

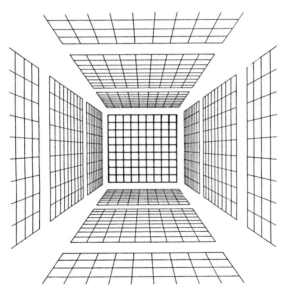

Robert R. Blake
Jane S. Mouton

The Managerial Grid ® III

The Managerial Grid (first edition), copyright © 1964
  1st Printing, February 1964
  2nd Printing, October 1968
  3rd Printing, June 1970
  4th Printing, September 1972
  5th Printing, April 1974
  6th Printing, April 1975
  7th Printing, February 1977
The New Managerial Grid (second edition), copyright © 1978
  1st Printing, February 1978
  2nd Printing, May 1978
  3rd Printing, September 1979
  4th Printing, November 1981
  5th Printing, July 1984
The Managerial Grid III (third edition), copyright © 1985
  1st Printing, January 1985
  2nd Printing, January 1987

Library of Congress Cataloging in Publication Data
Blake, Robert Rogers, 1918–
  The managerial grid III.
  Rev. ed. of: The new managerial grid. c1978.
  Includes index.
  1. Management. 2. Industrial management. I. Mouton, Jane Srygley. II. Blake, Robert Rogers, 1918– New Managerial grid. III. Title. IV. Title: Managerial grid 3. V. Title: Managerial grid three.
  HD31.B523 1984   658.4   84-10875
  ISBN 0-87201-470-3

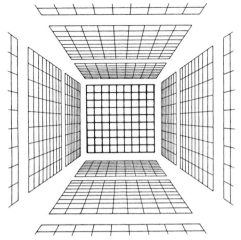

Contents

v

5

6

7

8

9

10

A 9,9-Oriented Approach to Management-by-Objectives and a Reward System to Motivate Productivity 127

Management-by-Objectives Through Goal Setting 127, Using Organizational Rewards to Motivate Productivity 135, Implications 139

11

Paternalism, Opportunism, and Facades 140

Paternalism/Maternalism (9 + 9) 140, Motivations 140, Managing Conflict 141, Behavioral Elements 142, Management Practices 144, Consequences 145, Recognizing Paternalistic Behavior 147, Suggestions for Change 147. **Opportunism** 148, Motivations 148, Managing Conflict 149, Behavioral Elements 150, Management Practices 152, Consequences 153, Recognizing Opportunistic Behavior 154, Suggestions for Change 155. **Facades** 155, Motivations 155, Managing Conflict 159, Behavioral Elements 161, Management Practices 167, Consequences 167, Recognizing Facadist Behavior 168, Suggestions for Change 168. **Wide-Arc Pendulum** 169, **Counterbalancing** 170, **The Two-Hat Approach** 172

12

Organizational Change 173

Are you the Person in Charge? 174, Three Approaches to Organizational Development (OD) 175, Phases of Grid OD 178, Summary 196

Appendices

A

Resolving Contradictions Among Leadership Theories 197

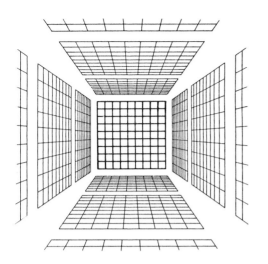

Preface

What is the route to managerial excellence? Students of management theory and management training have been searching for an answer to this question ever since they decided that management is an applied science rather than an art and that it can be learned. Invariably, the attention focuses on which style of leadership behavior produces excellence. Admittedly an organization's structure, plan, and concept are basic to its effectiveness, yet beyond these the greatest single variable lies with the behavior of the management team. Its members must act as leaders. They must accomplish their objectives through their ability to guide, motivate, and integrate the efforts of others. Therefore, a manager's job is to perfect a team culture that (1) promotes and sustains efficient performance of highest quality and quantity, (2) fosters and utilizes creativity, (3) stimulates enthusiasm for effort, experimentation, innovation and change, (4) takes learning advantage from problem-solving situations, and (5) looks for and finds new challenges. Such managerial competence can be taught and it can be learned.

We know some executives, managers, and supervisors are outstandingly successful in getting results and others are not. Leadership is one key.

Different approaches are advocated by one or another expert as to how sound leadership is exercised. This tells us that there is little agreement as to what sound leadership "is." An approach is needed that permits styles of leadership to be seen in systematic terms and to be assessed objectively.

The Grid identifies major theories about how to exercise leadership in the pursuit of production with and through others. Each is presented within a systematic framework that permits the reader to see similarities and differences among them, to identify their strengths and weaknesses, and to develop conclusions regarding sound and unsound ways of leading. The consequences for productivity and creativity as well as personal career success and satisfaction are of enduring importance.

ix

Through this self-convincing approach, a manager can learn the consequences and results from exercising leadership in various ways and decide personally what changes may be necessary in order to strengthen personal contributions.

The Grid has been under development and refinement since it took form twenty-five years ago when we were engaged by Exxon in a series of major experiments concerned with increasing leadership effectiveness. It has enjoyed widespread acceptance in many parts of the world in business, industry and government, colleges and universities, and in many functional areas—finance, manufacturing, R&D, marketing, and personnel.

Recent applications demonstrate how leadership is exercised most effectively by chief executives and by college and university administrators. Additional applications include those in the area of sales, nursing, social work, and secretarial and office support systems, as well as in dealing with the special problems that are encountered when the work involves technical information systems, professionals, and other knowledge workers. Insight from these new applications is included in this book.

The most recent major project involves use of the Grid to solve crises in the aircraft cockpit—commercial, military, and corporate. Aircrews are now using it to learn skills of teamwork essential for effectively mobilizing human resources. There are important implications for safety in the nuclear power plant, the surgical amphitheater, naval ships, and other high risk and high stakes environments that require problem solving and decision making under pressure.

Once organization members know how to use it, the Grid becomes a powerful management tool. It provides a basis for bringing about an integrated management approach whether within domestic or international companies. Since the Grid has been translated into twelve languages, it is available for bringing about the needed strengthening of leadership across companies operating in different countries as well. Once all personnel have learned it, they can use it to improve selection, training, development, and coaching; to strengthen the direction of work and participation, involvement, and commitment; to set goals, solve conflicts, and so on.

Part I presents the Grid. It is introduced by a self-administering instrument in Chapter 1. An overview of the Grid framework is presented in Chapter 2. The next chapters, 3–7, discuss five different theories of leadership—9,1, 1,9, 1,1, 5,5, and 9,9.

In Part II, the 9,9 leadership orientation is examined in greater depth, starting with Chapter 8 where the principles underlying a 9,9 orientation are introduced. Chapter 9 discusses when others should and should not be involved in decision-making activities and issues of critique. Chapter 10 focuses on specific aspects of a 9,9 orientation: management-by-objectives and the use of organizational rewards.

Against this background, it is then possible to examine the three additional leadership theories—paternalism/maternalism, opportunism, and facades—that are presented in Part III, Chapter 11.

Part IV is concerned with change. Chapter 12 explains how the Grid can be used to increase organizational effectiveness on an in-company basis. Appendices A and B report a conceptual analysis of current leadership theories and research evaluating the validity of the 9,9 orientation. Earlier literature, not included here, is referenced in the 1964 edition and extended in the 1978 edition.

Robert R. Blake
Jane S. Mouton

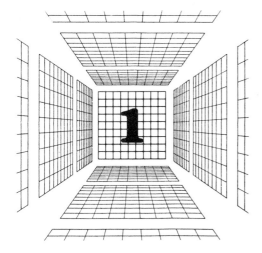

Managerial Styles

The character of leadership is a significant factor in organization success or failure. Strong and effective leadership creates high involvement and shared commitment that stimulates people to overcome obstacles to achieving maximum results. Active participation is possible because members have a clear sense of purpose. They give one another mutual support of the kind characteristic of outstanding teamwork. As team members gain experience, they qualify themselves for promotion and advancement. The result is that the organizational need for results is satisfied, personal benefits from involvement and commitment are gained, and opportunities for advancement are increased.

This book provides guidelines for effective leadership by comparing it with what it *is not*. It helps you answer fundamental questions about how to exercise leadership in achieving results. You will learn about things you are doing that limit your effectiveness and about things you are doing that are sound. The benefits to be gained include strengthening your contribution to your organization and increasing the likelihood of your having a successful and rewarding career in management.

The best way to study the Grid is to compare what is being discussed in the text with your own ways of leading. In reading each chapter, ask yourself, Is this me? Do I do this? Is it a sound way to lead or not? Should I do less of it or should I do more?

This book is a map for helping you to be more objective in seeing ways to increase your own effectiveness and be more self-analytical about your present ways of exercising leadership. What you are studying is you.

Elements of Leadership

While leadership is a complex process, it can be described by identifying its main elements, each of which is an ingredient, a component, a facet of leadership that can be isolated and examined. These elements are

1

initiative, inquiry, advocacy, conflict resolution, decision making, and *critique.** All six elements are vital to effective leadership because none can compensate for the lack or overabundance of any other.

The elements of leadership are briefly described in the following sections. Within each section are six statements that describe different leadership approaches. You will notice that all of the "A" statements reflect the same leadership approach, all the "B" statements reflect the same leadership approach, etc.

The statements provide benchmarks for describing leadership as a process of people working together to achieve organization objectives, so as you read these statements, ask yourself, "Do I know someone—a boss, colleague, or subordinate—who manages in this way?"

Initiative

Initiative is exercised whenever effort is concentrated on a specific activity, to start something that was not going on before, to stop something that was occurring, or to shift direction and character of effort. A leader may take initiative or avoid taking initiative even when others expect action.

A. I put out enough to get by.
B. I initiate actions that help and support others.
C. I seek to maintain a steady pace.
D. I drive myself and others.
E. I stress loyalty and extend appreciation to those who support my initiatives.
F. I exert vigorous effort and others join in enthusiastically.

Inquiry

Inquiry permits a leader to gain access to facts and data from people or other information sources. The quality of inquiry may depend on a leader's thoroughness. A leader may have very low personal standards of thoroughness and thus ignore the need for inquiry. Alternatively, a leader may have high standards of thoroughness and be keenly interested to learn as much as possible about work activities.

---

* Source: *Grid Team Building.* Austin, Texas: Scientific Methods, Inc., 1984. Element descriptions used by permission.

A. I go along with facts, beliefs, and positions given to me.
B. I look for facts, beliefs, and positions that suggest all is well. For the sake of harmony, I am not inclined to challenge others.
C. I take things more or less at face value and check facts, beliefs, and positions when obvious discrepancies appear.
D. I investigate facts, beliefs, and positions so that I am in control of any situation and to assure myself that others are not making mistakes.
E. I double-check what others tell me and compliment them when I am able to verify their positions.
F. I search for and validate information. I invite and listen for opinions, attitudes, and ideas different than my own. I continuously reevaluate my own and others' facts, beliefs, and positions for soundness.

Advocacy

To advocate is to take a position. A leader may have strong convictions but think it risky to take a stand. Alternatively, the leader may not advocate because of low or nonexistent convictions. The leader also may embrace a point of view simply to oppose someone or to win.

A. I keep my own counsel but respond when asked. I avoid taking sides by not revealing my opinions, attitudes, and ideas.
B. I embrace opinions, attitudes, and ideas of others even though I have reservations.
C. I express opinions, attitudes, and ideas in a tentative way and try to meet others halfway.
D. I stand up for my opinions, attitudes, and ideas even though it means rejecting others' views.
E. I maintain strong convictions but permit others to express their ideas so that I can help them think more objectively.
F. I feel it is important to express my concerns and convictions. I respond to ideas sounder than my own by changing my mind.

Conflict Resolution

When people have different points of view and express them, disagreement and conflict are inevitable. Conflict can be either disruptive and destructive or creative and constructive, depending on how it is handled. A leader who can face conflict with others and resolve it to their mutual understanding evokes respect. The inability to cope with conflict constructively leads to disrespect, even to increased hostility and antagonism.

A. I remain neutral or seek to stay out of conflict.
B. I avoid generating conflict but when it appears I try to soothe feelings to keep people together.
C. When conflict arises I try to find a reasonable position that others find suitable.
D. When conflict arises I try to cut it off or win my position.
E. When conflict arises I terminate it but thank people for expressing their views.
F. When conflict arises I seek out reasons for it in order to resolve underlying causes.

Decision Making

It is through decision making that leadership is applied to performance. It may involve solo decision making, in which the leader alone is the ultimate decision maker, or delegation of responsibilities for decisions (teamwork), in which all available resources are brought to bear on making and implementing decisions.

A. I let others make decisions or come to terms with whatever happens.
B. I search for decisions that maintain good relations and encourage others to make decisions when possible.
C. I search for workable decisions that others accept.
D. I place high value on making my own decisions and am rarely influenced by others.
E. I have the final say and make a sincere effort to see that my decisions are accepted.
F. I place high value on arriving at sound decisions. I seek understanding and agreement.

Critique

Critique describes a variety of useful ways to study and solve operational problems that members face either singly or collectively as they carry out their assignments. It is a process of stepping away from or interrupting an activity to study it, to see alternative possibilities for improving performance, and to anticipate and avoid any activities that have adverse consequences. A person may or may not consider work experience as a basis for learning and may or may not make reactions known to others through feedback. Without such learning, future activities are unlikely to be improved. Through learning from experience, critique and feedback provide the basis for working more effectively with and through people.

A. I avoid giving feedback.
B. I give encouragement and offer praise when something positive happens but avoid giving negative feedback.
C. I give informal or indirect feedback regarding suggestions for improvement.
D. I pinpoint weaknesses or failure to measure up.
E. I give others feedback and expect them to accept it because it is for their own good.
F. I encourage two-way feedback to strengthen operations.

The six leadership patterns from which the statements are drawn rest on certain *assumptions* about how to achieve production with and through people. The way in which assumptions guide behavior is discussed in the following section.

How Assumptions Guide Behavior

Whenever leaders approach a situation, they act on subjective appraisal, which may or may not be close to objective reality. This appraisal includes assumptions about what is true or reliable. The objective reality and the subjective appraisal of it can be close together or far apart.

There are several different sets of assumptions, and the assumptions a leader acts on may or may not be based on what appears to be sound. Sound or unsound, assumptions become part of a manager's beliefs or attitudes. They guide behavior. They constitute a personal leadership theory. If a person were to act without assumptions, behavior would be random, purposeless; it would not make sense or be predictable.

There are many examples of how assumptions shape behavior. Assumptions about illness, for example, in one culture lead to treatment by magic and cure through medicine in another. Some cultures assume that dictatorship is the way to organize the activities of people. The belief of others is that constitutional democracy or limited monarchy is best. The point is that assumptions organize our relationships and our ways of conducting affairs. When an assumption we make is also being made by those around us, for practical purposes it becomes an absolute not to be questioned. Other possible assumptions are ignored. The "absolute" eliminates courses of action that are inconsistent with those assumptions and blinds everyone to options that might produce sounder results.

Leaders seldom verbalize their assumptions, but they do act on them. Because some assumptions lead to good results and others lead to poor ones, not all assumptions are equal as a basis for exercising effective leadership. The idea that various sets of assumptions are "equal but different" has appeal because it permits a leader to avoid making a choice. The choice of assumptions, however, becomes an important issue for leaders to consider since some assumptions produce negative consequences and others produce positive ones.

A comprehensive theory of leadership is possible because only a limited number of assumptions about how to achieve performance with and through others are available. It is important to understand one's own assumptions because they operate silently and their central role in controlling our behavior is likely to be unseen. Understanding our assumptions about leadership can help us to see the impact of our behavior on the production efforts of those with whom we work.

Assumptions Can Be Changed

How are unsound assumptions changed? A first step is to become aware of them. Sometimes we explain something we did by saying, "I assumed that . . . " or " . . . that assumption didn't work." Far more often we are completely unaware of the assumptions that underlie our conduct. We are as baffled about why we do things as others are in trying to explain our actions. Without new experiences to challenge our assumptions, we have difficulty identifying them. With new experiences and feedback from others regarding our actions, assumptions on which they are based can be reexamined and change becomes possible.

The Grid helps us examine assumptions about leadership. Once we become aware of the depth and character of our assumptions, we can analyze them and identify the positive and negative consequences of actions based on them. We can consider alternative assumptions that may provide a sounder basis for our actions and practice applying them until they become characteristic.

Summary

The Grid is useful for helping leaders identify the assumptions they make as they work to get results with and through others. By using theories to identify assumptions, leaders see themselves and others more objectively, communicate more clearly, understand where their disagreements come from, see how to change themselves, and help others toward more productive and rewarding experiences. The more skilled a leader becomes in using a sound theory, the more capable that person is in reducing frustration, resentment, and other negative emotions. The shift away from these feelings toward enthusiasm and dedication promotes a sense of contribution and reward of personal fulfillment.

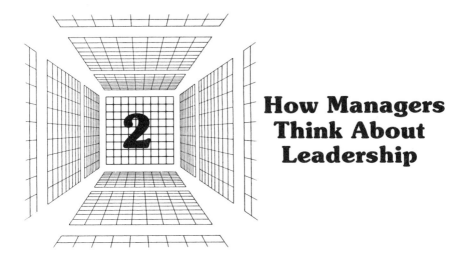

How Managers Think About Leadership

Since management takes place within organizations, it is important to determine what an organization *is*. Then the possibilities for improving competence in leading an organization toward improved performance can be seen.

Organization Universals

Several characteristics of organizations are constant. They are present regardless of the type of work. Effective management of these universals is the key to efficient production.

Purpose(s)

This is the first universal. It is difficult to imagine a purposeless organization. Admittedly, it is not always easy to identify *what* the purpose is. Furthermore, the purpose for which an organization exists may or may not be the same as the purpose for which it was formed originally.

It is easier to describe the purpose of industrial organizations than it is educational, governmental, hospital, military, political, religious, and family organizations. Industrial organization purpose is profit. The profit and loss statement defines how well effort has been applied in the short term and returned to the shareholder in the long term. Even though such financial measures may be unavailable for other institutions, such organizations also have purposes that are usually consistent with results-oriented motivation. Often the purpose is to supply service(s) at minimum expense. For this discussion, the equivalent of profit, that is, the production of *goods or services,* is regarded as the aim of organization activities. Production then can be regarded as an indication of organization purpose(s). It is a universal applicable to all organizations.

People

Another characteristic of organization is *people*. No organization can exist without them. Some say it would be desirable to replace people with technological procedures, automated processes, robots, etc. so that human energy is not wasted in doing work that machine systems can do. If it were possible to create a peopleless arrangement, it is unlikely that the word *organization* would be used to describe it. Even an automated factory requires some organization of people to plan operations and to maintain it.

Organization purpose, then, cannot be achieved without people, nor does it exist under circumstances where one person is acting alone. Others need to be drawn in to achieve it. Needing more than one person to achieve a result leads to organization.

Power (Hierarchy)

The third universal is *power*. Some organization members are supervisors; others are supervised. Some supervisors have more power than others. This is hierarchy or rank.

The process of achieving organization purpose (the first universal) through the efforts of people (the second universal) results in some people attaining authority to set direction and coordinate effort; that is, to exercise the responsibility for the activities of others. The foundation for understanding managerial leadership is in recognizing that a boss's actions are dictated by assumptions regarding how to use authority to achieve organization purpose with and through people.

Organization Culture

An organization is not simply a collection of individuals. Rather people work in groups and experience feelings of *organization membership,* the fourth universal. Organizations have norms and values that influence how members conduct themselves. These norms may prevent members from applying a maximum effort or may encourage them to do so. The boss has to think about how to get several people working together with people feeling that they are members, that they belong, and that they share production objectives in common, with some degree of mutual responsibility for one another. Thus, organization culture is the broader framework within which feelings of membership are experienced. The significance of organization culture is discussed further in Chapter 12.

The Grid

Various ways to use authority in exercising leadership are represented visually on the Grid. *Concern for production,* getting results, is one dimension of the Grid. A second is *concern for people*—subordinates and colleagues. "Concern for" is not a mechanical term that indicates the amount of actual production achieved or actual behavior toward people. Rather, it indicates the *character* and *strength of assumptions* present behind any given leadership style.

Concern for Production

This concern, which includes *results, bottom line, performance, profits,* or *mission,* may be represented, for example, by a key executive finding new directions for organization growth through acquisitions or by launching or expanding innovative research and development. Covering both quantity and quality, concern for production may be revealed in the scope and soundness of decisions, the number of creative ideas product development converts into salable items, accounts processed in a collection period, or quality and thoroughness of services provided by staff.

When work is physical, concern for production may take the form of efficiency measurements, number of units produced, time required to complete a certain production run, volume of sales, or attainment of a specified level of quality. In a hospital, it may be patient load, number of diagnostic tests completed, or length of hospital stay. In a government agency, productivity may be delivery time, number of forms correctly processed, or number of union-management conflicts in business brought to successful resolution through government mediators. Results may be measured in a university by the number of students graduated, students per faculty member, teaching load, research papers published, or graduates in any given year who complete advanced degrees at a later time. Production, in other words, is whatever an organization hires people to accomplish.

Concern for People

Since managers exercise leadership with and through others, the assumptions they make about people are important in determining effectiveness. People are people regardless of the context in which the work takes place—industry, government, educational and medical institutions, or the home.

Concern for people is revealed in many different ways. Some leaders' concerns are shown in their efforts to ensure that subordinates like them. Others are concerned that subordinates get their jobs done. Though different from each other, getting results based on trust and respect, obedience, sympathy, or understanding and support, is a manifestation of *concern* for people. Working conditions, salary structure, fringe benefits, job security, etc. are other ways in which concerns for people become evident. The degree of concern includes both character and intensity. Depending on the *character* of concern, subordinates may respond with enthusiasm or resentment, involvement or apathy, innovative or dull thinking, commitment or indifference, and eagerness or resistance to change.

How These Concerns Interrelate

These two concerns are pictured visually on the Grid in Figure 2-1. They are shown as nine-point scales, where *1* represents low concern, *5* represents an average amount of concern, and *9* is high concern. The other numbers denote intermediate degrees of concern. They signify steps between low and high just as the gauge in an automobile indicates the relative amount of fuel from empty to full, rather than specific quantities.

The manner in which these two concerns are expressed by a leader defines how authority is used. For example, when high concern for people is coupled with a low concern for production, the leader wants people to be well-related and "happy." This is far different from when high concern for people is coupled with a high concern for production. Here the leader wants people to be involved in the work and to strive enthusiastically to contribute.

While there are numerous ways of uniting these two concerns, only a few are important for understanding the exercise of leadership. Each of these theories or orientations rests on a different set of assumptions for using power and authority to link people into production. An orientation is a way of thinking about or analyzing a problem that is subject to change to another orientation as a result of increased understanding. Thus, an orientation is not a trait which is fixed and unchanging.

Motivations include what a person strives to reach as well as what a person seeks to avoid. Therefore, they can be described by a scale with end points of plus (+) and minus (−) and with varying degrees of intensity between them. The motivational end points differ as is pointed out in each of the Grid style chapters.

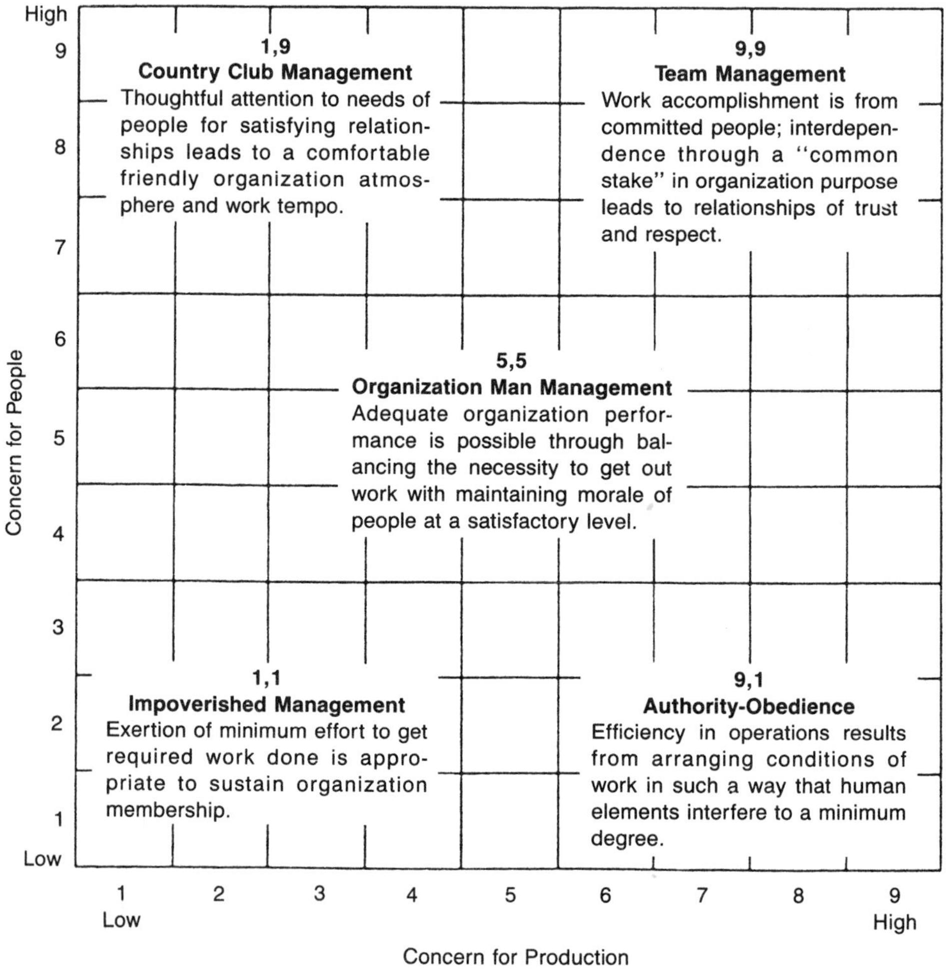

High
9   1,9
Country Club Management
Thoughtful attention to needs of
people for satisfying relation-
8   ships leads to a comfortable
friendly organization atmosphere and work tempo.

7

9,9
Team Management
Work accomplishment is from
committed people; interdependence through a "common
stake" in organization purpose
leads to relationships of trust
and respect.

Concern for People

6

5,5
Organization Man Management
Adequate organization performance is possible through bal-
5   ancing the necessity to get out
work with maintaining morale of
4   people at a satisfactory level.

3

1,1
Impoverished Management
Exertion of minimum effort to get
2   required work done is appropriate to sustain organization
1   membership.

Low

9,1
Authority-Obedience
Efficiency in operations results
from arranging conditions of
work in such a way that human
elements interfere to a minimum
degree.

1   2   3   4   5   6   7   8   9
Low   High

Concern for Production

Figure 2-1. The Managerial Grid.®

The important point is that to increase managerial competence and productivity in people, a leader must know of alternative leadership styles and be prepared to select the soundest. From the range of orientations, five display such significant differences in characteristic actions and outcomes they are readily identified as benchmark styles:

9,1 In the lower right-hand corner of the Grid a maximum concern for production (9) is combined with a minimum concern for people (1). A manager acting on these assumptions concentrates on maximizing production by exercising power and authority, and achieving control over people by dictating what they should do and how they should do it. The D statements in Chapter 1 represent this leadership style.

1,9 The 1,9-oriented leadership style is in the top left corner. Here a minimum concern for production (1) is coupled with a maximum concern for people (9). Primary attention is placed on good feelings among colleagues and subordinates even at the expense of achieving results, as indicated by the B statements.

1,1 A minimum concern for both production and people is represented by 1,1 in the lower left corner. As seen in the A statements, the 1,1-oriented manager does only the minimum required to remain within the organization.

5,5 The center depicts the 5,5 orientation. This is the "middle of the road" theory or the "go-along-to-get-along" assumptions, which are revealed in conformity to the status quo as reflected in all of the C statements.

9,9 Represented in the upper right corner of the Grid, this style integrates production and people concerns. It is a goal-centered, team approach that seeks to gain optimum results through participation, involvement, commitment, and conflict solving of everyone who can contribute, as characterized by the F statements.

Other Grid Styles

Three additional theories of significance are combinations of the previously described "pure" styles. *Paternalism,* as seen in the E statements, is a combination of 9,1 direction and control coupled with 1,9 rewards through praising compliance. *Opportunism* is a combination of any or all theories based on whatever will advance the manager's personal gain. *Facades* involve role playing a 9,9 orientation to hide true motivations.

These are further explained in Chapter 11. Other mixtures could be pictured as intermediate degrees, such as 9,5; 5,9; 8,3; or 4,4. Any benefits that might be gained from theories at intermediate locations are not worth the complexities involved in specifying their characteristics.

Factors that Determine Dominant Grid Style

The dominant managerial assumptions for a given person under a particular circumstance are influenced by any of the following conditions.

Organization. Managerial behavior frequently is influenced by organization membership. Some organizations' rules and requirements are so rigid that the individual manager's style cannot be exercised. The leadership style exhibited may reflect less of one's preferred assumptions and more about the organization beliefs regarding "the right way to manage."

Values. A manager's assumptions are based on values, beliefs, or ideals regarding the way to treat people or the way to manage results. Any set of assumptions can have personal values attached to them concerning the desirability of a managerial style.

Personal History. The dominant managerial style may, to an important degree, result from deep-rooted personal history. An individual is predisposed to one approach over another because that style may have been experienced so frequently in the past. Grid style is not the same as personality.

Chance. Managerial assumptions may guide a person's behavior because they were adopted without considering their consequences. Such individuals may not have discovered or have been confronted with other sets of assumptions about how to manage. "Chance," so to speak, has not helped them learn.

It is unreasonable to expect that a Grid style can predict every feature of managerial behavior for any given individual. Managers are likely to be aware of their own dominant Grid style and also to be able to recognize inconsistencies that do not fit the assumptions of the dominant Grid style. What can be expected is explicit patterns of basic behavior for which the Grid style is an apt description.

In reading what follows, it is important to understand that there is no relationship between IQ and Grid style. A 1,9-oriented manager may be no less intelligent than a 9,1- or a 9,9-oriented manager. The Grid is a set of theories about how people *use* their intelligence and skills in working with and through other people for results.

Dominant and Backup Styles

Granted that a manager's Grid style may be consistent over a range of situations, it is also true a manager shifts and adapts Grid styles according to the situation. How can the concept of a dominant set of assumptions be reconciled with managerial styles that shift and change? Most managers not only have a dominant Grid style, but also a backup style; sometimes even a third and fourth. A manager's backup style becomes apparent when the dominant Grid style cannot be applied. In other words, a backup style is the style a leader reverts to when under pressure, tension, or in situations of conflict that cannot be solved in a characteristic way.

Relationships between dominant and backup styles are easily seen in how a supervisor deals with a recalcitrant worker. First, logic and reason are tried in a 9,9 way, but it doesn't work. Then, a get-tough approach is applied, possibly with a touch of ridicule. Both are 9,1 ways of attempting to get the worker's obedience. Since resentment and rejection have been created, there is a switch-over to friendliness and encouragement with the hope that a 1,9 attitude will bring the worker around. Finally, still unable to elicit cooperation, the supervisor either returns to a 9,1 strategy of threats and punishments or withdraws in a 1,1 way and says "It's not worth worrying about."

It is important to remember that the style or styles employed by managers as they work can be complex. The dominant or most characteristic style is the one most central to understanding how a person manages. The dominant style may not always be the *first* one used in a given situation. For example, a manager might begin a meeting with subordinates in a friendly and casual way but quickly utilize a 9,1 approach when they get down to business. Even though the friendly, casual beginning might be 1,9 in character, the 9,1 approach is the dominant one. The backup is the one used next most often as the basis for actions. To really understand one's dominant and backup approaches it is necessary to observe behavior over time and over a range of situations. Some managers shift frequently and others less often.

Any Grid style can back up any other. For example, a 1,9-oriented leader prefers to yield and defer, but may become stubborn and demanding (9,1) when the pressure becomes too great. A leader who seeks control and mastery in a 9,1 way and meets continued resistance from subordinates may shift to a 9,9 teamwork basis of cooperative problem solving. A dominant to backup shift also may be observed when a manager works with subordinates in a 9,9 manner in everyday situations, but then switches when a crisis arises. A 9,1-oriented backup appears when the manager takes over an operation without utilizing the resources of those who may be best able to contribute to a solution. This great array of dominant-backup combinations is what makes each manager such a unique individual.

In the final analysis leadership is everything. The latest equipment, the best product design, the finest facilities, and the most highly qualified people may count for little or nothing if leadership is ineffectively exercised in taking advantage of these potentials. Leadership is what converts the resources available to an organization into effective results.

Benefits and Limitations

Benefits

There are many benefits from using the Grid framework as a conceptual infrastructure on which to build leadership excellence.

Inclusive. The Grid identifies all significant approaches for exercising leadership.

Comparative. Grid theories permit comparison of similarities and differences of leadership styles.

Evaluative. The Grid permits an evaluation of the consequences of each leadership style for productivity, creativity, career success, and satisfaction.

Subjective Appraisal. It is a self-convincing approach that permits the reader to draw personal conclusions as to what constitutes effective leadership.

Objective Evidence. Fifty years of research on leadership style and operational consequences provide a basis of empirical assessment of the validity of the 9,9 orientation in comparison with others, thus providing an independent source of confirmation. The Grid structural framework has been independently assessed for its conceptual vigor and found to meet the highest standards for conceptual logic. The 9,9 orientation presents a scientifically derived theory and therefore is a sound alternative to rejected models of the past.

Shared Concepts and Language. Since the Grid provides a standard language for thinking about and discussing leadership, it permits managers to discuss and agree among themselves how leadership should and should not be exercised.

Organization Development. The Grid provides a basic model for developing an organization into a system characterized by effective leadership that stimulates sound participation-based teamwork throughout its membership.

Useful for Selection, Coaching, and Performance Appraisal. Once the Grid is understood, it can be used as the basis for selection, coaching, and performance appraisal. This framework provides a management tool for an integrated system of human resource utilization.

Wide Applicability. Once learned, the Grid has applicability to any situation of achieving results with and through people.

☐ It is pertinent wherever work is being done in business, industry, government, education, or human service organizations.
☐ The Grid can be used constructively by persons of any technical background, at any organization level or level of experience. Application includes first line through the executive suite; management of operations, finance, R&D, maintenance, construction; business of high technical content or otherwise.
☐ The Grid is applicable for organizations of any size since sound leadership is the same whether exercised in a five- or five-thousand person organization.
☐ The various Grid styles of exercising leadership are present in cross-national organizations; therefore, the Grid is useful for strengthening problem-solving leadership across cultures.
☐ The Grid framework has pertinence for family life, child rearing, and in other community settings; in other words, wherever problems arise that need resolution with and through others.

Limitations

Some think that learning how to lead effectively is next to impossible; some believe leadership is a natural ability and either you have it or you don't; and still others think that you can learn it but you can't teach an old dog new tricks. Accepting any of these propositions precludes the possibility of learning to become more effective. Though they are value-based beliefs, they rest on false assumptions about human learning. It is as practical to learn to lead effectively as it is to learn arithmetic or to referee a game or to perfect any other applied skill.

Overview

The following chapters provide a comprehensive analysis of each of the major Grid styles, examples of their use, and suggestions for what a person might consider doing to strengthen leadership.

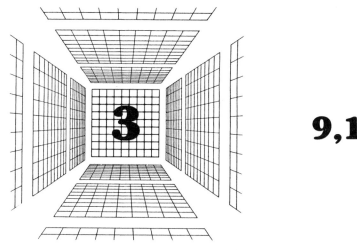

9,1

The 9,1 orientation is located in the lower right-hand corner of the Grid where a high concern for production, *9,* is coupled with a low concern for people, *1.* The 9,1 leadership style rests on the assumption that there is an inevitable contradiction between the organization's needs for productivity and the needs of people. Production objectives can be met when people are controlled and directed in a way that compels them to complete the necessary tasks. A 9,1-oriented manager is characterized as an exacting taskmaster who already knows what is best and whose actions and concerns are focused on one thought—getting results. The manager's mental gyroscope maintains a constant direction in a single-minded way.

The effort is to arrange conditions of work in ways that diminish subordinates' needs for exercising independent thought and judgment. "Human" elements are prevented from interfering with efficiency and output by close supervision. When people do as they are told, results can be achieved without wasting time to solve conflicts or confer with others. The 9,1 orientation is summed up in the phrase "produce or perish."

Motivations

A 9,1-oriented manager's sense of strength comes from feeling powerful, submitting to nothing and to no one, and expecting unquestioning subservience from subordinates. A 9,1-oriented manager is hardworking and prepared to spend whatever time it takes to grapple with problems for which responsibility is felt. However, the emphasis is on will-power exercised by an inflexible determination to master, control, and dominate. To do this, it may be necessary to demand, "Do it or else." When production is high, the manager feels in charge and little appreciates others' contributions. This manager also does not request suggestions, recommendations, advice, or guidance. To do so would admit a need, which in turn would indicate weakness or incompetence. The same would be true about sharing credit for success. The goal is to rely on no one. The 9,1 assumption, then, is: "When I have sufficient strength, I can impose my will regardless of opposition."

9,1-oriented acquisitiveness is far broader than just seeking to accumulate money or other external indicators of power. The accumulation of control may be just as important. Approving spending authorizations, signing paychecks, double verifying merit evaluations, or demanding direct reports are all ways of acquiring control over others. This accumulation of control may in fact so overload the 9,1-oriented boss that it is self-defeating. Rather than giving the mastery and domination that is wanted, it may create the dreaded condition of failure.

Sometimes a 9,1-oriented manager's close supervision is resisted. Then the greatest dread is to falter, lose control, or be defeated. Fear of failure is the negative end of the motivational scale. When failure occurs, the 9,1-oriented manager's mastery, control, and domination have broken down. Blame for the failure is placed on colleagues and subordinates, leading to, "Next time I'll watch them more closely." The general conclusion is, "I am the reason for my successes; failure is caused by the actions of others. Never trust them."

Anger is often experienced when domination, mastery, and control is threatened. Then the focus is on eliminating the obstacles that triggered the anger rather than studying the causes of losing inner composure. This means determining what others have been doing wrong and then checking to see that they do not repeat it. Over time this can produce an angry attitude, with a chip-on-the-shoulder readiness to take corrective action even when it may be inappropriate. Even though unprovoked, this surplus of anger and hostility may stimulate a search for situations where it can be unloaded. Someone with this kind of free-floating anger is described by such phrases as "looking for a fight," "going on the warpath," or "having a short fuse." The 9,1-oriented manager's reaction is likely to be, "I've found I can't get anything worthwhile without fighting for it." As a result, the manager may be so overpowering and involved in getting production that he or she unwittingly runs roughshod over others.

When a 9,1 orientation spreads throughout an organization, it can produce an atmosphere similar to a guard-prisoner culture. Guards are also prisoners in the sense that they are controlled from above yet they control those under their charge. This guard-prisoner mentality leads to a lack of candor coupled with suspicion and distrust. One common reaction of subordinates is to salute, to say "yes" even though it covers up a "no." The idea is, "Don't get caught," and this often means hiding one's thoughts, feelings, and actions. When people are closed and hidden, it becomes even more important for the 9,1-oriented manager to remain vigilant and alert to what they may be doing so that failure is avoided.

Managing Conflict

When subordinates have different points of view or fail to carry out instructions, the 9,1-oriented manager faces the dilemma of either putting up with the situation or correcting it. Since conflict threatens control, the approach is to anticipate and prevent it or, when control has broken down, to reestablish compliance.

Preventing Conflict

There are many ways a 9,1-oriented manager anticipates and prevents conflict. Once a boss establishes an objective and has a plan for accomplishing it, the next step is to implement the plan. A 9,1-oriented manager communicates precisely what subordinates are to do. The manager might say, genuinely meaning every word, "I'm going to tell you what I want done, and then I'm going to tell you again, and then I'm going to tell you what I told you. By the time I get through I expect you to have a full understanding of what I want you to do."

The manager often gives instructions one step at a time, assuming that this will reduce the likelihood of confusion or error. This also ensures that the manager is the only person who has an overview of the entire project. By limiting the instructions and focusing attention on who, what, where, when, and how, the manager hopes to prevent subordinates from asking *why* a task is to be done in the assigned way. Though the boss may ask, "Do you understand?" the subordinate is expected to answer "yes." Even when subordinates don't understand, they have learned it is in their own best interest not to admit it.

Handling Conflict When It Appears

While such one-way supervision and step-at-a-time instructions are calculated to eliminate conflict, this approach is not sufficient to totally eliminate it.

Since a 9,1-oriented manager likely views disagreement the same as insubordination, the primary approach to resolving conflict is to suppress it by forcing his or her view onto others and rejecting their counterarguments as unacceptable. Believing that rank is power permits the boss to use this rank more or less arbitrarily. Subordinates are told what viewpoint prevails and are expected to comply with it. They may even be prevented from talking about matters they disagree with. Whether they privately disagree is beside the point. "What you *think* is your business. What you *do* is my business." Suppression is a powerful means of extracting compliance and is widely practiced in the name of maintaining direction and ensuring control.

Suppressive methods may produce side effects that are not immediately apparent; for example, they communicate a lack of confidence that others are able to act responsibly and thus deny people the opportunity to make a useful contribution.

A boss may unwittingly assume that when a disagreement is suppressed, so is resistance. This may not be so since a person's convictions are seldom changed by forced compliance. Therefore, suppressing disagreement will likely lead to subordinates withholding information that might otherwise serve as valuable feedback.

Suppression also results in counterattack. Such an activity may not always be "anti-organizational" but might be in the form of a "protest," which, despite constructive intentions, is rejected because it does not conform to the 9,1-oriented boss's view of accomplishing the job.

Some counterattacks do reflect genuine anti-organizational creativity. These obviously are not carried out in the open. It might be a shipment of bad quality where the culprit cannot be identified, the breakdown of equipment due to tampering, or no more than the "failure" of someone to tighten a screw. Slowdowns and foot-dragging are other typical responses designed to deny 9,1-oriented managers their objectives.

When a disagreement arises with peers, a 9,1-oriented manager ends the conflict by proving them wrong. Since rank cannot be used, the approach is to win by forcing colleagues to back off. What matters is to win; being liked is irrelevant. The fact that colleagues may be frustrated or feel degraded is not considered.

A 9,1-oriented manager usually perceives a challenge as a win-lose situation. The manager personalizes the conflict by saying, "You think I'm wrong," not "You think that my position is wrong." Such a person has difficulty distinguishing between the issue and the ill feelings for the person who is disagreeing.

When Conflict Remains

Because of the resentment and resistance that suppression and win-lose fighting provokes, people either "go underground" to continue the fight for their position or rely on other ways, such as withholding their cooperation. The 9,1-oriented manager may then try to reduce the intensity of conflict by indirect means.

Undermining the Other Person's Sense of Confidence. By belittling a person or raising reservations about a proposal or recommendation, though none of these reservations may make it wrong, a 9,1-oriented manager can create such a heavy burden that the advocate is likely to give up. For example, such dogmatic, flat statements as "You don't know what you're talking about," "We've tried that before and it doesn't work," "I wouldn't do that if I were you," are ways of bringing someone into line.

The use of hard-hitting humor and sarcasm may be used by a 9,1-oriented manager to suppress an adversary. Humor can be a potent weapon and this manager's humor frequently carries a sting. On reflection, the manager may try to excuse this hard-hitting humor by saying, "I was only trying to get your attention."

Use of Threat and Punishment. A boss can threaten bad consequences if noncompliance continues. When threats don't work, punishment and reprisal usually are available and come in several forms. Punishment may be as indirect, for example, as not inviting a person to an important meeting, or failing to include someone on the circulation slip for an important memo. Transfer is another way of getting rid of someone who resists accepting an authority-obedience relationship. Revenge or other forms of retribution may be as obvious as demotion or firing, or less obvious, such as assignments to unpleasant jobs or to undesirable shifts.

Techniques of leverage are disguised forms of punishment and can be used to accomplish the same result as punishment. This is possible by creating dilemmas that force the subordinate to submit or face some worse consequence. Typically, a job may be declared no longer necessary. When firing is out of the question, an equivalent job elsewhere is offered which, for some reason (family, etc.), cannot possibly be accepted. The only real option is to resign. Such leverage strategies are widely used to bring an end to differences and to eliminate those who do not conform. The thinking behind them can range from subtle coercion to deliberate manipulation. The resort to leverage techniques stems from 9,1-oriented assumptions regardless of how they are justified.

Behavioral Elements

We can now examine how these motivations and approaches to conflict solving shape the manner in which 9,1-oriented leadership is daily exercised.

Initiative

Initiative sets the direction for others to follow; therefore, the unilateral exercise of initiative is important to the 9,1-oriented manager. It is telling others to do something, to stop doing something or to do something in a different way. The word for initiative in the 9,1 context is "hard-driving," i.e., "I drive myself and others." The manager places a premium on productivity and on shouldering this pressure just as it is put on others. Effort may even be increased when a 9,1-oriented manager feels in competition, for now the stimulus of win-lose increases the readiness to take the initiative away from others.

The flavor of how a 9,1-oriented manager maintains initiative by shutting out help or advice is in the following. Mary (the 9,1-oriented manager) says to Joe, her subordinate, "Joe, this is what I want done and this is how I want you to do it." Joe replies, "But what about doing it my way? It will take less time and bring about the same result." Mary answers, "I didn't ask for your advice, I asked you for an action." Joe has been shut out and he knows it.

This manner of exercising initiative rests on three questionable assumptions: (1) telling others what to do is strong; (2) asking for suggestions is weak; and (3) people want to be led. The unilateral exercise of initiative may go against the grain but that does not mean it is always rejected. People are often relieved to see someone try to do something that needs to be done and therefore respect that person's concern for making things happen. In this case, it is *not* the exercise of initiative itself that is resented, but the 9,1-oriented way of exercising that initiative.

Another reason why a 9,1-oriented exercise of initiative may sometimes be accepted is that some people want to be led. They want to be told what to do. People have worked under the assumption that they are followers for so long that they have ceased thinking of acting autonomously or of taking responsibility in the work place. Being told what to do is expected and accepted as normal. To be asked to do anything other than comply is contradictory. In a sense they have become good soldiers, willing to execute a command, but nothing more.

Inquiry

The phrase "knowledge is power" aptly describes knowledge as one of the important tools for exercising domination, mastery, and control.

Questions are one means of acquiring knowledge about operating situations; a 9,1-oriented manager is more than likely to constantly interrupt, interrogate others for information, and take little at face value. The questions asked, however, are likely to be direct and limited to factual information. Numbers, volume, whether on schedule and up to specifications are acceptable contributions but thoughts, opinions, feelings, or recommendations are not. "Just give me the facts." In this way, the 9,1-oriented manager reserves the right to evaluate and interpret. By doing so, others are prevented from exercising judgments that might obligate the manager to acknowledge the wisdom of someone else and therefore lose domination.

When asking questions, the 9,1-oriented manager does not know the meaning of backing off and has little or no concern for the feelings of others. This approach helps acquire important information, but undermines subordinates' security. The manager often seeks information regarding problems, errors, or failures in order to find weaknesses or pin responsibility on the one who "did it."

Sometimes this direct approach does not gain the information sought. Then a trap may be laid by posing a leading question. By answering the question, the person denies the existence of some adverse situation. This is seen in the following situation where Charles is talking with Sue. Charles, who already knows of a customer complaint and the circumstances surrounding it, says to Sue, "Have you had any customer complaints in the last week?"

Sue says, "No, not as far as I can recall."

Now the questioning becomes accusative. Bill says, "Wait a minute. What about the damaged shipment to Toronto? They were angry with us on the phone yesterday, and you know it. Why did you let it happen?"

Such a question is not really intended to promote problem solving but to pin down the victim. If the answer is "yes," the victim is in trouble. If "no," the trap can be sprung. The "yes" answer exposes the victim to a reprimand or some other form of punishment. The "no" answer not only results in punishment but also identifies someone whose word can no longer be trusted. The 9,1-oriented manager can then justify increased surveillance to ensure obedient compliance.

A 9,1-oriented manager is likely to listen defensively, alert for indications of trouble. This is understandable because the 9,1-oriented manager fears failure and therefore must remain on guard to prevent it or to discover it quickly. While defensive listening keeps a person alert, concentration may be so focused on being ready with the answers that other critical information isn't heard. This kind of one-track mind makes a manager deaf to available information that could lead toward a different conclusion.

Advocacy

A 9,1-oriented manager has little hesitation in letting others, regardless of their rank, know where he or she stands on particular issues. Being straightforward with respect to convictions and saying it as it is are obvious characteristics. As a result, such a manager is likely to be open and candid.

In this orientation, however, most things are viewed in black and white terms. Absolute statements that convey the notion "all," "never," "impossible," "everyone," and so on are made. Positions are taken with no room for argument. Tentativeness is a sign of weakness whereas certainty is strength. This manager does not express convictions in a way that invites discussion; conversely, alternative possibilities or counterarguments are resisted. This may mean marshalling evidence to support his or her position and ignoring contradictory information that might lead to a different definition of the problem.

The 9,1-oriented manager does not listen for understanding and is likely to be mentally rehearsing the next point while someone else is speaking. Interrupting others to make one's point is also common. A 9,1-oriented person may be heard to say to a colleague who was trying to reestablish a give-and-take basis of discussion, "You shouldn't be talking when I'm interrupting." As a result, the manager is seen as closed-minded. Subordinates may also stop presenting their positions, saying, "What's the use? Why beat my head against a wall?" This means the benefits possible from thrashing through disagreements are lost, and the 9,1-oriented manager sacrifices good results while being unaware of doing so. However, if someone were to confront the manager with that possibility, it would most likely be rejected.

Decisions

A 9,1-oriented manager says, "I place high values on making my own decisions and am rarely influenced by others." This approach to decision making is influenced by the belief that he or she alone has the required knowledge, experience, and authority. Thus, others are not likely to be involved except for carrying out the decision. A frequent rationalization for such actions is, "There isn't time to consult." Often a 9,1-oriented manager will cause such time constraints to prevent outside involvement, when in fact with better planning or a greater desire to do so, there is sufficient time to involve others.

Rather than being regarded as confident and self-reliant, the 9,1-oriented manager is more likely to be seen as rigid and heavy-handed. Once he or she makes a decision, it is seldom reexamined. If the decision is incorrect and yet the manager proceeds, he or she risks being regarded as stubborn, bullheaded, or blind. Persistence is likely to mean shutting out needed input as well as cutting off others who become increasingly less inclined to offer contrary evidence or information.

Regarding delegation, the 9,1-oriented manager makes a sharp distinction between planning and doing. Planning is retained, doing is delegated; thus production is accomplished by telling subordinates what to do without involving them in planning the best means for doing so. This approach is found at all levels of management. The president designs the plan and announces it as a finished program. The supervisor designs the work project of the day and gives it to those who report to him or her for their assignments. The manager feels compelled to act in this solitary way regardless of whether others are in a position to contribute. The division of labor between planning and doing is vital.

The 9,1-oriented manager thinks teamwork is merely having complete assignments. Each person is held accountable for the results achieved. When done well, this is a hammer-to-nail kind of relationship; however, a contradiction can occur under these circumstances. For example, Helen, the boss, thinks, "I have a top-notch team. We're all in it together." Richard, the subordinate, thinks, "Team? What do you mean? We're not a team. I'm told exactly what to do and it's set up so that any coordination needed is *through* the boss, not directly. Any information I need I have to get from the boss rather than from the source of the information. The boss thinks this is good teamwork because she's on top of everything. In fact, we have poor teamwork because she's overloaded. She's in it up to her neck and works 18 hours a day."

Critique

Checking on performance is an indispensable tool of 9,1 management because the boss wants to know that things are being done in the manner expected. Thus the boss gets information by direct observation, inspection, and interrogation of others. This kind of reporting to the boss is single-loop vigilance and surveillance to be sure activities are proceeding according to plan.

Once the boss receives the information, critique is in the form of criticism and correction of wrongdoing. For example, Dan (the boss) says to Bill, "Look, you made a mistake, and I want you to know why. I gave the directions, but you decided to act on your own rather than doing it as I asked. This is unacceptable to me. I expect you to do it the next time as I tell you and with no excuses. To be sure that you have learned your lesson, I want you to tell me when you have successfully completed each step before you take the next one."

This is a one-way, judgmental evaluation. The subordinate is not involved in thinking through the activity as a way of learning. It is intended to induce guilt and weakness without helping the "guilty" person feel ownership of the actions in question and accept responsibility for solving similar problems in the future.

Management Practices

A 9,1-oriented manager views managerial responsibilities in ways that are distinctive to that orientation.

Planning: "I plan by setting production requirements and detailing plans to achieve them."

Organizing: "I make assignments and tell subordinates what to do, how, when, and with whom."

Directing: "I keep in close touch with what's going on to ensure that what I have authorized is being followed."

Controlling: "I ensure that schedules are being met and move people along faster if progress permits. I criticize, assign blame for deviations, and impose corrective actions."

Staffing: "I choose obedient people and force out malcontents. Management development is probably okay but concentrating on selection is what really counts."

Management-by-Objectives: "I let subordinates know where they stand relative to requirements, clearly and without qualification. Then they know what I expect of them."

Performance Appraisal: "My obligation is to evaluate subordinates and point out ways in which they are not measuring up, concentrating on weaknesses and what to do to correct them. After that it's the person's responsibility to shape up."

Active resentment or at best grudging respect is more or less inevitable when a boss manages in these ways. The 9,1-oriented manager comes to expect little more, justifying that getting production and moving the organization forward requires close supervision, even at the expense of stepping on toes.

Consequences

Several consequences of 9,1-oriented managerial behavior vis-á-vis corporate orientation and an individual's career are discussed in the following sections.

Impact on Productivity

In the short term, a 9,1 orientation is likely to have a favorable outcome for productivity, particularly when compared with other managerial styles where there is a low concern for productivity. Close supervision can keep people focused on achieving results because there is no other option. Sometimes production may be at a high level, not because of a 9,1 orientation but in spite of it. This can occur when the needs for production are evident to everyone.

Over the long term, a 9,1 orientation sows the seeds of its own difficulties. Morale and cohesion are likely to deteriorate as subordinates become resentful and resist being pushed around. They may go through the motions of being productive but in fact show their disrespect for such leadership through failure to maintain quality or through withholding initiative. Then the 9,1-oriented manager "solves" the problem by increasing the pressure, sometimes even adding staff to tell people what to do. Absenteeism may become excessive or subordinates may seek job opportunities elsewhere.

Impact on Creativity

A number of different sources provide evidence that a 9,1 orientation produces creative responses, but unfortunately these tend to be anti-organizational in character. These reflect innovative thinking about ways to undermine the organization or to avoid being trapped into the system rather than how to contribute constructively to organization purposes. Anti-organizational creativity is seen in industrial sabotage, including the destruction of equipment, "lost" reports and other documents, disregard of customer complaints, excessive waste, and stealing.

Impact on Satisfaction

Although the boss manages by edict, few problems arise and subordinates feel little tension if his or her decisions are good ones.

Some subordinates comply because it is easier than disagreeing. They tell the boss he or she is right, regardless of whether this is so. Other subordinates do not anticipate being involved and therefore are not disappointed when nothing more than obedience is expected. If what is demanded of them is dull compliance, subordinates may tend to become less interested in the work itself. Eventually they center attention on private thoughts or engage in discussions on social topics such as sports, politics, or the weather. These activities replace what otherwise would be unbearable boredom in the absence of involvement in the work itself.

When a subordinate resents *fait accompli* decisions and feels anger at not being consulted, he or she may retreat into a withdrawn (1,1) attitude. The subordinate views his or her own ideas as excellent but unappreciated and justifies withdrawal by saying, "I'll not help them any more by offering my ideas. Then they'll come to see what they've lost by not using them."

Another way to escape 9,1-oriented disfavor is to hide actions that violate practices and procedures. For example, subordinates may protect themselves in the short term by filtering and muting information about quality control problems to the point that, when it does reach the top, much of its validity has been lost.

A disgruntled subordinate who bows to authority may vindicate his or her position by encouraging slowdowns, making careless errors, misinterpreting instructions, and similar events that can cause the boss's course of action to falter.

Another common reaction is righteous indignation and a readiness to rebel against the system that dehumanizes but demands. Open hostility is more or less out of the question, but antagonisms take the form of feelings of dislike, even rage. These are expressed in a subordinate's finding something wrong whenever an occasion arises by complaining, backbiting, ridiculing, and so on. The more intense the frustration, the more likely a subordinate is to strike back by fair means or foul. The most extreme form of rebellion is to leave the system, which explains high turnover in some 9,1-oriented organizations.

Impact on Career

Extensive research has led to the conclusion that the careers of 9,1-oriented managers are average in terms of career success. Fewer populate the top of organizations than one might expect. On the other hand, they are more often operating in higher levels of organizations than are the 5,5-, 1,9-, or 1,1-oriented managers where concern for results is lower.

Unions

Subordinates who find themselves ignored or offended by arbitrary treatment and unable to redress what they regard as injustices or wrongs may pursue other, more militant, ways of correcting problems. Given effective leadership, they can achieve through numbers what they are unable to accomplish individually. Recognizing their individual helplessness, workers, supervisors, and professional employees (engineers, etc.) join together to force upon employers the recognition of their common strength. There are many stated reasons why people join unions, but such a commitment is often anti-organizational, a way of *resisting* the organization's attitudes and treatment of its employees. To the degree that 9,1-oriented leadership is continued into the future, unionization among white-collar, high tech, school teachers, and government employees may be expected to continue.

The Management of Crises—A Special Case

Conventional wisdom would say that 9,1 would be the only effective way to deal with crises. Recent applied research, however, questions whether this assumption is as valid as some feel it to be.

It is necessary to evaluate what a crisis is as background for understanding these dynamics. Crisis conveys the notion of a problem for which there is no immediately available solution and there is only a limited time period available for taking action. The 9,1 assumption disregards the possibility that a crisis can be anticipated and therefore planned for.

Solving such dilemmas involves getting the best thinking available from those in the situation. Teamwork brings this knowledge into focus. However, conventional wisdom tells the 9,1-oriented manager to take over and solve it, which can result in a less than optimal resolution than is possible when the manager is open and responsive to the thinking of others and factors their contributions into the final solution. This has nothing to do with *who* makes the decision.

These generalizations apply at all levels of management and supervision. In many respects avoiding this kind of 9,1-oriented response is of even greater importance at higher levels. Part of the reason is that decisions at the top have a wider impact on the organization as a whole. Also, decisions at higher levels are usually more complex and the executive responsible may need to gather information in order to reach the best decision. He or she may not be aware of how a 9,1 orientation toward "taking over" in a crisis may block getting the needed information from those who have it.

Recognizing 9,1 Behavior

Many words and phrases are used in describing 9,1-oriented behavior. No one of them captures the whole, but examined as a group the words and phrases give an idea of how everyday language is used to depict this style of leading:

- Controlling
- Cuts people off
- Decides and then tells people what to do
- Decisions are final
- Demanding
- Expects Compliance
- Fault-finding
- Gets into win-lose fights
- Hard driving
- Has all the answers
- Impatient
- Interrogates
- Others keep their distance
- Overpowering

- Pushy
- Quick to blame
- Sees things in black/white terms
- Stubborn
- Taskmaster
- Tells people what to do but not why

Suggestions for Change

The significant motivation to change is for managers to see the adverse consequences of their Grid style behavior. Below are suggestions a 9,1-oriented leader might want to consider.

Motivation

☐ If subordinates think it wise to either salute you or stay out of your way, increase their involvement by getting them to open up and participate in solving problems. Utilize your subordinates as resources who can contribute more if your leadership mobilizes their energies more fully.

☐ Try to prevent your fear of failure from causing you to hold information inside yourself, as this keeps people from acting until you tell them what to do.

Initiative

☐ See if you can evoke improved involvement by inviting others to take initiative in areas where you have ordinarily called the shots.

☐ Think before you start. You may see a needed action and immediately move to fill the void. Diagnose why it is that others don't seem to move when the need is obvious. Help them to do so.

☐ Check out what you do on your own. Test whether a better result could occur if you were to consult others. You may be underconsulting and therefore not gaining the support that is otherwise readily available.

Inquiry

☐ Consult others who may have information you need for doing a better job.

☐ Resist the tendency to discount information that comes from someone you may dislike. Remember that IQ is independent of Grid style, meaning that no one operating in any particular Grid style has a corner on the truth, and no one is a dullard just because of Grid style.

☐ Listen to ideas different from your own; otherwise you may be cutting off information that is of critical significance for finding sound solutions. Try listening more to see what you learn.

Advocacy

☐ Try promoting others' advocacy by getting them to say what they think before stating your own position.

☐ After you have presented your own position, ask others to react to it rather than demanding they accept any of it as final.

☐ Listen for understanding when others are advocating a position. Find out what they really mean rather than mentally rehearsing your counterarguments.

☐ When advocating a position, you can help others understand and support it by expressing your own reservations about it.

Conflict

☐ If almost every difference of opinion ends in a "fight," take a closer look at whether you are needlessly arguing just to win.

☐ Listen to understand others' points of view before telling them "why they're wrong." It may be that their thinking and analysis are at least as good as your own, even better.

☐ Suppressing differences does not cause them to "go away" but it increases resentment and limits your ability to exercise effective supervision. Get them out in the open rather than reject them.

Decisions

☐ Slow down your decision making. Consult with others. Find out where they stand prior to announcing a decision. Try to take reservations or disagreements into account, or at least explain why you cannot.

☐ Communicate the rationale behind your decisions rather than stating the conclusions only.

☐ Realize that asking for help and thereby support may not be a sign of weakness but rather a sign of strength.

Critique

☐ Realize that feedback can be objective when it describes what you observe others doing and the consequences. Critique does not have to be blame-inducing or fault-finding.
☐ Feedback should be a two-way street. Others may be able to contribute to strengthening your effectiveness if you allow them to tell you what they think about your leadership—and why.

9,1 Orientation Summary

"I drive myself and others. I investigate facts, beliefs, and positions so that I am in control of any situation and to assure myself that others are not making mistakes. I stand up for my opinion, attitudes, and ideas even though it means rejecting others' views. When conflict arises I try to cut it off or win my position. I place high value on making my own decisions and am rarely influenced by others. I pinpoint weaknesses or failure to measure up."

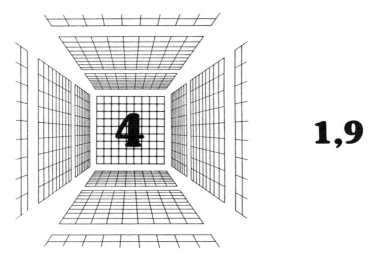

1,9

The 1,9 managerial orientation is shown in the upper left-hand corner of the Grid where low concern for production, *1*, is coupled with high concern for people, *9*. It is based on the premise that production requirements often interfere or conflict with the needs and desires of people. The 1,9-oriented way of thinking about it is, "People are not human commodities to be weighed on a scale of values; therefore, their attitudes and feelings are of primary importance." Conditions are arranged so that personal and social needs can be satisfied on the job. When these needs are jeopardized by production concerns, it is production that suffers.

A 1,9-oriented manager leads in ways that promote friendship and camaraderie but, perhaps unintentionally, deemphasize productivity. The key is establishing a congenial atmosphere. This manager avoids imposing on others, saying, "I'd rather lead than push." The attitude is reflected in the statement, "You can't pressure people; if you do, they'll resist." What this means is, "I find out what they want or think is okay and then help it come true. People should be helped, not goaded." 1,9 supportive management unintentionally turns attention away from the task in the interest of warm and friendly relations.

Motivations

One of the motivations underlying this style of managing is the desire for acceptance and approval. A person feels secure when relationships are positive. A 1,9 assumption is, "If I am nice to people, they will like me." This means being nice, helpful, kind, and sympathetic. These feelings are communicated and convey the fact that the 1,9-oriented manager is tenderhearted. The manager is likely to be very sensitive to what others think and feel and therefore eager to accept signs of appreciation. When others show their appreciation, there is a general feeling of oneness. For these reasons the boss seeks to create an atmosphere of warmth, caring, and approval. The words "deferential" and "ingratiating" are apt descriptions of the 1,9 attitude.

The negative side of the 1,9 motivation is fear of disapproval or rejection. Feelings of rejection leave a 1,9-oriented manager "deeply wounded" and dejected. Since criticism is one step away from rejection, a 1,9-oriented person is constantly alert to it so that the possibility of experiencing it can be avoided. A typical reaction to this fear is flight, escape from the situation, which results in separation from those whose acceptance and approval is sought. Since a 1,9-oriented manager enjoys being with others in preference to working alone, the aim then is simply to avoid conflict with them.

When a 1,9 orientation spreads throughout an organization, a country-club atmosphere comes to exist. People work at an easy tempo and with whom they like. Attention is concentrated on areas where people feel agreeable or express satisfaction. Creativity and innovation may suffer because these are stimulated by and thrive on challenge and controversy.

Production may suffer in this kind of an atmosphere because problems that need to be solved to maintain or improve productivity are put aside "until tomorrow." Remaining unsolved they result in lowered productivity, unnecessary expenses, or both.

Managing Conflict

Conflict is disliked because it threatens warmth and approval, the main staples in the 1,9 emotional diet. A fundamental basis for understanding this dislike is that a 1,9-oriented person finds it difficult to distinguish between an idea being rejected on the one hand and experiencing personal rejection for expressing an idea on the other. It is safer to be mild-mannered and avoid taking a position or to agree with what others are saying.

Preventing Conflict

Letting Others Express Themselves First. Conflict is avoided by staying in close contact with what others—boss, colleagues, and subordinates—are thinking and agreeing with them. Differences cannot arise when one's thoughts parallel those of others. This is done by listening to what others think before expressing one's own point of view.

Creating a Climate of Pleasantness. A 1,9-oriented manager is interested in others, seeking to be friendly with bosses, colleagues, associates, and subordinates—everyone. The manager courts acceptance and approval of others by extending acceptance and approval to them. Harmony comes from keeping relationships informal, becoming overly involved in the progress of associates' children, showing excessive interest in someone's vacation trip, showering people with compliments, and so on. Such acts promote a sense of togetherness and help ward off the potentially disgruntled subordinate who might otherwise be disruptive by expressing unhappiness. This also can make it possible to ask people to do things that are burdensome, anticipating their good-natured readiness to help.

People are encouraged to interact by discussing things they enjoy talking about rather than revealing differences. Because differences do not become apparent, the manager can deal with others in ways unmarred by tensions or frustrations. This tendency to over-politeness, over-graciousness and over-solicitousness can be readily understood. The 1,9-oriented person says "I can show my high concern for others by being sensitive to their feelings and appreciative of them." The underlying state of mind is, "Don't say anything if you can't say something nice." When the boss gathers a group of subordinates around who are inclined to encourage and accentuate the positive, the result is likely to be that problems needing solutions continue to accumulate since they cannot find expression. Eventually a crisis that was not anticipated explodes.

Informal chats allow a manager to be aware of the state of morale and to pay attention to those who are left out and lonely, bringing them in by positive interest in their well-being and by giving favorable reactions to specific requests. Work is more enjoyable and life more pleasant with an appreciative pat on the back, a friendly word, or a smile. These gestures create an attitude of sharing, a sense of warmth, a balm of security.

Holding Back Disagreement. There is a reluctance to propose a different point of view when it might be challenged. A 1,9-oriented manager avoids making statements such as "I disagree," or, "You're wrong." He or she is conscious of even unintended slights but is likely to think, "This isn't worth making an issue over." Therefore, the manager does not express opinions that might result in his or her taking a fixed position. For example, instead of saying, "I saw a new model today. I think it's time we changed ours," the question is likely to be, "Have you noticed the noise our equipment is making lately?" The latter opens up a discussion without the manager having to take a stand.

Shading the Truth. When asked to explain something that might cause feelings of rejection or hurt, the 1,9-oriented manager is unlikely to give all the facts. Bad news is glossed over or played down. When there is no way to avoid it, the conversation may start with an apology that softens impact, "I know it's not your fault, but. . . ." Although the manager may not actually *lie*, the truth is molded to make it as palatable as possible.

Handling Conflict When it Appears

Yielding One's Point of View. A 1,9-oriented manager is quick to accept the position expressed by someone else when conflict does arise. Any opposing view one has crumbles by accepting others' views at face value in spite of the fact that private reservations may remain. Agreement and harmony, however, is restored. "On second thought, I think you're right," or "That's a better way of putting it," or "Your way of thinking on this is better than mine," or "That's a new wrinkle I hadn't thought of" are said in the absence of genuine convictions.

Explaining Away Negatives. When others react angrily or in a hostile manner, the manager is more likely to be soft-spoken, even meek, when criticized. Failure of subordinates to cooperate is explained away— "Mary is under terrific pressure" or "John must not be feeling well." Someone's absenteeism is not shirking; it is sickness or possibly family illness, never contrariness or laziness.

Apologies and Promises. Sometimes the manager gets caught in situations where differences are unavoidable; for example, production records indicating a downward trend for the last quarter. A way of reducing the risk is through apologies and promises of "I'm terribly sorry. It will never happen again." To relieve feelings of rejection, the manager may even ask for additional assignments and in this way hope to regain acceptance that has been jeopardized.

Smoothing Over Differences. Ideas are expressed in such general terms that *everyone* can agree with them. Yet differences are bound to arise. Reconciliation comes from saying the issue is not too important. Smoothing over discontent is done by suggesting how good things are compared to how bad they might be. The attitude is, "Every cloud has a silver lining," "Every day things are getting better and better," or "Count your blessings, things could be worse." Oil is poured on troubled waters by the plea, "Let's come together on those things that we agree on and not dwell on those matters that we cannot resolve."

Using Humor to Reduce Tension. The 1,9-oriented manager's humor diverts attention away from the issue. Funny stories help to shift the focus of thought. A new topic of discussion is then introduced to shift to a less tense issue. In other words, this humor has no particular connection to the issue itself and is intended to help shift from it rather than to inquire into it more deeply.

Downplaying Pressures. The manager often is disturbed by pressures to achieve profit-based goals and objectives because these force one to make demands on others. Pressures frustrate subordinates and rarely bring about the desired results anyway. On the other hand, increasing profit by reducing expenses, that is, taking away conveniences or privileges, also annoys people. The result is that productivity may be further reduced.

Often pressures from above that must be passed down disturb the possibility of managing in this approval-seeking and friendly way. The dilemma is that disregarding the wishes of one's own boss can hurt that relationship; yet, if the pressures are passed directly to subordinates, the manager risks losing their acceptance. One way of dealing with this is to reinterpret production requirements and gently persuade subordinates to work on the problem. Coaxing and cajoling move subordinates effortlessly in the wanted direction. What might otherwise have been posed as an inflexible command thus becomes an appealing request.

If a problem must be dealt with even though resentment is anticipated, the manager may explain it a little at a time. Explaining it all at once might produce an explosion. Also, those required inconveniences that cannot be prevented are made more appealing by "sugarcoating."

When Conflict Remains

How does a 1,9-oriented person deal with tensions when conflict can neither be avoided nor harmony easily restored?

Letting Off Steam. Frustration and tension are discharged by complaining to colleagues, family members, or friends. While venting to third parties may relieve tensions, it does nothing to correct the problems that produced the tensions. Much gossip takes place in interactions between people who are operating in 1,9-oriented settings.

Forgetting. Forgetfulness is possibly more noticeable in 1,9-oriented managers than with other Grid styles. Here is how it can happen. To gain affection and approval, particularly from someone feared, a 1,9-oriented manager accepts a request to do something when in fact resentment results from being asked. The mind says "No" and the result is failure to follow through. The manager is excessively contrite when forgetfulness is pointed out. 1,9-oriented people are sometimes difficult to rely on because they may fail to deliver when the task is unpleasant or when they disagree with the requirement.

Behavioral Elements

The following elements shape the manner in which 1,9 leadership is exercised on a daily basis.

Initiative

A 1,9-oriented manager is eager to be helpful and many actions are taken under this premise. Senses are fine-tuned, and ears and eyes pick up impressions and filter them through 1,9 attitudes to determine whether an action might gain quick acceptance. A 1,9-oriented manager is alert to initiatives taken by others, wanting to respond in order to gain approval. This is not initiative in the self-starting or stopping sense because it is following others rather than leading them.

There are two kinds of actions that are particularly difficult for a 1,9-oriented manager to initiate. One is to bring up an issue with which others may disagree and recommend an alternative. "I don't have the heart to say no" explains the reluctance. Also, when an initiative is taken it may be misunderstood and therefore it is preferable to avoid accusations of being "pushy." A rationalization is, "Sometimes it is difficult to see what actions should be taken so it's better to let the situation develop until it becomes clear what is the best thing to do." The manager may also be convinced that the situation will take care of itself as others become aware of the problem.

Why does a 1,9-oriented manager fail to exercise initiative? The manager may see the problem and feel worry, anguish, or the need to do something, but the real underlying reason is his or her difficulty in starting something or, on the other hand, stopping something.

The other difficulty in exercising initiative is in bringing a discussion to a close when others might misinterpret such action as disinterest or impoliteness—"If I end the conversation, I will be indicating that I am not interested, and I would feel hurt if someone felt that way toward me" or "If I were to do that it might prevent the other person from making some additional point." Finding it difficult to bring matters to a close means that other things tend to pile up. Then, as a 1,9-oriented person falls behind, feelings of pressure or overwork mount. Others become frustrated or disappointed because their expectations are not met. Thus, a contradiction exists because the 1,9-oriented person, ever thoughtful, is unable to see the consequences of this reluctance to terminate a conversation, keep on schedule, and so on.

If the low exercise of initiative exists under the 1,9 orientation, then how does this reconcile with the fact that many managers who lead in this way seem to be quite active and busy? The answer is that 1,9-oriented managers may be quite reluctant to exercise initiative on their own responsibility but very active in responding to initiative originating in others. Others may be bosses, colleagues, or subordinates, and the 1,9-oriented manager may be as eager to respond to a subordinate's request as to a request from the boss. The point is that the responsibility for the initiative is lodged in someone other than the 1,9-oriented manager.

Inquiry

The 1,9 approach is to keep abreast of what is going on, but this is particularly difficult for a 1,9-oriented person because a likely feeling is that there are so many ways for questions to be misunderstood. Sometimes inquiry is thorough; at other times shallow. It is thorough and complete when it is felt the approval gained from the person requesting the information is important. No effort at getting to the facts is too much, particularly when inquiry is from impersonal information sources.

Inquiry is shallow when the 1,9-oriented person's request is based on his or her own interests and responsibilities. This is particularly true when asking for information that might be embarrassing. The risk of embarrassment makes it preferable to hope that the information will be volunteered. When it is not, that's the end of it.

Questions that are characteristic of the 1,9-oriented person are ones that find out what others want, or what may be expected—"When would you like this report? How long and detailed would you like it?" These questions relate to what another person is thinking or desires and are unlikely to bring rejection. When a 1,9-oriented person asks a question that does not have an obvious answer, however, then the person to whom the question is put is likely to react negatively. The answer may be contrary to what the 1,9-oriented person wishes to hear, or the question may force others to acknowledge they don't know the answer or lead to unpleasant admissions. Any of these reactions cause the 1,9-oriented manager to feel uneasy.

The manager is also likely to be a good listener, alert to what others are saying, thinking, and feeling, even though taking what they say at face value.

Any reading done by a 1,9-oriented manager about business-related matters may be thorough or shallow. It is thorough when the topic is positive or the manager expects to be questioned about it. It is likely to be shallow when the content is negative; this may be so even when the person expects to be questioned. For example, some 1,9-oriented managers find it difficult to study information that reveals a competitor's advantage. Thinking about it arouses anxiety. Concentration is difficult. The reading material is put down with the intention of picking it up later, but later never becomes here and now. Even if read, the goal is only to get the gist rather than to examine it thoroughly. The attitude is to learn a little about the situation; not what to do about it.

Advocacy

When a person expresses convictions as to what should or should not be done, others are stimulated to take counterpositions. The resulting discussion may lead to feelings of being misunderstood. An important consequence is that knowledge or convictions about the soundest or best way to handle some problem may not be made known to others. Regardless of the strength of convictions, a 1,9-oriented person is likely to be reluctant to speak up, particularly on controversial issues, and appear unassuming, timid, or shy. Advocacy lacks force and when undertaken it is likely to be tentative, nonspecific, or indirect in order not to have a negative effect on others. A point may be qualified so that attention others pay to it is diminished. "Of course, I'm probably wrong, but could it be that . . . ?" These qualifiers are to preserve good relations and facilitate a friendly interchange. This is why 1,9-oriented people tend to be seen as gullible or undirected. Common descriptions are "He's a 'yes man,'" or "She's too quick to agree." Problems that might have been solved remained unsolved or solutions reached are less than sound.

Decisions

Making decisions can be a pleasure when they are likely to be endorsed. A 1,9-oriented manager sees decisions as opportunities for sharing. When decisions affect several people, group discussion is encouraged in order for them to consider and recommend or make the decision they prefer.

Even though some decisions must be unilateral, extensive consultation may precede them. Delegating is done whenever possible. Not only does this relieve the manager of potentially unpleasant actions, but he or she may even be seen as a good delegator.

Decision making is particularly difficult when the person pressing for the decision is the boss. The best way to stay in the boss's good graces is to do what is wanted and let it be known to subordinates that the decision was made at a "higher" level and that no other options are available.

The immediate boss has to make the decision when the problem falls between the responsibility of someone at a higher level and ones that can be delegated. Then postponing decisions may be preferable to taking unpopular action and the manager cannot be challenged because a decision has not been made. By delay it may become clearer to the manager which alternative is the more favored by those whom it will affect or the situation may develop so that the proper decision becomes obvious or unnecessary. Others may see this as procrastination.

Critique

The tendency is to look on the positive or bright side by making comments that avoid disturbing aspects. Positive reinforcement through compliments or encouragement creates a climate of approval conducive to better working relationships. One justification for shifting away from negatives is the premise that people probably already know their limitations and faults. Calling attention to them only increases frustration.

Negative feedback to others may be given to sidestep personal responsibility. When the need to do so cannot be avoided, the idea is to attribute the thought to someone else: "The boss asked me to tell you that. . . ."

Management Practices

How management practices are carried out shows how 1,9-oriented attitudes influence day-to-day performance.

> *Planning:* "I suggest assignments and convey confidence by saying, 'I'm sure you know how to do this and that all will go well.'"

> *Organizing:* "Subordinates know what to do and how to coordinate. If they need suggestions, I'm ready to listen and offer whatever help I can."

Directing: "I see my subordinates frequently and encourage them to visit me. My door is always open. I get them the things they want or need without their having to ask. That encourages people."

Controlling: "I rarely check on subordinates since they try their best. I place emphasis on congratulating good effort. Our discussions usually end by talking about why we did as well as we did and how we can help things go as smoothly or more so in the future."

Staffing: "Even though it's not possible to please everyone all the time, I try to see to it that subordinates are in the jobs they like best and working with others they enjoy being with."

Management-by-Objectives: "It is a good approach. The aim is to help each subordinate establish goals. Through free and unguided discussions, there might be ways in which the subordinate can increase effort. These self-set and self-managed goals guide everyone's efforts and relieve me of the need to check and control. A subordinate who is self-directed is not likely to have hostile feelings toward the boss."

Performance Appraisal: "Performance appraisals are geared to help people feel and realize that their past efforts are appreciated. These informal chats touch on personal matters and communicate the fact that I am interested in their personal needs and well-being. I treat subordinates with the care and attention needed to help their growth and fulfillment.

While a boss who manages in these ways is not likely to be deeply respected, he or she is most certainly liked and appreciated. The harmonious atmosphere encourages people to be pleasant, friendly, and thoughtful of one another. Productivity may be somewhat lower, but the decisions that favor people are felt to be well worth it.

Consequences

Several consequences arise from 1,9-oriented supervision. These can be viewed from both the corporate and the career point of view of the individual.

Impact on Productivity

Production standards and norms tend to be set at low levels in a 1,9-oriented environment. Because of this, conflicts and pressures that might otherwise be present are infrequent.

Pricing decisions usually favor the customer rather than the company, leading to loyal customers but to reduced profit margins. A decision to deal with a favored supplier may be made rather than undertaking competitive bidding. Unnecessary expenses are absorbed rather than avoided. Absenteeism is likely to be permitted rather than investigating the cause actually behind it, with production maintained by relying on overtime. These loose practices arise in a 1,9-oriented atmosphere and can contribute to lowered productivity and reduced profit margins.

Impact on Creativity

Changes required to implement new methods are considered unsettling and likely to promote differences and disagreement. Task-based tensions are sometimes misinterpreted as interpersonal antagonisms. When such tensions arise, it is preferable to smooth over or yield one's point of view, even though a price is paid in lessened creativity from doing so.

Impact on Satisfaction

Personal reactions range from feeling safe and secure within a warm and friendly atmosphere to feeling smothered, stifled, unchallenged, and wanting to escape from it.

When the 1,9 approach is seen as supportive and helpful, those working in that atmosphere say, "We would not want to change jobs. We enjoy the people we work with and couldn't ask for better conditions." The 1,9-oriented manager remarks, "Many departments here have a high turnover. We don't. I have been with the company thirty-three years, and most of my people have been with me for years. Commitment is high because of the low-key, accepting atmosphere we have been able to create." These people are happy in a sheltering organization.

Other may resist and find little satisfaction in a 1,9 team. These are people who find challenging work rewarding. Unchallenged, frustrations arise because, even though they may be paid well, they may feel they are wasting time and making little or no contribution. They become resentful of the way they are being managed and contemptuous of the apparent lack of interest in organization objectives.

Impact on Career

A country-club atmosphere congenial to the 1,9-oriented manager may prevail because the organization is able to move along in a more or less trouble-free manner, living with its troubles without having to solve them, at least on a short-term basis. The 1,9-oriented manager can look forward to an enjoyable career as long as organization pressures for productivity are not intense. He or she may not advance up the organization, but this is of less concern since ambition is not high.

Recognizing 1,9 Behavior

The following words and phrases characterize a 1,9-oriented manager's actions and indicate how this Grid style is described in everyday language:

- Agreeable
- Appreciative
- Avoids negatives
- Can't say no
- Deferential
- Dislikes disagreement
- Excessively complimentary
- Overly eager to help
- Over trusting
- Remorseful at unintended slights
- Says nice and thoughtful things
- Sensitive, easily hurt
- Supporting and comforting
- Sympathetic and soft
- Thrives on harmony
- Uncontroversial
- Unlikely to probe
- Waits to hear what others think before speaking
- Withholds controversial convictions
- Yields to gain approval

Suggestions for Change

The following are suggestions for change that a 1,9-oriented leader might want to consider.

Motivation

- ☐ Being polite and solicitous of others makes you feel good about yourself but others may see it as overdone. They may feel uneasy when it obscures real issues that need solutions.
- ☐ When a person acts according to high standards and expects the same of others, it is possible to achieve both acceptance and respect from them.

Initiative

- ☐ Don't stop yourself before you start. Instead of discounting an opportunity by thinking "I had better not," replace it with "I should."
- ☐ Take initiative when you ordinarily tend to back off. See if you do not receive increased respect.
- ☐ You may have been overchecking, waiting to get an okay for routine actions. Assess what you can do on your own, and give yourself permission to do it rather than ask for your boss's okay.

Inquiry

- ☐ Increase your preparation before attending meetings. This can help you feel more self-assured when you advocate a point of view.
- ☐ Strengthen inquiry by asking questions that invite explanations of "why" and "why not." Others usually are ready to contribute what they know.

Advocacy

- ☐ Rehearse your own convictions in a way that makes them clearly understood and then express them.
- ☐ Be among the first to speak when opinions are being presented. Don't wait to see what others have to say before deciding they might not like your opinion.
- ☐ Let people know where you stand by saying, "I think. . . ."
- ☐ Be as specific as possible regarding what you advocate: not "I think the B alternative is wrong," but "I think the B alternative is a limited possibility because it omits the following. . . ."
- ☐ If you have a tendency to get wordy when you speak, cut to the heart of the issue.

Conflict

- ☐ Assume that conflict is inevitable. Differences can be examined without creating tensions or risking personal rejection.
- ☐ Realize that smoothing over a difference doesn't solve it but does cause others to see you as weak.
- ☐ If others disagree with you, restate your position and ask them to explain their reservations.

Decisions

- ☐ Do not postpone embarrassing or unpleasant decisions. The problems are as likely to increase as to decrease if they are put off until later.
- ☐ Don't consult others about decisions if they see you as wasting their time or see no reason to be involved.

Critique

- ☐ Realize that feedback does not have to be painful. Describe what you observe others doing and what you believe the consequences to be.
- ☐ Others want to be helpful when you seek feedback from them. They will tell you as much as you want to know.
- ☐ Realize that feedback can be a two-way street and when problems arise others may expect you to let them know how things look to you.
- ☐ Point out barriers to good performance. Correcting negative situations is as important as reinforcing positive ones.

1,9 Orientation Summary

"I initiate actions that help and support others. I look for facts, beliefs, and positions that suggest all is well. For the sake of harmony, I am not inclined to challenge others. I embrace opinions, attitudes, and ideas of others even though I have reservations. I avoid generating conflict, but when it appears I try to soothe feelings to keep people together. I search for decisions that maintain good relations and I encourage others to make decisions when possible. I encourage and praise when something positive happens, but avoid giving negative feedback."

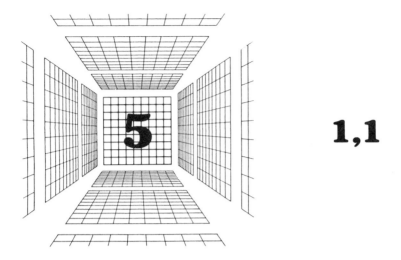

1,1

The 1,1 leadership pattern is located in the lower left corner of the Grid. The leader experiences little or no contradiction between production requirements and needs of people since concern for both is low. Being more or less "out of it" while remaining "in" the organization, the leader expects little and little is given.

Motivations

Though uninvolved and withdrawn, the 1,1-oriented person's positive motivation is to stay in the organization by going through the motions of being a manager. This means doing the minimum necessary, or even a little bit more in order to build seniority, but with little regard for making a contribution that benefits the organization.

On the negative side, the motivation is to "hold on" and avoid becoming the center of attention. Although bored, drifting, and listless, a 1,1-oriented person hides these feelings from others. By being visible yet inconspicuous, it is possible to avoid being controversial, having enemies, or getting fired. Appearing somewhat preoccupied tends to keep others at a distance and aids in maintaining a bystander position. The degree to which one remains unobtrusive and nonresponsive is governed by the minimum that others are prepared to tolerate without a disturbance.

Maintaining this low-key and colorless presence is the key to not being resented by others because of noncommitment. Thus a 1,1-oriented "leader" occupies the position only superficially. The nonchalant attitude leads to the motto, "See no evil, speak no evil, and hear no evil, and you are protected by not being noticed." He or she passes through the organization, leaving no permanent mark. But the organization may have left its mark by "pushing" or letting the manager drift from some other Grid style into the 1,1 corner, merely waiting for retirement.

Managing Conflict

By holding the title of boss, but not acting like one, 1,1-oriented managers remain relatively uninvolved in conflict. This is the "ostrich dynamic," keeping one's head buried to avoid problems. Disagreeable situations are noticed but ignored and frequently disappear for lack of attention. However, situations of potential conflict do arise from time to time and these must be faced in some way.

Preventing Conflict

Receding into the Background. There may be differences between the observable and unobservable behavior of a 1,1-oriented manager. Observable behavior conforms to the requirements of the job description and affords protection by making the manager unnoticeable. This means being on time if on-time performance is important, displaying an unperturbed, studious attitude, avoiding leaving early, fitting a vacation to the convenience of others, not taking sick leave when possible, and filling out required reports promptly. Occasional expressions of mild interest divert attention from the apathy the manager feels. These give the appearance of involvement in the deeper objectives of the organization so that the manager does not appear to be a loner.

Actual behavior is likely to be different when it is not observed by others or subject to their review, and likely reflects the depth of resignation and indifference. One way to stay out of the line of fire is always to return a call but not to place one unless explicitly requested to do so. The memo that does not demand a response is not answered.

When participation is expected, the tactic is to be seen but not to be active. When present in a group, a 1,1-oriented manager seldom participates spontaneously. Comments are made from time to time, but nothing is said to reveal thoughts (or lack of them) regarding what is being discussed. "Could be," "Possibly," "I guess so," acknowledge some point with little or no commitment intended or conveyed. Though they may not quite realize it, others have little or no idea about what is or is not important to the 1,1-oriented leader. This nondemonstrative way of "participation" is acceptable when others either fail to notice it, interpret it as thoughtful attention to what is being discussed, or believe that a passive acknowledgment means implicit agreement.

Message Passing. This is another approach that avoids personal involvement. Orders are moved down the line from above so as not to get caught "holding the bag." Also, messages from below that need to go up are faithfully repeated to the boss to ensure that the 1,1-oriented manager is not recognized as a missing link in the communication chain. The procedure is neither to add to nor to take away from what others have said. By repeating, one passes the message without becoming entangled in interpreting the contents.

The flavor of the 1,1 orientation is seen in the following example. John has just returned from a weekly staff meeting where changes in procedures and policies were discussed and where members were to initiate appropriate changes within their own areas of responsibility. John's behavior appeared commendable in the meeting itself; he had listened and taken notes, both indicators of interest to his own boss.

John calls his five subordinates to his office and proceeds to carefully read the notes and conclusions so that no one can say later that he has not "communicated." He files his dated notes in his desk drawer after this recitation.

Without looking up, he says, "I'm going to the plant. Who has the company car keys?" As he turns to leave, a subordinate asks how and when a particular change that was reported is to be effected.

"They didn't comment further on that," is the manager's reply, "I may hear more next week."

Another raises a question about fifteen large boxes of materials in the hallway.

"They said to order them. They didn't say what to do with them when they got here. I mentioned they'd arrived. Let 'em sit." With that he departs.

This incident describes the 1,1 approach. The "facts" as this manager had heard them from above were carried to his subordinates. When accountability is unavoidable, he is able to report, "I told them what to do. If they haven't done it, it's because they didn't listen. It's not my problem." When a subordinate does something wrong, he is likely to say, "Oh! *They* are always causing trouble, but what can I do?" Responsibility is impersonal and calls for taking no action.

Handling Conflict When It Appears

Maintaining Neutrality. When conflict arises, there are many ways of appearing to respond without presenting one's views. This is maintaining neutrality in order to be safe.

A grunt is the best reply of all. "Hmm" means more or less "Okay, so what, it's not an issue with me." If a 1,1-oriented manager should come straight out with, "It's not an issue with me . . ." it might be taken as an affront, but "hmm" is a deadender. It leaves the other person with no certain way to respond, only to think "Might as well drop it."

There is an infinite variety of neutral answers when asked what other people think or do: "I'm not a mind reader . . . I haven't heard . . . I don't know . . . I wasn't there." Equally adept answers are provided when pressed further: "It's up to you . . . Whatever you say . . . It's your problem, not mine . . . I'm no expert." This is communication that evades controversy. When challenged, the manager might respond with, "You never asked."

The 1,1-oriented manager gives up easily in an argument, yet avoids the appearance of backing off. Neutrality is maintained by responding to disagreement with "Fine, that's your opinion and you're entitled to it."

When directly asked, the 1,1-oriented person answers in vague, abstract, and general terms that reveal little or nothing. A statement such as, "It takes all sorts . . . I suppose," is one way to pass on a contentious point and leave no enemies. While some feel mollified by having been answered, the answer itself has not obligated the manager to any particular course of action. Saluting is preferable whenever the price of agreeing is less than the expense of resisting. The standard salute is, "Whatever . . . " There is apparent agreement without explicit commitment.

When someone complains about something, the 1,1-oriented manager either ignores it or implies that the displeasure has been noted. Issues are likely to be downplayed and delayed with, "It'll probably work itself out." The "it" becomes, "Out of sight, out of mind." The issue is unlikely to reappear.

The way to deal with a disturbing memo is to file it and "forget" where it is filed, or have a subordinate answer it. To a query about some past memo, the answer is, "We will have to research that one and it will take time."

A 1,1-oriented manager cannot help but observe from time to time that others are working at cross-purposes. The approach is to ignore them and keep out of the way unless the conflict is severe enough to pose a threat to his or her future. The manager shrugs and hopes that subordinates will not be called to account.

Local option. Even though the 1,1-oriented manager might see the benefits from sorting out disagreements, hopelessness of trying to do so is also considered. The manager can choose local options in order to permit actions to be taken, but not be personally responsible for them by saying in an even-tempered way, "Look, each of you regional managers faces a different and unique set of circumstances. There probably is a solution for each different location. Take whatever action you see fit on a local basis." Disregard of similarities from one plant to another may result in duplication of effort, but it doesn't really matter.

Double-talk. This tactic is useful when two points of view exist, each supported by an important faction, and the manager is called on to express a point of view. Wishing to offend no one and speaking to both sides without taking a position, a response is given: "Alternative A may be best for the reasons that have been given, but on the other hand, there are strong points on the side of alternative B." "It's possible to do X but it's also possible to do Y." Each side in the controversy, furthermore, feels the manager understands and has a sympathetic appreciation for the point of view expressed. The manager can go either way once a final course of action falls in place.

Mental Walkout. One way to live with conflicts is to free oneself of the burden by mentally walking out on them. If others press for solutions, the manager defers, saying, "Everything will work out in a few days . . ." and the few days turn into weeks.

These and other ways of dampening resistance allow the 1,1-oriented manager to live with conflict and keep its intensity low.

Behavioral Elements

Initiative

A 1,1-oriented leader is apathetic and unlikely to develop, much less initiate, new ideas. The intent is to stand pat and let things run their course. Any action taken is passive and unassertive, mainly to avoid being conspicuous. For example, the manager will usually either delegate when asked to do something or try to get out of the situation.

When avoidance of action doesn't work, a 1,1-oriented manager still tries to get the problem taken by someone else. For example, if a complaint is filed by a customer, the 1,1-oriented manager takes several actions. One is to acknowledge receipt. Another is to take it back and to find out how the boss wants it handled. Alternatively, it can be taken to a subordinate with instructions, "Look into it and either answer it directly or offer a recommendation for disposing of it."

Whenever a 1,1-oriented manager is responsible for several facilities, visits to various locations are necessary. The manager's rationale for inaction is, "I can't get to them all, so if I visited some they would feel more important and the others would feel ignored. So it's wiser not to visit any plant."

Inquiry

Here, the attitude is, "The less I know about it the better. I can always plead ignorance." It is better to stay in a shell and look neither to the left nor right.

That attitude may not be acceptable to others, however, and therefore inquiry is carried out, even though on a minimum "need to know" basis. A 1,1-oriented manager wants to know in order to avoid ignorance and potential problems regarding matters that should be known about. Under these circumstances, the manager risks being seen as retiring or less well-informed than desirable. When asked a question that can't be answered, the manager does not admit it, but responds "I'll find out." In other words, this reaction avoids the criticism that would come from saying "I don't know" and relieves tensions the other person might feel.

In summary, a 1,1-oriented manager is rarely well enough informed to be able to respond effectively. If it becomes necessary to deal with an immediate problem, the actions taken are likely to be perfunctory since the manager's knowledge of the issue is so limited.

Advocacy

The 1,1-oriented manager is noncommital and reticent, avoiding spontaneous comments when possible. The private attitude of the manager might be something like this: "Since subordinates weigh your words, they should not be spoken without the most careful and painstaking thought. They weigh each word to discover its meaning and any possible hidden implications. To avoid adverse consequences, it is better to keep counsel with yourself or to speak only when it is essential to let others know you are not raising objections."

If someone asks, "What's new?" the answer is "Nothing," or "Not much." If the question is, "How are things going?" the answer is "Okay." Further discussion is not encouraged by this kind of answer, yet there is nothing negative about a nice, bland "okay," particularly when it is not followed up with, "How are things with you?" Asking might expose a problem and commenting on it might start an argument. Then a person is expected to stand behind a conviction. Thus, the 1,1-oriented person is more likely to drift along, subscribing to the opinions of others.

When required, convictions can be expressed in terms that do not hold the manager to a fixed point of view. On close examination, phrases such as "perhaps," "maybe," "I'm not sure, but," "I guess you're right," "I'm not too certain about . . . " proliferate and are statements that provide the opportunity to go either way if forced to take a position. The same is true with phrases like "That's not a bad idea," and "I kind of like that." Both of these enigmatic statements appear to be endorsing the position of another person and yet one can always say later, "I didn't say I really liked it," or "I didn't say it was a good idea."

Decisions

A typical 1,1-oriented remark is, "I don't make decisions, I only work here." It communicates a sense of withdrawal from responsibility. Many times problems take care of themselves if decisions can be postponed or delayed. The approach is to patiently let circumstances dictate the decisions. Once a decision is made or forced by circumstances, it enters the realm of being a *fait accompli*. In modern jargon it's "history" and not subject to further deliberation whether it was right or wrong, good or bad, sound or unsound.

A 1,1-oriented manager defers rather than decides. The idea is to leave well enough alone. One way is to cast the issue into the future to avoid dealing with it now. "It would be useless to try to answer that question in advance. I want to decide each issue when it arises on its merits," or "I'll be able to get to that tomorrow or the next day," or suggest "More time is needed; I'll think about it." It may be a real and necessary effort that someone is making to anticipate a future problem and how to handle it, but the 1,1-oriented leader can leave it untouched by deferring or by asking a question that deflects the problem to someone else, such as, "What does the procedure manual say about this?"

"Good delegation" is considered a virtue. The 1,1-oriented manager can then act as a figurehead. It is not delegation but abdication when decisions are based on the other person's likes and wishes. The rationalization is, "Giving subordinates problems helps them grow," and it can work perfectly when tasks are not too difficult or when subordinates are competent.

The boss may subscribe to "teamwork" when others expect it. The group is brought together and told, "Here's a problem for you to thrash through and decide. I don't want to influence you so I'll listen." The group may fall apart without sufficient leadership but, on the other hand, if a member of the group provides leadership it may be possible to reach quality decisions. The manager accepts them as self-evident and it may even appear to his or her own boss that a good job is being done.

An example of the 1,1 orientation to delegation and teamwork is found in the following self-portrayal of Beth, a manager of a large management information system. "Department meetings are held at ten-thirty on Tuesdays and Fridays. These are informal. Members are asked if they have problems to bring up. There are rarely any differences of opinion. They should not disagree among themselves as their duty is not to argue or to advise each other but to advise and recommend to me. After discussion, I announce the decision. I rarely fail to accept their recommendations."

While Beth may extol the virtues of teamwork and delegation, she in fact has effectively removed herself from responsibility by abdication and has eliminated any real possibility of teamwork.

Critique

It is unlikely that the 1,1-oriented manager engages in much introspection because his or her mind is not on the task to be done. As a result, feedback to others is unlikely. This behavior can be taken by subordinates to mean that they are allowed to do what they want and therefore actions they take are endorsed and agreed to by the manager. If the manager offers feedback to a question, it is vague and shallow.

Management Practices

A 1,1-oriented manager assigns subordinates whatever tasks must be done and gives them free reign in completing them. The flavor of this abdication is shown in the following.

Planning: "I give broad assignments though I avoid specifics when possible. Subordinates are responsible for themselves."

Organizing: "Subordinates carry out assignments since they know their own jobs and capabilities better than anyone else. I expect them to coordinate with one another."

Directing: "I carry the word from those above to those below. I pass the message and with as little embellishment or interpretation as possible."

Controlling: "I make the rounds, but I take little on-the-spot action if I can avoid it. They like it that way; I do, too."

Staffing: "I take whomever they give me."

Management-by-Objectives: "My boss decides my goals. I prefer that subordinates set their own goals; I avoid interfering because they need to learn to think ahead from their own perspectives."

Performance Appraisal: "I expect people will do whatever is necessary and will learn from their own mistakes. However, I go through a perfunctory performance appraisal if required, rating subordinates more or less the same."

Consequences

The consequences resulting from the 1,1 style of managing include the following.

Impact on Productivity

How is it possible for an organization to persist in ignoring its "deadwood?" It is common in organizations that guarantee job security after a few years so that any manager is safe until retirement. If low productivity exists, it is tolerated or ignored. For example, a manager, once the president of a subsidiary company, was promoted to the legal department in headquarters. The reason was that legal issues facing the corporation had become more complex, and an executive with legal background and broad business experience had become a necessity. This executive was seldom seen in the headquarters for twelve years before his retirement. He delegated technical problems to subordinates, studied their conclusions, and forwarded their studies as appropriate, often sending subordinates to meetings about implications of their recommendations or conclusions. He quietly came and went, unnoticed, and traveled quite a lot. His secretary, who rarely did typing except for cover letters, saw him infrequently but knew where he was but not the reason why. Incoming and outgoing correspondence and calls were few in the beginning and continued to shrink as executives who needed legal assistance eventually contacted his juniors directly. His attendance at meetings was regular but more as a listener than as a participant. He had shelved himself, and the organization carried his dead weight for years without much notice of it.

A 1,1-oriented individual usually rationalizes nonproductivity by blaming something or someone else. For example, "Government has become so huge that nothing can be done about it." "The rapidly advancing technology can be blamed for bringing about a dehumanizing way of life," adding, "I want nothing to do with it." "The money-crazed corporation where profit is the sole aim," or "The vicious, competitive rat race for promotions that chews up people," or "The university, which fails to provide education pertinent to today's requirements"—all may be complaints. These rationalizations serve to justify indifference, passivity, and a "can't do" spirit. They make it unnecessary for the manager to admit uninvolvement and the contentment to treadmill through life as an onlooker.

Inherent in the 1,1 approach is "inertia." To the degree that the 1,1 style is present throughout an organization culture, the organization performance drifts toward less and less. Necessary actions are not taken and the long-term outcome is failure.

Impact on Creativity

It is unrealistic to expect creativity from a leader with a 1,1 orientation. The reason is that creativity demands involvement and commitment. It rests on thoroughness and inquiry and it calls for conviction and advocacy in pursuing a possibility to its limits. These are deficient.

Impact on Satisfaction

A person with a 1,1 managerial orientation is unlikely to feel gratified or disheartened with his or her situation. There is little or no basis for experiencing either, thus neither satisfaction nor dissatisfaction is likely to be strong.

Impact on Career

Research has consistently shown that 1,1-oriented managers have the slowest rate of advancement in organizations where managers with other Grid styles are present. When promotion is based on a straight seniority system 1,1-oriented managers do "fail" upwards.

Some managers whose careers are characterized by some other dominant Grid style may later shift into the 1,1 orientation. They can be heard described as, "He had a brilliant career and made important contributions for many years. Now no one wants to be harsh. Anyway, he has only a few more years to go." Or, they might say, "She has no enemies and is not doing anyone much harm. We can live with it a little while longer." Months may turn into years. Or, "We'd have to find someone else to fill that slot and it's pretty dull business. Let's let it go at that."

Origins of a 1,1 Orientation

A dominant 1,1 orientation does not always originate at an early point in life. Its origins may be in the adult years and related to the work situation itself.

Consider John, who does well in elementary school, high school, and in the first years of college. Then he becomes an academic vagabond for the next two or three years. People say, "He will never amount to anything." Understanding a 1,1 orientation, however, we can appreciate that something may have happened in his sophomore year that caused him to cease striving. For a period of time he has been thrown from a dominant 9,9, 9,1, 5,5, or 1,9 style into a 1,1 orientation.

Time passes and he returns to college, picks up where he left off, graduates with flying colors, and enters a career where he does well. How can we understand this interruption? There are several possible reasons. One is that during the vagabond period John was probably avoiding a threat to his image of self. Also, greater maturity provided the capacity for understanding and insight that permitted him to proceed with his career without facing the same threat. He is now able to grasp quickly what, as a sophomore, he had been unable to comprehend. Values associated with his sense of personal adequacy, which existed at an earlier time, may have shifted so that now the same performance has a different meaning. He can now engage in the activity without feeling undue risk. His dominant orientation has shifted again, either back to the original style or to some other, but in either event, he has shifted away from the dominant 1,1 approach.

Another example occurs when managers get in over their heads. Wayne has had an outstanding record, resulting in several promotions. Now responsible for a section or a unit, his quality of supervision is visible to everyone. Personal competence to operate with initiative is exposed, possibly for the first time. At this point he becomes immobilized, unable to move. Formerly operating under precise instructions as a subordinate, Wayne was acting in behalf of someone else rather than under personal motivation and initiative. Now the risk of being incompetent is too much to deal with and he is unable to perform productively.

Because of unusual qualifications or academic or technical preparation, a manager may be assigned as an assistant to a corporation president or some other senior executive. Talent in carrying out assignments is conspicuous. Performance draws attention, and an important line appointment results: the young manager arrives at a high position years before peers. Things go well during the period while learning the ropes is in progress; that is, while the manager still is *not* personally responsible for the line performance. The more the manager comes to feel greater personal responsibility for decisions and results, the less he or she is able to initiate. Decisions are postponed until "further studies are completed." When completed, additional unanswered questions that must be explored remain. Decisions are never put to the test.

Still another example is Carol who was highly committed but has now withdrawn and is presently managing according to 1,1-oriented assumptions: the case of a backup style becoming dominant. Carol had a dominant 9,1 style and rather than face defeat and failure, withdrew from the fight, rationalizing that her contributions were not appreciated. It is a case of a person performing quite well up to some age such as forty, forty-five or so, then "burn out," with interest lost in a job that is empty and no longer challenging.

The actual causes of burnout are usually quite varied. During the early years of successful performance dreams of control, mastery, and domination were far removed from what was achieved in day-by-day performance. The years have gone by, and now, the middle level manager faces middle age, never to be president. How can one avoid recognizing that performance has been inferior to aspirations? The 1,1 approach is to back off and rationalize, "The challenge has gone out of the job . . . I've lost interest . . . I want to spend more time with my family." Dominant style has receded, and a 1,1 orientation has replaced it.

Still another explanation of how a 1,1 backup orientation may become dominant concerns a leader in some other orientation. Withdrawal can result when a person can neither fight back nor afford to leave and seek employment elsewhere. The 1,1 corner is a harbor that protects one from having to sail against unfavorable winds.

The 1,1-oriented manager maintains organizational membership and continuity for personal advantages yet withdraws from active participation. In doing so, however, the cast and form of acceptable behavior is maintained. There is a vacuum from within, but exterior trappings remain as they were. The physical and functional appearances that put behavior into conformance with that of many others is present. The organization becomes the means for maintaining a socially acceptable role of citizen by discharging the very minimum of requirements. Position, status, and pay come from within the organization with minimum effort given in exchange.

Recognizing 1,1 Behavior

There are many words and phrases that are commonly used in describing 1,1-oriented behavior. The phrases below depict in everyday language this style of leading.

- Apathetic
- Bystander
- Defers
- Delays
- Disclaims responsibility
- Feedback doesn't register
- Gives up easily
- Hands-offish
- Inconspicuous
- Indifferent
- Keeps out of the way
- Lets things run their course
- Likely to miss new things that need to be done
- Neglects task responsibilities
- Neutral
- Noncommital
- Noncontributor
- "Putting in time"
- Resigned
- Stays out of the line of fire
- Volunteers few opinions
- Waits for others to take action
- Weak follow-through
- Withdrawn

Suggestions for Change

The following are suggestions for change that a 1,1-oriented person might consider.

Motivation

☐ A first step might be to imagine the kinds of changes that would permit you to snap out of the 1,1 orientation.

☐ If you find yourself saying, "Why bother, it doesn't matter . . . ," reassess your degree of uninvolvement or indifference. Is this an enjoyable way to spend eight hours a day or would you find greater satisfaction from strengthened commitment?

☐ You might examine the consequences of being fired. It is always possible that a 1,1-oriented leader is riding for a fall and you may not have focused on this possibility. Thinking it through may be enough to reactivate doing a better job of leading.

☐ Many who have slipped into the 1,1 corner or who have gotten there via burnout have discovered they do not like what they see once such a self-diagnosis has been made. The contrast between what they admit to be true and what they wish to think about themselves is sufficient for rearousing interest and involvement.

Initiative

☐ It is safe to say your subordinates are aware of your uninvolvement. It is also likely true that they will encourage you once they see your interest increase. You may already see ways to take actions since you probably possess considerable skill in exercising initiative when you are motivated. It's more a matter of will than skill.

☐ You might talk with your boss. Ask for more assignments.

Inquiry

☐ Asking more questions of subordinates is invaluable as a step in rebuilding your knowledge base.

☐ Pick up pertinent literature, articles, new reports, and so on. See what they have to say. Use them as a background for further inquiry with subordinates.

Advocacy

☐ Answer questions straightforwardly.

☐ If asked questions on topics you haven't thought about for some time, give the questioner your pledge to investigate the answer. Set a time when you will get back on it and keep that schedule.

☐ Take positions so that others know where you stand.

Conflict

☐ Stop taking mental walkouts when people disagree. Explore and resolve your differences. This is a most important step toward establishing a stronger basis of teamwork.

☐ Simply avoiding disagreement is less rewarding than reaching agreement. Others are usually ready to go more than halfway to find a mutually acceptable basis of agreement.

☐ Others may disagree because you have not stated your case clearly. Make your convictions known so others understand your position and can react accordingly.

Decisions

☐ You might answer the question before you hand a project over to someone: "What can I do to help get this project completed in a successful way?"

☐ You may see how to involve several subordinates in solving complex problems. Coordination by you will strengthen the practice of sound teamwork.

Critique

☐ Once you have started doing things on your own initiative, this may be the time to get feedback. Ask subordinates how you are doing. Give them straightforward readings on how you see productivity, creativity, and so on. Overall productivity may be increased by working together as a more closely knit team.

1,1 Orientation Summary

"I put out enough to get by. I go along with facts, beliefs, and positions given to me. I keep my own counsel but respond when asked. I avoid taking sides by not revealing my opinions, attitudes, and ideas. I remain neutral or seek to stay out of conflict. I let others make decisions or come to terms with whatever happens. I avoid giving critique."

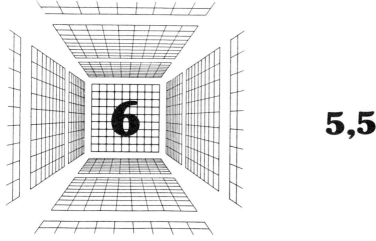

6

5,5

The 5,5 orientation is represented in the middle of the Grid where intermediate concern for production, *5,* is linked with moderate concern for people, *5.* A contradiction between production and people needs is also presumed by this Grid style; that is, the 5,5 solution to the production-people dilemma is to trade off, to give up half of one in order to get the other half. The manager with a 5,5 orientation assumes that people needs are realistic but that *some* effort is expected and must be exerted. Also, by reducing the push for production to a moderate level and giving some consideration to attitudes and feelings, people accept the situation and are more or less "satisfied." The underlying assumption is that extreme positions promote conflict and should be avoided. Steady progress comes from compromise and a willingness to yield some advantages in order to gain others. The result is that a 5,5-oriented manager is unlikely to seek the best position for either production or people, but to find an equilibrium that is in between both.

Motivations

The positive motivation of the 5,5-oriented manager is to make progress within the system in order to belong and be a member in good standing. "I want to look good, to be 'in' with my colleagues." Being popular means putting together a package of qualities that are sought in the management market, including whatever is appropriate in dress, topics of conversation, being up on the latest in what's new in management techniques, being informed about the latest popular management books, and technical jargon related to the work itself. In order to be affable and companionable, he or she strives to become an interesting conversationalist in order to make many friends. The 5,5-oriented manager might be described as sociable, outgoing, a good mixer, and a glad-hander.

A manager who is motivated to be "in" tends to keep things on a superficial level and takes cues from the actions of others. Prevailing opinions become personal opinions. What others reject is rejected. The inclination is to embrace the traditions, precedents, and practices of the organization in a non-critical manner because "that's the corporate way" or "that's how things are done around here." The motivational motto is, "If I think, look, and act like everyone else, but a little more so, I will be a manager in good standing." People with a 5,5 orientation tend to identify with wealth and power or with those who have it, and try to gain prestige by association.

The negative motivation is to avoid being separated from the main-stream or becoming a target of ridicule. When the 5,5-oriented manager is unsuccessful and feels unpopular, out of step, and isolated from others, the experience may range from embarassment to shame. Being out of step can lead to ostracism, loss of friendship, jeopardizing one's group status, and ultimately anxiety. Typically this anxiety can build up and become constant. A key indicator of such anxiety is being uncertain which way to turn, and this is why what others think is so important to a 5,5-oriented manager.

Managing Conflict

The 5,5 approach is based on an internal logic that says, "No person or movement has ever had its exclusive way. Rather, skill is needed to adjust to the inevitable conflicts that occur in daily management."

Preventing Conflict

How has it been done in the past? Conflict related to independent judgment is avoided by carefully adhering to established routine and thereby feeling safe and secure. A 5,5-oriented manager often venerates traditions, long-established practices, or unwritten procedures. These criteria, which are embedded within the status quo, are taken for granted. As long as performance conforms to them, everything is regarded as moving in an appropriate manner. When history can be relied on, no personal decisions have to be made. When traditions are unavailable, a precedent may serve as guidance. The 5,5-oriented manager then assumes a "better to be safe than sorry" approach, thus appearing to others to be anything but a careless risk-taker.

Organization Protocol. Diplomacy and protocol are used to prevent conflict by structuring the relationships of people according to pre-set conventions. Protocol tells people what to do when they are uncertain about what is appropriate and sound. This relieves uncertainty and avoids embarassment at doing something others may criticize. These points of protocol have much to do with maintaining or enhancing status within the hierarchy. Thus self-expression and spontaneity are curbed by organization conventions that honor status, hierarchy, and seniority.

Rule-Making. A rule establishes what is regarded as acceptable or desired behavior. Rules reduce the necessity for people to act at their individual discretion; therefore, disagreements are likely to be diminished when everyone behaves consistently with them.

Rules also help relieve existing conflicts by bringing unacceptable behavior to the attention of those "nonconformists" who might resent being corrected by the boss. A 5,5-oriented manager can post rules on the bulletin board or write "To whom it may concern" memos about them in order to inform everyone of what is authorized without singling out anyone. These methods may also serve to bring colleague pressure to bear on violators to toe the line.

Making rules or emphasizing existing ones reduces the likelihood of person-to-person conflict; however, rules also contain the roots of bureaucracy. When relied on as a substitute for direct management, enough rules can be produced to cover everything. Once made, rules tend to take on a life of their own over time, and their excessive propagation can stifle initiative, which is important to achieving organization results.

Avoiding a Public Stand. Since taking a stand can put one at odds with others, a 5,5-oriented approach is to discover in advance whether disagreements with a position are likely to be encountered. If a position will spark disagreement, it can be modified or abandoned. This can be done by pulling punches, equivocating, or approaching issues in oblique ways. Task forces and pilot projects also can be motivated by the desire not to be linked to controversial positions.

Trial balloons ascend when a 5,5-oriented manager cannot gauge what others expect and yet must act or take a position. An unpopular position risks resistance, so signals are put out, anonymously if possible, to see how people might react to some decision or action. The skill of a 5,5-oriented manager lies in being able to float the balloon without holding the string that might "tie" him or her to a potentially unpopular decision.

Deemphasizing differences and emphasizing similarities are characteristic of the 5,5 orientation when agreement is essential to action, because they reduce the need to confront underlying disagreements that might provoke conflict. The opposite is true when agreement is not needed and one's membership status is not in question. Then the 5,5-oriented manager is likely to appeal to each person's unique qualities, playing down underlying similarities and emphasizing surface differences, such as distinctiveness of thinking and originality. Nothing is lost and much is gained by letting subordinates know that, "We don't regiment people around here. We're a democracy."

Another similar tactic is seen when an issue arises that involves the vested interest of several people. The 5,5 approach is to avoid having a meeting until the issues can be discussed with each person on a one-on-one basis. Once several have expressed themselves, the manager knows whether a basis of agreement exists or disagreement will be provoked if the topic is brought up in public. If agreement exists, it can be brought up as an agenda item in a future meeting. If not, the issue can be dropped or discussions can be continued on a one-to-one basis until points of contention can be ironed out.

Not only can this sequence be time-consuming because the same discussion has to be repeated with several people, but the creative thinking that the clash of ideas can stimulate in open discussion has no chance to occur. The advantage is that problems do get solved, if not in the soundest, speediest, or most creative way, but at least in ways acceptable to those who have a vested interest in the outcome.

Handling Conflict When It Appears

It is seldom wise to confront conflict directly because when a disagreement becomes polarized, someone wins and someone loses. The loser then becomes a potential enemy when the next disagreement arises. So when possible, the 5,5-oriented manager prefers to back off and let tensions in the situation cool.

Compromise. When a seemingly unresolvable problem arises, several people are asked to contribute their ideas and come up with an answer. The trouble starts when a definitive decision is needed and one suggestion must be chosen over the others. The 5,5-oriented manager's approach then is to take some part of everyone's ideas and come up with a halfway solution. It may not be perfect, but it sells. This kind of accommodation leads to progress when each side gives something to get something. The final position may not meet the full requirements of anyone, but it does provide a middle position that people with different views can accept in preference to continuing to fight.

There are some situations in which the middle ground is the soundest solution, but a 5,5 orientation is not aimed at this position because it is the best one. Rather, the 5,5 motivation and effort to find the middle ground will likely leave the reservations and doubts that led to the initial differences.

The true goal of managerial competence is to achieve the best result in terms of production through people. The best is rarely defined by something that is in the middle, intermediate, or represents a splitting of differences between divergent points of view.

A distinction is sometimes drawn between compromise when it relates to matters of principle and compromise when it relates to situations of applied decision making. The view is that compromising on operational matters reflects reasonableness. This distinction may be a useful one, but it is clear that principles undergird practices and that managerial practices derive their validity from principles. Therefore, it is "easy" to compromise on matters of operational practice by simply not considering the underlying principles that may be violated. This is known as being adaptable and tolerant of other positions.

Sometimes, what the manager's boss wants and what subordinates would be willing to go along with are two different things, and the solution cannot be had by opting for one or the other. Because of the protocol of hierarchy that says you don't bring three levels together, the intermediate becomes a go-between manager, running between the higher level boss and subordinates, testing a course of action, first from one side, then from the other. This allows a position to finally emerge through a series of accommodations that is more or less acceptable to everyone: a middle ground solution rather than one that is objectively "best."

Separating Those in Disagreement. When two subordinates are in conflict, a 5,5-oriented boss may prefer to talk with each one separately to find points on which the two subordinates can both agree. This is likely to result in finding some basis of agreement that can be lived with. Unfortunately, subordinates usually do not learn to come to terms with one another and future disagreements are likely to be handled in the same time-consuming manner.

Physically separating persons who are antagonistic to one another is another 5,5 tactic. The splitting strategy may be no more than suggesting that subordinates move their desks to opposite sides of the room if they are in a large work area. This reduces the tensions between them because they are not close enough to fight. Thus the subordinates are helped and, at least on the surface, the whole situation appears more congenial.

Splitting may also take more subtle forms such as "taking turns," agreeing in advance on agenda from which one may not depart, using mechanical rules and time limits to ensure orderly procedure, and so on.

Another way to separate people is to arrange a transfer; an assignment in another location "solves" the problem. Redrawing the organization chart is still another separation tactic. Reporting lines are redrawn so that two disagreeing parties no longer report to the same boss.

These approaches reduce tensions but fail to solve the problem that was causing the conflict in the first place.

When Conflict Remains

A 5,5-oriented manager may have several ways of reacting to conflicts that persist, and although any of them may calm the situation on the surface, the disagreements remain.

Accepting Impasse. A 5,5 practice for living with disagreement is expressed in the idea "we agree to disagree." This says that since skills of conflict solving do not exist, it is easier to avoid areas of disagreement than to try to find the reasons for them and relieve underlying causes. Having expressed one's position and found it unacceptable to others, the "agree to disagree" maxim provides a rationalization for inaction.

Distancing. When conflict remains unsolved, tensions can be avoided by increasing the distance between oneself and others. This is done by avoiding the other person directly or by discussing only topics that do not provoke disagreement.

Compartmentalization. An example of this is seeing production as one thing and quality as another. Production is measured in units and is the responsibility of the line; quality is measured in terms of errors and is the responsibility of inspectors. Thus, tensions between the two different aspects of a product are dealt with by splitting the responsibility for the various facets.

Solving production problems is regarded as a line manager's job. Solving personnel problems is assigned to the human resources department. Planning involves a different set of skills; execution another. Therefore they are assigned to different departments.

The front line of supervision frequently is viewed as the dividing line between managers and employees. A 5,5-oriented supervisor said, "My job is to ride the fence between management and the work force," not seeing the desirability of eliminating the concept of "fence."

Compartmentalization is sometimes justified by the inherent complexity in the whole activity. Too often it is arbitrary, providing a convenient rather than a sound way of relieving differences or reducing tensions.

Behavioral Elements

It is easy to grasp the 5,5-oriented manager's approach as revealed in the following behavioral elements when it is understood that the motivation is to be popular on the one hand and to avoid embarassment on the other.

Initiative

The status quo situation defines the arena of action. The objective is to make operations within it work in an acceptable and orderly manner. Effort is maintained at a steady pace. The exercise of initiative is limited; novel or experimental approaches are seen as untried and risky. Creative ideas often lead to remarks such as, "Better not," "Not me," "A word of caution . . . ," "A little too radical . . . ," "I like it myself, but . . . ," "We tried something like that once . . . ," "It's just not us . . . ," "I wish it were that easy . . . ." If others persist, the 5,5-oriented manager feels free to act if precedents are found—"Has it been tried elsewhere?" or "How do they do it?" Unless strongly pressured otherwise, he or she may continue to say, "Too risky."

When traditions, policies, and regulations are ambiguous, the 5,5-oriented manager turns to others for direction but in such a way that hides uncertainty. This may be done by tactfully asking for guidance from the boss. Then the manager may even be seen as initiating and exercising responsibility.

Inquiry

Beyond the rule book, inquiry is likely to be cautious and shallow because of noncommitment to personal standards of thoroughness. To keep updated, the 5,5-oriented manager frequently uses the informal organization, which has its own norms, standards, and rules of conduct; its leaders and followers; its conformists and deviants. Its channels of communication—gossip, and rumor—are a gold mine for inquiry concerning morale and satisfaction. It lets the manager know how people are reacting to moves such as expansion, layoffs, or union and management tensions.

A 5,5-oriented manager uses the informal organization to keep a finger on the organization's pulse, constantly observing others and listening to them. He or she is seen by influential members in the informal organization as a good guy who lets people in on what is going on. As one manager says, "You have to use your sixth sense, that is, your radar, to know what's going on." As a result of all this, the 5,5-oriented person can usually keep in step, rarely missing the cadence created by those considered to be important in the organization. Relying on the status quo is preferred to searching for deeper understandings that might point to more fundamental solutions.

Questions are formulated tentatively or indirectly so that if they are unacceptable, they can be appropriately modified. This may lead to problems though. For example, Mike is trying to find out if Sarah is responding to a customer complaint that placed the company in a difficult position. Rather than ask Tom outright if Sarah is handling the problem, Mike says to Tom, "Where is Sarah? I haven't seen her today. Do you know anything?"

Tom might answer, "I think I heard someone say she's taking a day of vacation." Or he could say, "I saw her just this morning." Mike is left hanging since Tom did not catch the intent of the question, which was to find out whether Sarah had followed instructions.

5,5-oriented listening means staying alert to clues in order to stay in the know. For example, Mike is alert to learn who was included in an important meeting, who is accompanying the boss to the conference in Chicago, who is in line for a raise, who is being considered for transfer to San Francisco, etc. All of these constitute clues to who is "up and coming" vs. who is "down and out," and provide guidelines for what might be done to get positive and to avoid negative attention.

Other information sources such as technical documents are likely to get attention only when one anticipates being held accountable or to score a one-upmanship point. Otherwise, they are given a cursory review. Technical documents are handed to others with the request for a synopsis of the main points, with a summary or an abstract relied upon as the sole basis for reaction.

Advocacy

It is unlikely that a 5,5-oriented manager will strongly advocate unique positions. When challenged or disagreed with, the manager is likely to become evasive or back off, sometimes allowing the convictions of others to override private judgments in the interest of "progress." Convictions are unlikely to be deeply held, definite, or clear.

A 5,5-oriented manager may advocate in a reasonably strong manner when speaking in the name of the top person, or on behalf of the company, or when reflecting a point of view previously announced by the boss. For example, Jennifer says to Tom, "The boss wants us to come up with a lean budget and I'm all for it." Tom says to Jim, "This company has stood for quality and product satisfaction for 77 years and I know of no better basis for doing business than that." In other words, when there is an established position or party line, the 5,5-oriented manager feels free to express convictions in support of it. While these are not personal convictions, they may be interpreted as such by others.

Often advocacy is not determined by one's convictions but by what is politically safe, salable, or workable. Expedient positions are embraced, frequently at the expense of a sounder way. Expediency has come to have important implications for corporate ethics. A 5,5-oriented manager may feel under no particular ethical compulsion beyond "to do what everybody else is doing." This can result in an erosion of corporate ethics and morality. The foundation of equity and justice is undermined when no one is prepared to question prevailing attitudes that are ethically unsound.

Bending the truth, half-truths, or white lies may be seen by the 5,5-oriented manager as acceptable tactics for getting results. Candor is sacrificed as a way of getting cooperation. Over a period of time, however, such distortions are likely to form a patchwork of contradictions. Yet the 5,5-oriented manager feels this is the practical or realistic approach: the end justifies the means as long as no one is caught. This is not conscious manipulation of the sort associated with a facade or outright lying. A 5,5-oriented manager is not likely to realize how tailoring of information in order to persuade others colors their understanding. They may go along, but often it doesn't feel right.

Shading differences can sometimes be used to escape advocating for a position that may be wrong. One way this can be done is in the concept of "equal but different" applied to situations that are unequal and different. The purpose is to make them appear balanced, which reduces the need to advocate one position over the other.

Decisions

The 5,5-oriented manager has little difficulty in making easy and quick decisions based on previously established expectations, precedents, or job descriptions. Decision making becomes difficult when the decision being considered might be unpopular, result in unpleasant job assignments, or lead to new and untested actions.

While opinion polls and surveys may provide useful evidence, they may also be leaned on as sources of information when making decisions. Managers can use them as courses of action without exposing their own thinking or putting their own judgment on the line. They can rely on the opinion poll without "sticking their necks out." If the decision turns out badly, it was due to "bad" market research.

Delegation may be premised on equity and fairness, which means that responsibilities or problems are carved up with each subordinate given a fair share. No one is expected to shoulder more of the burden than anyone else. This may be sound when the solution to a problem is purely mechanical, but the solutions for many problems call for different contributions based on different abilities.

Emphasis on a majority orientation places an equal weight on each person's convictions. Popularity is used to decide what is right or valid rather than objective evidence. This means that several people may agree on the same perhaps faulty assumptions, or base a conclusion on the same incorrect data. The greater the popularity the greater the risk of accepting such majority agreements as being based on objective facts. "Groupthink" is a special case of a 5,5 orientation. Unsure of themselves or their facts, such individuals prefer to go along and to give their support rather than to engage in thorough inquiry, advocate for their real convictions, or create opposition to an emerging plan. Under this kind of decision making, the plan snowballs and rolls over what few reservations may remain. No one wants to be out of step. Everyone seems together. Agreement is reached. An action is taken. A fiasco results.

Critique

The 5,5-oriented approach to critique and feedback is based on the notion of positive reinforcement. This means encouraging subordinates by passing along compliments heard from others or expressing his or her own good reactions to their performance.

Negative feedback is risky because it can backfire. In spite of a dislike for telling people unpleasant things, a 5,5-oriented manager realizes the importance of doing so since people do need to be aware of their weaknesses in order to improve. It is, however, approached in a restrained manner. One way to deal with negative information is indirectly, by asking a person a question which, if answered objectively, forces the person to acknowledge weakness. Another way is more oblique. The manager might ask a subordinate, for example, who is preparing a technical report, "Would it be better to frame these conclusions this way?" The boss hasn't openly told the subordinate that the way the report is written is unacceptable, but when the subordinate takes the suggestion it shows that the message has been received. Another way to make a negative or critical reaction more acceptable is to sandwich a criticism in between two compliments. This makes it easier for the subordinate to accept it.

This approach to feedback is not candid, open, and straightforward. It can result in misunderstanding by subordinates because the message is not likely to be clear.

Management Practices

A 5,5 orientation to managing is "responsive" leadership. The way to move forward is always to be in step with others and never too far out in the lead. The philosophy is *gradualism,* where change is a step at a time, not by goals-oriented direction or experimentation. The result is not chaotic, but neither is it coherent. It is more likely to be conformity-centered and to come out piecemeal and makeshift. The 5,5-oriented leader, in this sense, is likely to be characterized as conservative, conventional, and acting with moderation.

According to this line of thinking, a manager does not *command* or *direct* to get the job done so much as to *communicate.* The approach is to request and to persuade people to want to work rather than to exert formal authority.

Planning: "I make my plans according to what I know my subordinates will accept and what they will resist."

Organizing: "After explaining goals and schedules, I make individual assignments. I double-check to make sure my subordinates think what I request is all right. I encourage them to come back if they don't understand."

Directing: "I keep up with each person's performance and talk about progress from time to time. If someone is having difficulty, I try to reduce the pressures by rearranging conditions of work whenever possible."

Controlling: "I touch base informally to discuss how things are going. I tend to emphasize good points and avoid appearing critical or negative, though I do encourage subordinates to be aware of their own weak points. My subordinates know I take their thoughts and feelings into account in my decisions."

Staffing: "I seek people who fit in."

Management-by-Objectives: "Objectives are scaled to what people are prepared to accept. I encourage subordinates to offer suggestions either to reduce the effort necessary to get a result or to decrease pressure and thereby reduce stress and frustration."

Performance Appraisal: "I try to bring to my subordinates' attention ways in which they are doing well. Positive suggestions motivate but criticism turns people off."

This approach to production avoids sacrificing people needs. It is a balancing act, giving up some of one to get some of the other. When the boss softens the push for production and considers attitudes and feelings, people are expected to accept the situation and be relatively satisfied. This orientation assumes that people are pragmatic in realizing that reasonable effort is to be exerted in the interests of production.

The 5,5-oriented manager prefers informal and easygoing, give-and-take discussions, one-to-one dealings with each subordinate. By touching base with subordinates, the manager appears to embrace participative values but in fact does little to lead subordinates into genuine involvement. However, there is a tendency to use meetings to solve problems and to rely on group decisions, special committees, or task forces to spread responsibility for unpopular decisions. The leadership role is seen as that of a catalyst or facilitator, one whose procedural skills help subordinates reach majority points of view. Keeping everyone in step becomes important in this kind of arrangement.

Consequences

The consequences resulting from the 5,5 style of managing include the following.

Impact on Productivity

Consequences of this approach are reflected in the constant buildup of bureaucracy, which establishes how things should and should not be done and precludes the necessity of exercising much thought or judgment. Rules and regulations govern status and prestige. Politics, favors, and trade-offs reduce the organization's capacity to change when change is needed or to make decisions that competition may require. Because bureaucracies tend to be slow to adjust to changing circumstances, they are likely to lose the capacity to compete or to provide services efficiently.

Impact on Creativity

A manager with a 5,5 orientation is unlikely to lead in a way that inspires creativity or innovation. Creativity requires thinking that is uncharacteristic of a person who is conformity-centered. A 5,5-oriented manager lacks the independence of judgment or divergent thinking essential for creativity.

Impact on Satisfaction

The 5,5-oriented manager is likely satisfied in a bureaucratic organization because his or her preferred ways of leading mesh with what the organization expects. The leader and the corporate culture are matched to one another, with conformity a reliable key to advancement. However, when career progression is based on merit, others in the same rank may be expected to advance more rapidly.

Impact on Career

When the system is built on seniority and bureaucracy, a 5,5-oriented manager stands as much chance to get to the top as anyone. 5,5-oriented managers in organizations that have not settled into a bureaucratic mode can enjoy moderately successful careers but are unlikely to advance above the middle of the organization before retirement.

Recognizing 5,5 Behavior

The following words and phrases give the flavor of the 5,5-oriented manager as described in daily activities:

- Accommodates
- Cautious
- Compromises
- Conformist
- Evasive when challenged

- Expedient
- Indirect
- Likes the tried-and-true
- Negotiates
- Prefers middle ground
- Prefers to act on precedent
- Pulls punches
- Sandwiches bad between good comments
- Soft-pedals disagreement
- Stays on majority side
- Straddles issues
- Swallows convictions in the interest of "progress"
- Tests the wind
- Waffles
- Waits to see where others stand

Suggestions for Change

Here are suggestions a 5,5-oriented leader may want to consider in order to change.

Motivation

☐ Consider whether the reactions you get from others communicate respect, or whether they simply reflect their approval of your conformity-based actions. Respect can be earned, but it involves the difference between speaking one's genuine convictions and what one thinks others want to believe.

Initiative

☐ When you find something that needs to be done, do it based on the logic of the situation and without overreliance on traditions, precedents, and past practices.

☐ Take on an obvious problem rather than waiting to get somebody's okay or approval before moving. This generates respect.

Inquiry

☐ It is necessary for you to be more thorough to avoid being uninformed. When you think you have learned something, ask additional questions to be sure your understanding is complete and that you are informed of essential details.

☐ When you write something, ask yourself why you wrote it in that way. Was it written to make it attractive or palatable? If so, what were you really trying to accomplish? Double-check your interpretations with those of others to see if they read it the same way.

Advocacy

☐ One way to break through excessive tentativeness is to express convictions on the premise that others are interested in knowing what you really think. Rather than editing or shaping your convictions to make them agreeable to others, you may generate spontaneity by saying what you really think.

Conflict

☐ Disagreement can lead to innovation and innovation is valuable. It is possible to disagree with someone and then to explore the background and rationale of the disagreement in an open and candid way. Disagreement is possible without being disagreeable.

☐ What produces hostility when a disagreement arises is the implied " . . . and you are wrong." What reduces it is to ask for background information or for reservations and doubts that the person might hold regarding his or her own position. Do the same for them without having to be asked.

☐ It is possible to weigh the soundest conclusion without regard for who will be the winner, gain points, or lose face. Openness and candor take the win-lose out of conflict.

Decisions

☐ It is important to realize that there are some decisions that only you can make. Although you may ask for input, the outcome is yours alone. It is inappropriate to ask others to share in it beyond input.

☐ You gain respect by making decisions without delay since others expect you to make them.

☐ When you make your decision known, others will better understand if you provide the reasoning behind it. It is also a good idea to let others know the alternative possibilities you examined and the reasons for their rejection.

☐ Be prepared to revise your decision to everyone's benefit if people disagree with the decision and can find flaws in the reasoning that led to it.

☐ It may be desirable to reexamine how much and to whom you delegate. Equity and equal burden are not to be disregarded, but the soundest criterion for effective delegation is that problems are handled by those with the greatest resources for dealing with them in an effective way.

☐ Teamwork based on majority thinking may be in the right direction because two heads may be better than one. However, two heads may very well be worse if teamwork is based on compromise and shading of differences. You might consider concentrating more attention on why those who agree on some direction think it is best and what the reservations and doubts are of those who disagree with it. Much is to be learned by exploring reservations and doubts.

☐ Majority-based decision making can be harmful when "go along to get along" is the basis of agreement. Decision making is based on the idea that several people thinking and analyzing together can express themselves in open and candid ways and can find the most valid solution. The two ought not be confused and the strong leader works to shift the basis of decision making from the former to the latter.

☐ Strive for unqualified consensus. When a member enters into teamwide consensus, he or she accepts responsibility for consequences. This means the member has a good understanding of what to do, how to do it, and with whom without having to be told and possibly not even checked upon. For these reasons, it is important to dig out reservations to reach an unqualified consensus.

Critique

☐ Feedback allows you to check out what you plan to do before you do it and therefore reduces or eliminates needless mistakes.

☐ Critique is particularly valuable when it is negative and raises doubts; possibly more so than when it is positive and strengthens confidence. One way to get good feedback is to ask for it, and then to listen to whatever is offered. Rather than accepting it publicly but rejecting it privately or ignoring it, ask yourself, "Is this the sound interpretation or am I kidding myself?"

☐ Indicating to people that you want feedback and critique is likely to encourage team members to solve the real issues that hamper productivity.

5,5 Orientation Summary

"I seek to maintain a steady pace. I take things more or less at face value and check facts, beliefs, and positions when obvious discrepancies appear. I express opinions, attitudes, and ideas in a tentative way and try to meet others halfway. When conflict arises I try to find a reasonable position that others find suitable. I search for workable decisions that others accept. I give informal or indirect feedback regarding suggestions for improvement."

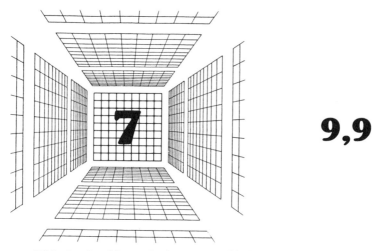

This leadership style integrates high concern for production, *9,* with high concern for people, *9,* as indicated in the upper right corner of the Grid. Unlike the other leadership approaches, the 9,9 orientation assumes that there is no inherent contradiction between organizational purposes of production and needs of people. Effective integration is possible by involving people and their ideas in determining the strategies of work and achievement. The highest attainable level of integration is possible only through leadership that meets the mature needs of people to commit themselves to corporate objectives through contributions that are beyond the ordinary. The needs of people are met through establishing sound and mature relationships with one another, which is essential to accomplishing organizational goals. The aim of a 9,9 orientation, then, is to promote participation, involvement, and commitment to teamwork.

Motivations

The 9,9 theory of managing presumes a necessary *connection* between organizational needs for production and the needs of people for full and rewarding work experiences. The leader's desire is to contribute to corporate success by involving others so that they too may contribute. Such a "can-do" spirit is contagious, inspires a "win" attitude in others, and promotes enthusiasm, voluntarism, spontaneity, and openness. Contribution with caring in the sense of a genuine desire to help others reach their highest potential is basic to creativity, commitment, and cohesion.

The 9,9 achievement motivation comes from developing the competence required to make a positive contribution and therefore pursue corporate goals and objectives with the same enthusiasm as if they were one's own. This is what promotes a high-spirited sense of gratification, enjoyment from work, and excitement from making a contribution. The closer one comes to success in advancing corporate goals, the greater the sense of personal fulfillment. When the organization reward system is geared to the same value system, the 9,9-oriented manager can expect to enjoy the benefits of financial gain made possible by organization success (see Chapter 10).

A 9,9-oriented manager avoids advancing selfish interests at the expense of others or the corporation. To do so would invite suspicion and distrust, and ultimately reduce candor in dealing with others. Guarded relationships impede progress and create those adverse conditions that permeate many organizations: politics, climbing over others, hiding information, and other ways of advancing oneself at the expense of others. A 9,9-oriented manager deals with his or her boss in the same way as with colleagues or subordinates.

The motivation to avoid self-serving actions may be referred to as enlightened self-interest or altruistic egotism. Managers who conduct themselves in this way enjoy the greatest gain as measured by career advancement and financial earnings. Furthermore, when the corporate capacity to compete is strengthened in these ways, personal security is greater than when corporate strength is retarded by actions that weaken competitive position.

Managing Conflict

Preventing Conflict

Many skills allow 9,9-oriented managers to have disagreements that lead to finding sound solutions to problems, but without creating animosity.

Getting Early Involvement. Involving others early in problems that affect them provides the opportunity for gathering additional information. It also allows alternatives to be identified, the pros and cons to be weighed, and sometimes even trial runs or experimental tests to be conducted.

Exchanging Background Viewpoints and Sharing Perspectives. This is particularly useful when people are sufficiently open with one another to be able to candidly share reservations and doubts. Getting differences into the open and thinking them through allows each person to assess the strength of each other person's convictions. It permits faulty logic and distorted perspectives to be identified and dealt with, and it helps eliminate incorrect information. Each of these decreases the likelihood of disruptive conflict.

Full Self-Disclosure Within the Framework of One's Job Description. Full self-disclosure means withholding nothing that might be pertinent to problem solving. This includes data and logic, but also involves attitudes, feelings, hunches, and intuition—all aspects that might improve others' insight. Self-disclosure is complete when everything of job-related evidence that needs to be said has been said. It includes personal or private information only as these bear directly on organizational performance.

Clear Communication. Some words and phrases are vague and difficult to understand; others are precise and descriptive. Some are neutral; others inflammatory. Some have a valid meaning in one context and have quite a different and even incorrect meaning when used in another. The choice of words can influence the interpretation of what is communicated and can significantly affect understanding, feelings, and attitudes.

If Craig goes to his boss with a proposition and comes back without approval, he might tell Ted, "The boss vetoed it," when the accurate description of what happened might have been, "The boss found a limitation I hadn't thought about so she and I agreed that the idea wasn't a sound one." These two descriptions depict the same event but in significantly different ways.

Developing Criteria. Getting agreement on what a sound solution might be before searching for an actual solution is an excellent way of avoiding conflict and of getting better solutions.

When Walt and James use different, unshared criteria to evaluate the soundness of a solution, disagreement can shift into conflict. For example, if James proposes a solution that would be valuable for the long-term, even though somewhat more expensive in the short-run, and Walt is concerned with costs only in the short-term, then each is evaluating with different criteria in mind. A disagreement might have been avoided had they agreed upon the timeframe in which to apply the best solution.

Handling Conflict When It Appears

Confrontation. Many conflicts cause people to withhold information, misread one another's motivations, and sometimes even deny the presence of tensions and antagonistic feelings. Confrontation helps avoid such reactions. There are two distinct meanings in the way the word confrontation is used, and because there is no good substitute for this term, it is important to distinguish between them.

One meaning of confrontation implies going a little beyond contest but falling short of actually battling it out. It rests upon the concept of bringing opposing points of view into sharp focus. This type of confrontation is intended to test one's strength against another's. The underlying assumption is that one person's view will prevail over the other. This is confrontation as combat and it is the 9,1 approach to ending differences.

Confrontation-as-comparison-through-contrast has quite a different meaning. It means solving conflict by focusing on differences. By being brought out into the open, differences can be resolved directly by those who are a party to them. Emotions that usually accompany conflict—anger, hostility, fear, anxiety, doubt, and disappointment—can also be dealt with.

Opposing viewpoints are brought into the same sharp focus so that discrepancies can be reviewed and removed by understanding. There is no commitment that either one viewpoint must prevail, although that may be the case because one party has learned that there are necessary and sufficient reasons for accepting it. However, it may be that neither viewpoint prevails. Out of the comparison and contrast, a position may emerge that incorporates something of both positions, but also may add elements of uniqueness, inclusiveness, etc. that make it superior to any of the prior ones. It is also possible that an entirely different solution is found.

Viewed by an observer, confrontation-as-combat and confrontation-as-comparison-and-contrast might appear highly similar. There is, however, an important underlying difference, often recognized only by those engaged in a confrontation. In the case of confrontation-as-combat there is a contest of wills—the holder of one view feels threatened by the holder of the other. To yield in this kind of confrontation means being forced by one's own weakness to accept the other position.

The meaning of confrontation-as-comparison-and-contrast implies mutual trust among those who are trying to resolve the difference. Trust implies goodwill, good intentions, and respect for others whether they agree or disagree. To prevail over the other person is unimportant; to find a sound solution is all-important.

Being open-minded to considering alternatives, well-disciplined in testing consequences, and forthright is critical in seeking sound solutions. Under these conditions, one person's yielding to the position of another is not capitulation. It entails no loss of face. It is no measure of weakness. Rather, it is a demonstration of commitment to a best solution achieved through logic and reason and removal of reservations and doubts.

The distinction between these two meanings of confrontation can be drawn simply and clearly: the first is based on answering the question "Who is right?" the second, "What is right?"

Being Aware of Personal Needs and Expectations. Many conflicts occur because one person is unaware of the personal needs or objectives of the other and thus unable to satisfy them. People can prevent some conflicts by making needs known to one another. The boss, Ann, feels that it is important for others to knock before entering her office. Thus, she is likely to feel antagonistic toward Bruce and react negatively when he bursts in unannounced. Bruce can't cooperate if he doesn't know that Ann expects this kind of respect.

By being aware of people's expectations, it becomes possible to factor them into the give-and-take of everyday relationships. However, it is also possible to confront them when such expectations are adverse to productivity.

When Conflict Remains

When other means have not been successful, additional steps can be taken that may end the conflict or at least bring it within manageable bounds.

Ventilation. One or both parties may seek to relieve the tensions within themselves through a process of ventilation. This means discussing frustrating, discouraging issues with a third party. Sometimes this reduces tensions sufficiently for increased efforts at problem solving to take place.

Review and Feedback from Neutrals. Disagreeing parties may be so enmeshed in the problem that they have lost objectivity, and must rely on a third party to get an outside reaction. The "neutral" may be another manager, a staff person, or a consultant—anyone who has no vested interest in the outcome.

When All Else Fails. When the conflict persists but action is required, it may be necessary to shift into a backup premised on prior understanding and commitment. Without agreement, or when the issue itself is of overriding importance, the only remaining option may be resignation.

Behavioral Elements

Initiative

In the 9,9 orientation initiative is exercised in a strong, pro-organizational manner. The leader is likely to be eager, vigorous, and able to sustain a significant capacity for work. Personal energy is focused on exercising initiative in an enthusiastic and spontaneous way that arouses the involvement and commitment of others.

Not all initiatives have equal priority in mobilizing effort, and so the 9,9-oriented manager plans, prioritizes, and then follows through, retesting along the way to ensure soundness. Two problems may be equally important but of different urgency, so this factor is also brought into consideration. Also, if two equally important problems exist, the one offering the larger payout gets priority. If two equal payouts result, the one that can be completed with lesser expense gets the priority. Initiative is exercised as a matter of membership. Initiatives may arise externally to the team or from any of its members, thus not relying solely on the team leader. Widespread and spontaneous initiative taking ensures that no one will say, "That's not my problem. Let someone else handle it."

Inquiry

Inquiry is comprehensive and in depth, ensuring that all bases are evaluated in an analytical manner that increases the likelihood real problems are fully understood. This manager might be described as "Knowing the score" or "Knows what he's talking about." A premium is placed on developing facts and data, and digging out contradictory as well as supporting evidence. Clear separation is maintained between fact and opinion. This enthusiasm for knowing the score is reinforced by curiosity.

Questioning can be a two-way process with subordinates as free to ask questions of the boss as the boss is with them. Questions are basic to inquiry but 9,9-oriented questions have a unique quality. They are open-ended. "How does the situation look to you?" "How can you make sense out of it?" "What do you know about it?"

One reaction to a question naturally leads to other questions, with the facts, data, and evidence examined for consistency with or contradiction to other data. This helps develop a framework of understanding as well as assemble isolated bits of information into a coherent whole.

Listening also is open and active, with the listener aware that his or her own assumptions can distort interpretations. Thus anything pertinent to the issue can be said without risk of being misunderstood. Understanding occurs when participants can paraphrase what others have said in an accurate manner. If misunderstandings are identified it is then possible to correct them. Studying sources pertinent to grasping the full complexity of the problem is another aspect of sound inquiry. Written documents are studied proactively. The reader is alert and asks, "Why did the author say this? I know of exceptions, why were they not presented?" "That point is made in a persuasive way, which leads me to think he is trying to convince me, not educate me." "That's a sweeping statement I can't let pass unchallenged." To double-check, a 9,9-oriented manager might hand the document to a subordinate and say, "Look, I've studied this but I'd like you to dig into it. Then I can double-check my understanding of what is said against yours to see what we can make of it. I won't tell you what I think until you have had a chance to reach your own conclusions."

A final consideration tends to be unique to 9,9-oriented inquiry. The approach to understanding is likely to be carried out on a team-wide basis with those who have something to contribute simultaneously engaged in digging out and testing facts, data, and evidence. This process enriches the quality of inquiry because it permits each participant to examine facts and see the problem from more perspectives than when thinking is undertaken in a solo manner.

Thoroughness and depth of inquiry are at the heart of 9,9-oriented management. "Prework is a prerequisite for participation" is another way of saying that problem solving can be no better than the thinking that leads to the conclusion, and thinking is limited by the available input of information. Additionally, everyone involved has access to the thinking and understanding as the basis for exercising initiative.

Advocacy

Information and ideas are presented quickly. This means that convictions are developed and expressed, and reservations are discussed in a direct, logical, and convincing manner. This tell-it-as-it-is approach rings true, and as a result the 9,9-oriented manager earns wide respect for his or her convictions, opinions, and values, which are held unless contradictory evidence makes them untenable. This readiness to advocate for convictions may result in a 9,9-oriented leader being seen as self-assured and strong-willed, but openness to alternative points of view makes it possible to distinguish this from cockiness and rigidity.

Strong advocacy increases the likelihood that every viewpoint receives the attention it merits. This means that Anne must convince Alan that what he is advocating is either unsound or there is a more sound position before Alan can be expected to shift.

Decisions

Decisions may be reached and made known in a way that may appear almost offhand. The reason is that by thorough inquiry and advocacy, a decision is self-evident rather than the leader's sole possession, waiting to be announced.

When a decision involves several people, 9,9 decision making seeks understanding and agreement among the relevant people. The coupling of the words *understanding and agreement* is important because action without understanding can be little more than obedience or compliance. Further, a person may have understanding without agreement and yet be committed to the course of action that follows. Understanding and commitment, however, do not make as solid a foundation for action as commitment based on understanding and agreement, because with the latter lingering reservations have been removed. When the basis is understanding and commitment, reservations and doubts must be overcome by the person who has them.

A phrase used earlier should be examined more closely, because appreciation of it is central to understanding the 9,9 orientation to decision making. The phrase is "Everyone who is involved . . . ," and superficially it implies that "*everyone* is involved in making decisions all of the time." This is unrealistic because some people have nothing to contribute to the solution of the problems and are not specifically involved in implementing conclusions. For them to take part is a misuse of human resources. While the typical 9,9 qualities of subordinate/boss involvement and participation certainly exist in 9,9 decision making, it must be emphasized that they in no way reduce the hierarchical authority and responsibility of the boss to achieve results. For example, let's look at a team of four members. Al is boss; George, Cathy, and Don are subordinates. Who participates in problem-solving activities is described.

One-Alone. Certain "team" problems involve *only* Al—or George, or Cathy, or Don—in the solution. The reasoning behind one-alone is that one member has the responsibility, the capacity, and the information to solve the problem. Then it's in the interest of teamwork for that person to solve the problem alone and then let others know of the solution as it affects their own responsibilities. Such team problems, in fact, are "one-alone." Individual effectiveness contributes to teamwork by moving the team toward its goals and avoiding duplication of effort. These solo decisions (1/0) may be ones the boss makes singly or ones the subordinate makes under delegated responsibility.

A special case of solo initiative occurs whenever one team member substitutes him or herself on behalf of another team member. An example of this kind of supportive teamwork clarifies what is involved.

> "I know you have to go to New York to arrange a loan. I'm going to see our R&D people there next Thursday. I could also deal with the loan people and make it unnecessary for you to be away at the same time unless something more is involved . . ."

Another is this:

> "George is away on an extended foreign trip, but I can act in his behalf and give you an answer."

The initiative rests with whatever team member takes the supportive action, but the responsibility for outcomes remains with the member on whose behalf the second team member initiated action. In this sense it calls for trust to a degree beyond that required in any other kind of situation.

One-to-One. Team problems that involve Al and George together are 1/1 team actions. It's up to them to work out the solution and to take actions that move the team toward its goals. These 1/1's between Al and George free Cathy and Don, who can contribute nothing, to use their time in dealing with other aspects of the team situation. These 1/1 actions between a boss and a subordinate are traditionally thought of as activities that are "delegated."

Delegation, from a 9,9 orientation, also has a training and personal development aspect. The boss aids subordinates to gain experiences that increase their autonomy and sense of achievement. Delegation in this way also frees the boss for other activities. One 9,9-oriented manager described her approach this way:

> "With subordinates who have less experience I identify the problem and discuss it with them, asking them to develop an approach to doing the task. Then I review their thinking to help with unsolved problems before okaying the next step.
>
> "After experience has been developed, I ask subordinates who have unsolved questions to consult with their colleagues to review plans and solutions and come to me only when a solution cannot be found or when a shift

in direction is called for. Getting help and critique from colleagues is critical to successful delegation and development.

"I conduct meetings all along in which the main projects of each subordinate are reviewed as part of teamwork. I emphasize uncovering resources which others can take advantage of when they are publicly acknowledged. Those who are frequently contacted for help know that it is appreciated by those who need the help. They are clearly the strongest contributors."

In this way, the boss-to-subordinate activities that are 1/1 in character are reviewed by all members in the team for their additional contributions as well as for cross-learning through critique.

Under a 9,9-oriented approach, 1/1 situations may also involve any member interacting with any other member according to that person's specific area of responsibility and need for help. Failure to bring in that other member on a shared responsibility premise of lateral coordination can be expected to have adverse effects.

One-to-One-to-One. This is more complex but no less important. What happens is that each member takes a certain action that makes it possible for another member to take a second action, and so on until everyone has contributed in sequence to the end result. Each team member's activity is indispensable to a successful sequence. For example, a salesperson writes up an order. Smooth coordination from the salesperson to those who receive the order, to those who fill it, to those who prepare the invoice, and to those who package and ship constitutes a complex sequence of interdependent operations. Done well, they satisfy the customer and build repeat business. Though there may be no face-to-face meetings, what they do links them together in a team effort. This is sequential teamwork.

One-to-Some. Here the work involves more than two people but not the total team. They fall between 1/1 and 1/all and differ in number of members involved rather than in the character of interdependence, whether simultaneous or sequential. Therefore, they are not treated separately. This category is maintained only to ensure that 1/some interactions are utilized when needed.

One-to-All. Some problems can only be solved by Al, George, Cathy, and Don working on them. Such "one-to-all" (1/all) problems bring together everyone involved in achieving a common purpose or dealing with a given problem that touches on everyone. This is simultaneous team-work. It occurs when (1) no member has knowledge, information, or experience enough to formulate the answer, but everyone working together can be expected to reach it; (2) coordination is required to get the job completed; therefore, each member's participation is significant to a sucessful outcome; and (3) all must understand the overall effort so that each can fit it into his or her other ongoing activities.

9,9 teamwork may occur under 1/all, 1/some, 1/1/1, 1/1, or 1/0 conditions, depending on three fundamental aspects. One is related to decision quality; a second is concerned with the acceptance aspect involving readiness to implement the action called for; and the third deals with management development. Guidelines to answer the question as to when 9,9-oriented team action should be 1/all, 1/1 or 1/0 are presented in Chapter 9.

Critique

The following distinction needs to be made between feedback and critique. A 9,9 orientation includes the idea of feedback but goes beyond it to incorporate the larger concept of critique. Critique refers to the continuous examination and reexamination not only of decisions but also the how and why. Sound critique permits examination of things that are going well and also those that are going badly. Analyzing a success frequently contributes more useful knowledge for achieving organizational purpose than analyzing problems. Continuous examination ensures that the process is as effective at all points as possible. Barriers to effectiveness arise from many sources, and no one of them is more or less important than any other because all can impede sound decision making. The most common of these barriers are faulty logic, vested interest, hidden agendas, jealousies, favoritism, blindness to options, fear-provoking remarks, poor timing, unwitting acceptance of low caliber goals, and overlooking contributions. Critique can eliminate many of these impediments by reflection and examination. It can also be used as a steering mechanism to avoid factors that distort decisions and thus reduce their effectiveness.

Critique is not restricted to the leader telling others what is being done well or poorly. As is true for everyone else, he or she is likely to have limited understanding of the complex situation and therefore no one is likely to be in the unique position of making a purely solo contribution by virtue of rank. The leader is self-critical and receptive to feedback from others. When critique is effective, the potential for strengthened decisions is great. This double-loop approach to feedback permits learning from experience to occur. Learning in and of itself also constitutes a source of 9,9-oriented gratification.

Effectiveness of critique is characterized by properties such as the following:

☐ Openness and candor prevail because team members recognize that they foster "best" decisions.

☐ Critique occurs throughout an activity or task, not just at points along the way or as a postmortem that reconstructs the history of that task.

☐ Critique describes what is happening and the consequences that result and therefore should be undertaken as soon as possible after the event being discussed so that cause-and-effect is not dimmed.

☐ While critique analyzes the consequences of actions, it avoids as much as possible evaluative judgments of good or bad or right or wrong.

☐ Social topics and observations are pertinent to critique insofar as they relate to accomplishing the task. Observations about individuals that are concerned with such outside matters as politics, religion, child rearing, social engagements, music, and friends are all personal and have no real pertinence. They are out of bounds.

☐ Critique should reflect connections between personal behavior and consequences. For example, the initiative of one person may impede success because it is not connected to the initiative by others. Highlighting consequences of the inappropriate exercise of initiative helps participants learn how best to exercise initiative in the future.

Management Practices

The 9,9-oriented Grid style determines how management practices are undertaken. Participation-centered teamwork is basic. The essentials for sound planning are present when all available data and perspectives for defining a problem are utilized. The full complexity of the situation is more likely to be comprehended when those who share responsibility for specific outcomes pool information and judgment. Then, alternative solutions can be assessed through collaborative thinking, and high-quality decisions can be made.

Participation-centered teamwork is necessary to the involvement and commitment of those who are responsible for implementing decisions. Resistances and reservations that are worked through in the process of discussion are no longer present to hinder successful implementation.

Planning: "I get the people who have relevant facts and/or stakes in the outcome together to review the whole picture. We formulate a sound model of an entire project from start to completion. I get their reactions and ideas. I establish goals and flexible schedules with them."

Organizing: "We determine individual responsibilities, procedures, and ground rules."

Directing: "I keep informed of progress and influence subordinates by identifying problems and revising goals or action steps *with* them. I assist when needed by helping to remove barriers."

Controlling: "In addition to critiques to keep projects on schedule, I conduct a wrap-up with those responsible. We evaluate the way things went to see what we learned and how we can apply it to future projects. I give recognition on a team basis as well as for outstanding individual contributions."

Staffing: "Work requirements are matched with personnel capabilities or needs in deciding who is to do what."

Management-by-Objectives: "Team and individual objectives are mutually worked out on a timely basis. They provide statements of what needs to be accomplished. These are motivating because each subordinate is willing to strive for and be measured against a model of excellence."

Performance Appraisal: "Criteria for evaluating performance are worked out at the beginning of a period and the concrete indicators of performance specified in advance. The subordinate lead the discussion and provides the boss another perspective by offering and receiving feedback and critique. When necessary, the boss confronts the subordinate with adverse effects of performance and seeks to gain a realistic assessment of inevitable consequences even when these involve demotion or termination. Once past performance has been appraised, new objectives for future performance, with concrete indicators, are agreed on as the framework for assessing performance and learning from the next cycle."

In each of the descriptions of management practices, the manager is *creating* conditions that help subordinates understand problems and that create personal stakes for reaching successful outcomes. When people are oriented toward achieving goals that are high but realistic, and ones they understand and agree with, behavior becomes more orderly, meaningful, and purposeful. The assumption is that when individuals who must coordinate their activities are aware of organization purpose and of their real stakes in productivity, it becomes possible to place greater reliance on self-control and self-direction. With effective leadership, individuals can mesh their efforts in an interdependent way.

Consequences

The impact of the 9,9 cycle of leadership is described in the following.

Impact on Productivity

Several conditions come together and ensure that productivity is maintained at a high level. A positive environment is created when participants have clear goals, thorough knowledge, and strong convictions. Thus, sound conflict solving and effective decision making are gained. When "who does what *with* whom" is made explicit, then 1/0, 1/1, and 1/all utilization of resources and sound critique is possible without waste of human resources.

Impact on Creativity

A high level of creativity, particularly with respect to synergy from effective teamwork, also can be expected. Strong initiative means that many different approaches for solving a problem are likely to be assessed before a final action is decided on. Deep inquiry ensures that the real problem has the maximum likelihood of being identified rather than shallow definitions being accepted. Advocacy means that members get ideas out into the open where they can be challenged or corrected. Conflict solving permits participants to have differences and yet, through the direct confrontation of the feelings associated with them, avoid antagonisms. Critique provides the possibility of learning how to increase effectiveness in contributing to corporate goals.

Impact on Satisfaction

The satisfaction derived by a 9,9-oriented person from contributing is fulfilling because this approach to management affords many opportunities to make a difference. Satisfaction is more likely to be long-lasting.

Impact on Career

9,9-oriented individuals are evaluated by those above them to be the most reliable and capable of advancing the interests of the corporation. Research evidence confirms that maximum rate of advancing within an organization is characteristic of those who manage according to a 9,9 orientation.

Recognizing 9,9 Behavior

Words and phrases that describe 9,9 behavior include:

- Candid and forthright
- Confident
- Decisive
- Determined
- Enjoys working
- Fact-finder
- Focuses on real issues
- Follows through
- Gets issues into the open
- Has a "can do" spirit
- High standards
- Identifies underlying causes
- Innovative
- Open-minded
- Positive
- Priorities are clear
- Reflective
- Sets challenging goals
- Speaks mind
- Spontaneous
- Stands ground
- Stimulates participation
- Unselfish

9,9 Orientation Summary

"I exert vigorous effort and others join in enthusiastically. I search for and validate information. I invite and listen for opinions, attitudes, and ideas different from my own. I continuously reevaluate my own and others' facts, beliefs, and positions for soundness. I feel it is important to express my concerns and convictions. I respond to ideas sounder than my own by changing my mind. When conflict arises I seek out reasons for it in order to resolve underlying causes. I place high value on arriving at sound decisions. I seek understanding and agreement. I encourage two-way feedback to strengthen operations."

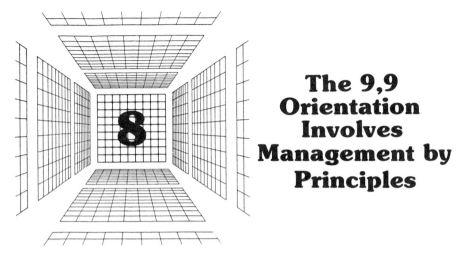

The 9,9 Orientation Involves Management by Principles

Managers are invariably confronted with unique situations. Even if the work itself consists of the same items—money, materials, machines and equipment, land, and buildings—an infinite variety of change can be expected in quantity, availability, quality, and even people, who change with each new experience.

Every Situation Is Unique

The essence of sound leadership is to treat each individual as unique and as one who needs unique leadership to become committed to the organizational needs for productivity and creativity. Commitment is enduring when it gives each individual a high degree of personal satisfaction and freedom from stress. Challenge and excellence are not compromised and each person feels *drawn* to a high level of contribution rather than being driven toward it.

The issue is that each situation—be it of things or people—is different and should be managed accordingly. Everyone "senses" that. This is common sense to most of us and is the appeal of schools of thought that advocate what has become known as "flexibility," "contingency," and "situational management," but these terms suggest that there are no basic *principles* for managing different situations. This contradicts experience in any field of endeavor. Are the principles of aerodynamics any different for a paper airplane than for a multi-engined jet aircraft? Are the principles of sound nutrition altered when feeding a six-month-old infant instead of a mature adult? If so, the paper airplane could not fly and the infant would risk ill health and poor development. The key is that the principles of aerodynamics are common to both the paper airplane and the jet aircraft, but the *application* of them is different. So too for the feeding of infants and adults. The basic principle is that protein, carbohydrates, vitamins, minerals, trace elements, and bulk are needed as a basis for life. The feeding bottle for the infant and a three-course meal for the adult are totally different, yet both represent the application of the same principles but to different situations.

Accepting that there is one sound way to exercise leadership is equivalent to accepting that effective behavior is based on scientific principles and is consistent with views held about other areas of scientific inquiry. We know that principles of physics underlie and explain a vast range of phenomena in inanimate nature. Principles of biology account for the phenomena of life and make them predictable. By analogy, principles of leadership underlie effective management, providing guidelines for soundness of action and making events predictable.

When basic principles of the physical, biological, or behavioral sciences are disregarded, it can be expected that resulting side effects and operational consequences will be faulty. Gravity is a constant physical principle, but it affects the engineering design of mechanisms used in space flights differently from how it affects those used in undersea exploration. Biological principles governing the transfer of oxygen to the blood can be violated by an excessive smoker, but not without shortening the expected life span. Managers who manage without attention to the principles of leadership soon discover that their tactics are likely to lead to lowered morale, creativity, and job satisfaction with resultant lowering of productivity and harm to the business as a whole.

Just as these principles of aerodynamics, nutrition, physics, and biology must be followed if results are to be sound, so must the principles underlying effective leadership behavior be followed in the practice of management. One cannot abandon principles just because one is faced with a new situation.

What, then, are the principles that underlie effective leadership in management? We can report those associated with superior performance of boss *and* subordinate(s), drawing on the work of researchers from more than twenty disciplines (Blake and Mouton, 1978).

Principles as the Basis of Action

An individual may understand behavioral science principles and employ them in a consistent way to achieve productive results with and through other people. *Versatility* requires using a range of skills to apply the same principles to various situations.

There is an important distinction between *principles* and *tactics*. Tactics dictate *how* the principle is applied in various situations. For example, a versatile leader recognizes that the soundest way to resolve conflict is to confront differences so that their causes can be identified and eliminated. There are two reasons why this is so. One is that disagreements are relieved by insight, and the other is that the tensions are relieved. Eliminating tensions arising from conflict in a given situation means that energy remains available for dealing with production problems. Resolving tensions is healthier than living with them.

Does this mean, then, that a versatile manager rigidly applies a principle without regard for the particulars of the situation to which it is applied? No. A versatile leader is concerned with applying a sound principle in a way that is appropriate to the particular situation. In dealing with a new employee, for example, discrepancies in opinion that might lead to conflict are dealt with in a different manner than conflict that arises with an employee of longer-standing. With the newly-hired subordinate, this leader might first examine the events leading to their differences. In this way causes of conflict can be identified that both boss and subordinate might otherwise fail to recognize. In contrast, the long-term employee understands quite well the activity being undertaken, and it would be wasteful to engage in the same procedure needed with a new person. It is possible to reach the core of their differences more quickly and explore the causes of its origin. *Confrontation* is relied on in both cases as the basis for a meeting of the minds. The principle remains constant but the application varies with the circumstances.

Principles as the Basis of 9,9-Oriented Management

What principles must be observed to ensure sound leadership? The following list is based on evidence from many applied disciplines, supported by research in social psychology, sociology, anthropology, mental health, counseling, psychiatry, political science, history, and by field studies of business effectiveness (Blake and Mouton, 1978). They are also validated in reverse by demonstrations of the negative behavior produced by their violation in the fields of criminology and penology, and by studies of the effects of colonialism, slavery, indentured servitude, and other forms of repression.

A background statement gives character to these principles. When they are brought into daily use, boss-subordinate interactions are characterized by mutual trust and respect. Trust and respect, in other words, are the end results of sound behavior. Sound behavior is also productive and creative in the operational sense. Productivity, creativity, personal satisfaction, and health are best served when these principles are applied. Adherence to these principles represents a different facet of a 9,9-oriented management strategy.

☐ *Fulfillment through contribution is the motivation that gives character to human activity and supports productivity and creativity.* When people are committed to the success of the organization, they are motivated to take the actions essential for its success. Fulfillment through contribution means to gain personal satisfaction by taking action which is useful, makes a difference, and is productively helpful to others. Fulfillment is derived from making such contributions. The gain in satisfaction from contributing seems to be a basic motivation.

☐ *Open communication is essential for the exercise of self- and shared responsibility.* When communication is free and open, organization members have access to the information that is pertinent to their interests and responsibilities. Organization members can make maximum contributions only when the information requisite for sound thinking is available to them.

☐ *Conflicts are solved by confrontation, with understanding and agreement as the bases of cooperative effort.* It is inevitable that differences will arise when people get together to openly share ideas. Choices must be narrowed and one selected from several. When conflict becomes intense, mutual trust and respect can be severely eroded, communication distorted, and feelings of personal responsibility substantially reduced.

Confrontation means taking a problem-solving approach to differences and identifying the underlying facts, logic, or emotions (prejudices, preconceptions, or antagonisms) that account for them. When conflicts are resolved through confronting and understanding their causes, people feel responsible for finding the soundest answer and exerting the necessary effort to do so.

Decisions that result in understanding and agreement are possible when members participate openly in resolving conflict. This in turn generates conviction and commitment to outcomes and stimulates the effort essential for realizing it.

☐ *Being responsible for one's own actions represents the highest level of maturity and is only possible through widespread delegation of power and authority.* The ability to make a maximum contribution depends on one voluntarily and spontaneously exercising initiative. The fullest exercise is possible only when authority for self-responsible action flows downward into the organization. Then opportunities to be more productive and creative can be acted on by those who see them.

☐ *Shared participation in problem solving and decision making stimulates active involvement in productivity and creative thinking.* Viewed in one perspective, participation is a human right, something that should always be honored as a condition of freedom, autonomy, and self-responsibility. It involves open, full involvement and commitment of one's resources. Participants feel they have a stake in the outcome of a decision or an action, leading to the notion that people support what they help create. When team-wide understanding and agreement have been reached, a consensus is present, which is supported without reservations. Such shared participation stimulates the kind of creative thinking that produces optimal solutions.

☐ *Management is by objectives.* Productivity and creativity are enhanced when individuals engage in achieving goals to which they are committed. Management-by-objectives is the operational way of bringing a goals orientation into widespread use. This means that managers identify and agree on the goals that are to be pursued and set in motion concrete activities for achieving them. When commitment is attached to the goal, then one is drawn to it, seeks to achieve it, thinks about how to reach it, and makes the effort necessary to attain it. When management-by-objectives through goal setting is done in a sound manner, the goals of individuals and the goals of the organization become more integrated and harmonious.

☐ *Merit is the basis of reward.* Two criteria for rewarding individual contribution include: (1) Does the contribution further the organization's prospects of success? (2) Does the contribution lead to the manager becoming a stronger leader? This is the meaning of reward based on merit.

When reward is based on merit, organization members experience the system of promotion and pay as fair and equitable. The important issue is that only when reward acknowledges personal contribution is the readiness to make contributions reinforced.

☐ *Norms and standards support personal and organization excellence.* Much of our behavior is regulated by norms and standards to which each of us conforms. When norms and standards are set at high levels, this stimulates the pursuit of excellence and contributes to the satisfaction people derive from work.

☐ *Learning from work experience is through critique.* Critique is a process of stepping away from or interrupting an activity to study it to learn what is going on, to see alternative possibilities for improving performance, and to anticipate and avoid any activities that have adverse consequences.

Critique is a more or less "natural" way of reflecting on what is happening or what has happened. When members have widespread understanding of and skill in utilizing critique, it becomes possible to accelerate the rate at which they learn and in this way to progress.

Summary

An organization can maximize its members' contributions by applying these principles daily, which will in turn help ensure relationships among members based on mutual trust and respect. Then it becomes possible to maximize the use of financial, technical, natural, and other resources.

Violate the principles of physics in the engineering of a bridge or a building, for example, and you get disaster—the collapse of the structure. Violate the principles of sound leadership and invite similar disaster—collapse of the organization.

This chapter has identified the principles underlying a 9,9 orientation and suggests that these principles are applied in tactically different ways depending on the circumstances. Chapter 9 illustrates tactics of 9,9 teamwork, including guidelines for who should be involved in problem solving, problem-solving steps, conflict-solving procedures, and using critique for increasing problem solving effectiveness. Chapter 10 deals with how management-by-objectives and organizational reward systems can motivate effort toward achieving organizational purpose.

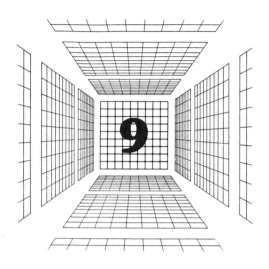

Tactics of 9,9 Teamwork

Leading effective teamwork is a significant aspect of the manager's behavior because the 9,9 orientation embraces the concern for integrating the needs and views of people into production.

Guidelines for Participation

9,9-oriented problem solving and decision making involves thorough inquiry and strong advocacy by everyone who is involved. As indicated in Chapter 7, the phrase "everyone who is involved" defines the need to examine participation more closely.

Guidelines that clarify when to use 1/0, 1/1, or 1/all are provided in Table 9-1. These guidelines answer the question, "Under what conditions are 1/0, 1/1, 1/some, or 1/all approaches likely to be most effective?" The left-hand column identifies criteria that help a manager decide if 1/0, 1/1, or 1/all is the soundest basis of action. The conditions for 1/some are so similar to 1/all that they are not separated for discussion, but these are actions that involve more than 1/1 but less than 1/all, where "all" means the entire membership of the team.

A manager should act without consulting others when the criteria for good decision making and problem solving, shown in the left column of Table 9-1, match conditions in the 1/0 column. When conditions match entries in the 1/1 column, a manager should consult one other team member, and when the circumstances match conditions in the right column, 1/some or 1/all actions should be taken.

The first six criteria relate most closely in one way or another to maximizing the quality of decision making by the effective and efficient use of human resources.

Table 9-1
Testing Actions for When They Should Be
1/0, 1/1, or 1/all

Criteria	Approach		
	1/0 if	**1/1 if**	**1/all if (1/some also)**
1. Whose problem is it?	mine	his or hers; both of us	ours
2. Time to contact	unavailable	available	available
3. Judgmental competence	full	low	insufficient
4. Pooling of information	unnecessary	vertical or horizontal	needed both horizontally and vertically
5. Synergy	not possible	possible	possible
6. Critique	no one else involved	problem belongs to two people	problem has implications for all
7. Significance to the team	low	low	high
8. Involvement-commitment of others	no significance	helpful-essential	necessary-essential
9. Relevance for others	none	present	present
10. Others' understanding of purpose/rationale of decision	no need or can be assumed	needed	needed
11. Coordination of effort	unnecessary	vertical or horizontal	horizontal and vertical
12. Change in team norms/standards	not relevant	not relevant	relevant
13. Representation of issue in other settings	none	pertinent	pertinent
14. Delegation	possible	unlikely	unlikely
15. Management development	none	present	present

Source: *Grid Team Building.* Austin, Texas: Scientific Methods, Inc., 1984. Reprinted by permission.

1. *Whose Problem Is It?* If, in viewing a problem, an individual can say, "That problem is my sole responsibility, and I have the capacity to handle it," then the problem calls for 1/0 action and the exercise of self-reliant initiative. If, however, the individual lacks the capacity for handling the problem or if it overlaps the responsibilities of two people, it represents a 1/1 situation. If the problem is superordinate in the sense that each individual has a piece of the problem but no one has all of it, then 1/all is the best interaction for solving it.

2. *Time to Contact.* If there is no time to involve others, for whatever sound reason, the individual takes the necessary action on a solo, or 1/0, basis. If consulting others will be advantageous and time is available to consult with one but not all, then it is a 1/1 situation. If time is available and there are advantages to several being involved, then it is 1/some or 1/all.

3. *Judgmental Competence.* A manager may have the depth and experience to exercise sound judgment. Other things equal, this is done in a 1/0 way. If the manager's experience with a certain problem is insufficient, however, and one other person is needed to strengthen the soundness of judgment, the situation is 1/1. If reaching a sound judgment requires the participation of everyone, then it should be carried out in a 1/all team manner.

4. *Pooling of Information.* When one person has all of the information needed to execute an action, 1/0 action is appropriate. If two people each have some of the information needed for the total understanding of a situation, then pooling of information may be required on a 1/1 basis. This may be a boss-subordinate relationship or it may be between equal-level colleagues. When all team members have unique aspects of information that need to be pooled to develop total comprehension, then 1/all pooling may be required.

5. *Synergy.* The term *synergy* applies when thrashing through of all the perspectives of team members results in a better solution than what any one, two, or several members might have developed. Teamwork may be needed because of synergistic possibilities from several or all team members studying or reviewing a problem. The leader who hears the opinions of subordinates in the presence of others gains the maximum opportunity for access to their thinking. Disagreements, rationale for positions, reservations, and so on are stimulated under this kind of open leadership. However, 1/0 is the rule if no synergy can be anticipated and 1/1 if only one other member can contribute.

6. *Critique.* Decision quality may be strengthened by discussions that study team skills in solving problems. A problem should be studied in a 1/0 way by self-critique if it has no team-building application; in a 1/1 manner if two people can learn something about teamwork effectiveness from it; and in a 1/all way if the full team can benefit from studying it. In addition, there are many techniques of critique that aid team members to study results relative to performance. These are detailed elsewhere in this book and others.

The next critical criteria, numbers 7 through 13, are more closely related to acceptance, i.e., the readiness of team members to implement a decision once it has been made.

7. *Significance to the Team.* If the action has no team implications beyond one member alone, unless he or she does not carry it out, it should be handled 1/0. If it has far-reaching operational significance, such as shifting the reporting lines in the organization, then the entire team should understand the issues. The more likely an action will affect team purpose, direction, character, or procedures, the more desirable the participation and involvement of all members.

8. *Involvement-Commitment of Others.* Understanding the problem and its solution may be necessary to achieve acceptance from those who must implement the decision. If the action to be taken does not involve other team members, it should be made 1/0. If it affects only one other, discussion with this team member is necessary (1/1). When the action has team-wide implications, all should discuss the pros and cons until those whose interests are involved have full understanding. Doubts and reservations are then relieved, and everyone is in a position of agreement and support.

9. *Relevance for Others.* Those whose future actions will be affected by a decision need to think through the issue and discuss its implications to see that it is understood and that they are committed to it. The larger the number of team members who have personal stakes in an action, the greater the need for them to discuss the decision.

10. *Others' Understanding of Purpose/Rationale of Decision.* There are some problems that do not require input from others, yet they can benefit from an awareness of the rationale employed in analyzing or solving it. When others already know the rationale or when it is not important to them, then the action should be 1/0. However, sometimes the rationale behind the action will benefit at least one other; therefore, it may need to be dealt with in a 1/1 way. All the others may not be in a position to

contribute to a solution but may need to know the rationale, and under these circumstances the rationale should be communicated on a 1/all basis.

11. *Coordination of Effort.* Often an action can and should be 1/0 because there is no need for coordination. When coordination is required, the matter should be dealt with jointly, on a 1/1 basis. Sometimes several if not all team members help implement a decision; in that case the strategies for coordination must be worked out on a 1/all basis.

12. *Change in Team Norms/Standards.* Norms/standards that influence team performance may need to be established, modified, or completely changed. All team members must be involved to know and be committed to the new norms/standards. Because each team member adheres to team-based norms/standards, it is unlikely that a 1/0 action would shift a norm/standard. The best condition for reaching such decisions is where a new team norm/standard is explicitly agreed to by all team members, particularly if the new norm/standard is intended to replace or modify an existing one.

13. *Representation of Issue in Other Settings.* Sometimes one team member serves as a representative in settings outside his or her own team situation. Other team members may contribute little or nothing to reaching a decision, but because they are in a "need to know" position, they are brought in to increase understanding.

These next two items are concerned specifically with using teamwork situations for management development.

14. *Delegation.* A problem should be solved by a person of lesser rank if he or she has the understanding and judgment necessary to deal with it, or if to do so would strengthen the subordinate's managerial effectiveness. Thus, capacity for exercising responsibility by dealing with larger and larger problems is increased. This shifts a 1/0 from one member to another. In addition, the boss is free to utilize this time on matters only he or she can solve.

A rule can be stated: Other things being equal, delegation should be relied on when (1) subordinates can deal with a given problem as well as or better than the boss; (2) the subordinate can strengthen managerial effectiveness; (3) delegation, not abdication, is the boss's motivation; and (4) the time made available to the boss permits the solution of another problem more important than the delegated one, provided the conditions are such that the subordinate has reasonable prospects of success.

15. *Management Development.* Team members participate in analyzing managerial issues, even though they may contribute little to quality of management by ways of information and their acceptance of decisions is immaterial. Their participation enables them to gain knowledge and to develop the judgment needed for dealing with such problems in the future. If a problem has no management development implications, it should be dealt with 1/0; if it has management development implications for only one other, it should be dealt with 1/1; if it has management development implications for all team members, it should be dealt with 1/all.

Matrix Teamwork

The matrix concept of organization has been of increasing interest in recent years. Under these conditions at least two differently structured arrangements are possible. In one a subordinate may have more than one boss, such as a line reporting relationship and a functional specialty reporting arrangement. In another any member may belong to more than one team, often on a temporary basis, but sometimes more or less permanently, such as a project team, a marketing launch team, or some other kind of interdepartmental grouping.

Matrix-centered structures place even greater emphasis on teamwork, as a member may contribute specialized expertise, then leave. If unable to work effectively with others, this member's contribution is likely to be limited. Additionally, the effectiveness of a member who cannot cope with having two bosses may suffer.

Matrix teamwork involving 9,9 skills of participation enables members to contribute significantly to organization effectiveness. The fifteen criteria for answering the question, "Who should participate?" all apply with equal pertinence when composing a matrix-centered team.

Problem-Solving Steps

A problem occurs whenever an existing condition prevents some desired outcome from happening or when a discrepancy is exposed between what "is" and what "should be." Many managers recognize the classic problem-solving model of defining the problem, developing alternative solutions to it, evaluating the alternatives, selecting the most desirable alternative; and finally, implementing that alternative. There are variations in how each of these steps is done, but they are relatively unimportant. This rational description of problem solving is useful as a sequence of tactics, but because it disregards the human side, it can be severely limiting in its usefulness.

The approach that results from applying 9,9 principles in a sound tactical manner is far different from the classic model because it focuses on additional considerations, which must be dealt with if the best solution is to be found.

Felt Problem or Real Problem

One of these considerations is being sure that the felt problem is the real problem. Frequently, the problem that managers feel a need to solve is not the real problem at all, and there is no assurance that solving the felt problem will contribute to solving the real problem.

An example of a felt problem expressed in many companies is communication difficulty. The attitude is, "If we could only solve our communication problems, many of our other difficulties would clear up." As a result, company after company has gone into media programs of various sorts: company papers, video cassette presentations, programs for aiding managers to acquire better platform skills, gripe sessions, seminars on listening, etc. Yet they find that no matter how much effort is put into solving communication difficulties, problems continue to exist. Difficulty of communication was merely a symptom.

The problem behind the communications problem is more likely to be the misuse of power and authority throughout the hierarchy, and trying to solve the real problem with a media blitz contributes little to its solution.

Another example is a company with a sizable real-estate holding that built various production units in one corner of the available space for economic reasons. It was simpler and less expensive to build a new unit onto an existing one and take advantage of utilities already provided. The felt problem in this case was conserving utilities, and this was done successfully.

But the wrong problem had been solved. The add-on produced such chronic congestion that the company was limited in expansion possibilities. The real problem, which had not been recognized, was how to provide for orderly expansion according to a basic plan and yet be in a position to take advantage of emerging opportunities. Providing a blueprint of the infrastructure for the long term would have solved the "problem."

The solution of felt problems as contrasted with real ones requires less diagnosis, less planning, and less short-term risk. If the real problem remains unsolved, however, adverse side effects are likely to appear. Eventually, the organization or its responsible individuals are "forced" to either abandon effort or to grapple with the real problem, usually after much unnecessary frustration and expense.

Identifying the real problem in the beginning is an invaluable managerial skill. On the physical side, this means effective utilization of various engineering and financial disciplines. On the human side the demand is for effective behavioral and organizational diagnosis.

When managers acquire skills of effective behavioral and organization diagnosis, they no longer will continue to solve problems that are immediately felt but will turn their attention to the real problems.

Whose Problem Is It?

A second important attribute in defining the problem is the ability to identify those individuals who have the know-how and responsibility for successfully grappling with it. The "Whose Problem Is It?" question is anything but simple, even though on the surface it may appear straightforward. If the "wrong" people solve the problem, it is less likely to stay solved than if the "right" people are involved in finding a solution to it.

The issue of "Whose Problem Is It?" is dealt with in Chapter 7 and elsewhere in this chapter where 1/0, 1/1, and 1/all participation were discussed. Only a brief reconstruction of the tactic needs to be reintroduced at this time.

The problem may belong to one person and this person may be the boss or a subordinate team member. In any event, that person working alone has the capacity and resources for solving the problem. Others can contribute nothing more to the solution, and drawing them in is a waste. The same basic logic applies to other groupings. The problem may involve only two members, a boss and a subordinate, or two colleagues. It may involve several, it may involve all team members; in some cases, additional people from outside the team may have the knowledge for dealing with the issue. Table 9-1 helps answer the question "Whose Problem Is It?" and indicates which approach to solving it is most appropriate. Thus, identifying the real problem and those who should be involved in solving it are the important first two steps.

The remaining tactics are involved in "doing it," but the process is more complicated than applying a series of steps. This approach is participative in character. It causes different points of view to appear which may create communication problems, arouse disagreement, conflict, etc. These "process" problems must be solved as the content problem is being worked on, which means that all participants must remember the importance of openness and candor, the significance of effective inquiry, strong and clear advocacy, confrontation of conflicts, decision making based on understanding and agreement, and of ongoing critique.

Developing Criteria of a Sound Solution

Before identifying alternatives for solving a problem, it is important to develop criteria against which to evaluate the various solutions in order to measure soundness and identify adverse side effects. When this step is omitted, vested interests surface that increase the difficulty of choosing the soundest alternative. Agreeing on the criteria for a sound solution encourages participants to focus on the character of the solution itself rather than on the extent to which the solution might be favorable or unfavorable from personal perspectives.

Developing Alternatives

Basic and sound examination of the full range of options, before deciding on a particular course of action, allows possibilities to be seen that might otherwise never be considered. For this reason the best solution is more likely to emerge.

Selecting the Best Available Solution

With explicit criteria for evaluating a sound solution and the right people engaged in searching for the solution, and with all available options and alternatives examined, the real test is whether the soundest approach actually can be agreed on and implemented.

Those responsible for solving the problem are still likely to disagree on the best solution. Some of this disagreement may arise from hidden agenda, vested interests, and, sometimes, simply from an insufficient background in "feeling" the most probable consequences of each alternative. The 9,9 way of dealing with this problem is to confront differences and air reservations openly.

Designing the Implementation

Difficulties likely to be encountered in implementation must be resolved in the problem-solving cycle.

While those responsible for implementation may have the capability and commitment, other ongoing problems may arise that draw their attention away from the implemention and implementation "dies." By anticipating time pressures from other demands, it becomes possible to search simultaneously for ways of dealing with other problems, as well as to implement the solution of the earlier problem.

Another barrier arises when resources for solving the problem may not be available and no effort was made to ensure that they would be provided. When this aspect of implementation is anticipated, it becomes possible to test for availability of resources. Contingencies can be introduced for dealing with unanticipated needs for resources should they arise.

Critique

Once the solution is implemented, the next step is to study how well it worked. All those who have been engaged in or concerned with the problem in any way are involved. Upon conclusion of the project they study the entire cycle to spot limitations in all phases of the problem-solving cycle. Such postmortem critiques are described more fully later in this chapter.

Conflict Solving

Even though the team consists of only the most capable and responsible people, it is still likely that strong, committed, well-considered viewpoints will result in conflict. A team relishes conflict— not from the joy of combat but from the stimulation of creativity toward further accomplishment. The possibility of heightened commitment challenges team members to develop ways to deal most effectively with conflict.

Resolving 1/1 Conflict

When a boss is involved in a conflict with a subordinate (or when team members are interacting 1/1 and find themselves in conflict), he or she should take the following concrete actions to confront and relieve the difference(s):

☐ Describe to the subordinate his or her own thinking in such a way that the subordinate does not feel personally attacked or denigrated.

☐ Take nothing for granted while listening to the subordinate's ideas and feelings. In answering questions, be forthright in order to avoid/relieve suspicions related to your position. Ask questions whose answers provide a true understanding of the subordinate's attitudes.

☐ Challenge the subordinate's thinking regarding different courses of action, but only after you and the subordinate have reached a shared understanding of the subordinate's basic values, needs, and assumptions.

☐ Probe for reasons, motives, and causes that give the subordinate a clear and possibly different perspective on the issue.

☐ Present and request data, logic, and counterarguments to help test your and the subordinate's objectivity.

☐ Help the subordinate explore the operational consequences of his/her preferred solution.

☐ Get help from the subordinate in exploring the consequences of your preferred solution. Stay with the discussion in a persistent way to get agreement and only conclude it unilaterally when no avenue of resolution has been found.

☐ Make sure that the process of deliberation regarding the outcome is open and not predetermined, thus allowing the subordinate to actually influence the outcome.

☐ Constantly search for new definitions of the problem that make its sound solution self-evident.

Conflicts often can be resolved on a one-to-one basis because they occur between and are limited to two people. This is not always the case, however.

Resolving 1/All Conflict

Sometimes the conflict is team-wide. This occurs when each person has a solution that no one else is prepared to accept. The situation becomes even more intense when Member A feels that it would be a personal defeat if Person B's solution was accepted. When such tension exists between A, B, C, D, and E, it is often assumed that the best that can be hoped for is compromise, and the worst is impasse. However, if conflict can be openly confronted by the team, resolution becomes possible, with advantages accruing from finding better solutions as well as retaining and strengthening the involvement of individual members.

Usually, this only occurs when the boss brings it about. The boss may begin by posing the dilemma: "Each of us has a different view, and we each have our own hip-pocket solution. There is a more objective view somewhere and a valid solution that can resolve the problem if we can find it. Our job is to step back and try to understand why we are locked in. Bill, how do you see the problem, and how does this differ from what you've heard me and others say?"

Starting with Bill and continuing until all have aired their views and have proved they understand the positions and views of others is the first step toward cutting through subjective feelings and creating a greater readiness on the part of each member to consider objectively others' points of view. Sometimes the blockage is caused by antagonisms that exist between one or more members. The "problem" becomes controversial, not because members are at a loss to deal with it but because they need the controversy to feed their emotional antagonisms. When this is so, the resolution is to get those who say "black" and the others who say "white" to recognize the antagonistic factor in their relationship; to examine openly what they are doing to foster it; to bring it to an end. Even when not directly involved in the controversy, the boss joins with subordinates to help the antagonists work through their differences, challenging those in disagreement to explain the reasons for it. Their reactions indicate whether they have understood the situation in the same way. If they have not, the boss keeps asking questions that allow them to confront their differences, presenting facts, counterarguments, and logic to help them test their objectivity. Once they come to understand their own values and assumptions, the boss can challenge their thinking and logic regarding the different courses of action available, probing for reasons, motives, and causes to give them a clear and possibly different perspective.

Conflict can erupt among members, not because of subjective attitudes or antagonisms, but because of a lack of team goals to which members are committed. Under these conditions each member pursues his or her distinctive version of the team goal as well as personal goals, and these may come into conflict. Now the solution is to get members committed to team-wide goals and to tailor their individual goals to the team goals in such a way that mutual support becomes first, possible, and then, a reality.

A more structured approach to narrowing the areas of disagreement is by using the 4,3,2,1 method. This involves asking each participant to write out a position statement. These positions are exchanged and a four-point system is used to examine each element of each position. Any one of the four points following may apply:

4—"I disagree with this part of the statement for the following reasons."

3—"I wish to ask the following questions for clarification of the meaning of this part of the statement."

2—"I agree with this part of the statement as rewritten in the following way."

1—"I agree with the statement as written."

The parties then exchange their findings. This activity is completed when as many of the 4's, 3's, and 2's as possible have been made into 1's, reflecting mutual agreement.

When team members are working effectively together it is often unnecessary to engage in more formal steps of conflict resolution. However, close examination of how people solve conflicts when they get sound results suggests that the approach approximates the 4, 3, 2, 1 method. They break the overall problem into its parts and then discuss how much agreement or disagreement is present for each component. Members are often heard to say:

"Well, look, I can agree with that proposal if we'll reword it slightly."

"I need more information about that aspect."

"I disagree with this part because of the following . . ."

These kinds of considerations make it possible to review complex issues and think in areas where disagreement persists, to supplement one another's factual information, to test and revise the logic relied on, and to get personal feelings into the open.

Though managers may realize that open confrontation is the most direct and valid approach to team and one-to-one conflict, they often avoid initiating such a discussion. There are several reasons, with the most important being the fear that the discussion may get out of hand; that conflict, openly acknowledged, might escalate out of control. Another is the worry that the boss who initiates such a discussion will look weak, or actually lose control and be unable to resolve differences in a quieter, more sophisticated, "private" way. Another source of reluctance stems from a different value orientation that says the manager should mastermind the solution he or she wants and bring it into use on a *fait accompli* basis or by "selling" it to all concerned.

A frequent reason is the belief that this approach takes too much time. Certainly, while the skills in using the techniques are being learned it may take more time because more facts, views, and alternatives are being considered. Because this type of discussion involves "causes" rather than mere "symptoms," sound, long-term solutions appear and problems do not keep recurring. With practice, sound solutions will be found in perhaps less time than currently applies.

All of these are "real," but they are not valid reasons for avoiding confrontation as a means of conflict resolution. Through the exercise of sound leadership, the discussion can be channeled and does not need to get out of hand. Once tensions are identified, the pressures and strains on those who feel them can be relieved. The boss who opens up such a discussion appears strong, not weak, because the boss shows confidence and skill in utilizing the resources of others in a problem-solving direction. Finally, by open discussion, rather than masterminding a solution, team-wide commitment is maintained and attention can be focused on consultation, exchange of viewpoints, and consensual resolution of differences.

Team Learning from Critique

Human values of candor, conflict confrontation, and an experimental attitude make it possible for a 9,9-oriented team to constantly learn how to improve its effectiveness. Such values open up the realistic possibility of using feedback, which is the critical factor in permitting team members to learn from critique. Critique denotes a variety of useful ways to study and solve operational problems members face either singly or collectively as they seek to carry out their assignments.

Participants in an experience frequently know that performance is below par and can usually describe what is going on, at least in mechanical terms. "We started at 10:00, and, though the project should have been completed by 12:00, we did not finish until 12:30." Or, "Even though I needed to exchange information with Bill and Tom, they never spoke to me, or to each other. Bill always asked Nan through Ralph. By the time it got to me it was useless." Describing it is a mental reconstruction of the event, involving awareness of the way things occur as they are happening. That is important, but it is only half the picture.

As a method of learning, critique usually occurs when two or more people exchange their own descriptions of an event both have directly experienced. If Bill, Tom, Nan, Ralph, and others had come together and answered the question, "Why is it that when the information gets to the last person, it's useless?" they would have been using critique to improve their situation. People also learn from critique when two or more people describe the actions of a third person and each pictures the meaning and intent of those actions as understood by each. By describing and discussing these similarities and differences with the third person, potential misunderstandings, errors of perception, or other unanticipated consequences of personal actions can be corrected.

When and How Critique Occurs

Critique can be used at the beginning of an activity, as it is taking place, or when it is over.

Beginning the Activity. Contradictory as it may seem, critique is an excellent approach to learning about problems even before the activity has taken place. Introduced before the beginning of an activity, critique helps team members think about the activity in which they are about to engage. Determining what each participant knows, what each expects to happen and how, and what each wants to see done, makes better use of human resources. In this way it is frequently possible to anticipate problems and thus to avoid them.

Consider the following. Shipbuilders routinely provide a warranty detailing the operating specifications they have built into a ship and the performance standards that the owner has a right to expect in sailing that ship. This is true for passenger ships, but it is also true for tankers, freighters, and even most pleasure craft.

The conventional practice of accepting a ship from its builder is for the captain to be designated and then for a crew to be drawn together. Before launching, the crew takes several days to become familiar with the ship's machinery and characteristics of its operation that can only be known through firsthand examination of the ship's construction and by studying its probable capabilities.

The ship is then taken on a shakedown cruise, and as many defects are worked out as possible. The fact that a warranty specifies performance standards is forgotten except when there is a gross malfunction. These malfunctions and significant departures from standards are reported to the captain. Many limitations in the ship are taken for granted, with the crew working around them as best it can.

Using critique methods under these conditions, the captain would be appointed and the crew drawn together, as in the conventional case. However, before boarding the ship, the crew, or team, would learn in detail what specifications for ship performance, machinery, and other subcomponents are written into the warranty. Then operating manuals that specify the proper operational approach to various pieces of equipment are consulted and critiqued for standard and unique features. Only at this point does the crew go aboard to learn about the actual properties of the ship and its equipment. During this phase, the ship and its equipment are to be tested to their maximum and minimum limits, rather than restricting their performance to an average range. The third step is taking the ship to sea.

Concurrent Critique. Critique can also occur, spontaneously or according to a plan, at any time during the activity. Here is an example of concurrent critique:

Frank to Sue: "Well, getting back to Sue here for a minute. Are you suggesting that we continue discussion and, as we see people get into a situation, that we stop and test then and there?"

Sue to Frank: "Well, yes. Take the opportunity to point it out just when it happens."

Frank to Sue: ". . . to observe each other as the discussion goes and see how things turn out. Is that right?" (General agreement)

George to Sue: "Let me try one on for size. *I just noticed you jump to an inference, real fast . . .*"

Sue to George: "That's right."

George to Sue: ". . . just a second ago . . . and what I meant was . . . and I can give you an example. All of a sudden you say, *'Well I've got the answer. It isn't that at all. It's this.'* You go too fast for the rest of us." (George spots a critical example and calls Sue's attention to it right after it happens.)

Sue to Group: "Well, do you deduce from that that I'm a woman of action?" (Laughter and some confusion) "But, seriously, I can understand why I look that way to you. I'll try to watch it, but when you see me doing it again, tell me about it."

Such feedback increases the likelihood of Sue coming to understand how to strengthen her own effectiveness. It increases the likelihood of each member examining his or her behavior and asking pointed questions, recognizing how habits might be changed to permit each member to contribute more to the team's problem-solving effectiveness.

The following is another example of how critique can replace behavior that inhibits goal attainment with behavior that supports a successful completion.

This group has several members, but the interaction is between Phil, Jim, and Barbara. The group had previously agreed that it would be better to critique events as they occurred rather than to wait until the end, as was the accustomed way of doing it. The rationale was that by stopping and testing occurrences in the here-and-now, improvements could be introduced on the spot.

Barbara to Jim: "It seems we are going around in circles. Jim, it doesn't sound to me like you're really hearing what Phil is trying to say. It sounds more like you're impatiently waiting for him to get through so that you can repeat the point you've made several times now."

Jim to Barbara: "I think you're right. I've gotten so committed to my own point of view that I've been trying to hammer Phil down rather than trying to understand why he keeps resisting."

Jim to Phil: "Phil, have you felt that I've been hammering you down?"

Phil to Jim: "You hit the nail on the head. I don't feel like you've heard a word I've said in the last several minutes."

Barbara to Jim: "Jim, repeat what you think that Phil has been saying, once he has restated his position, and see if Phil will buy the notion that you understand his position."

In this concurrent critique Jim had been talking past Phil. Without Barbara's intervention to examine what was really going on, two things were likely to occur. One is that Phil would eventually withdraw, feeling defeated. Another is that Jim, with self-righteousness, would feel that his view-point had prevailed over other view-points that were not forcefully expressed. Phil would likely harbor a deep resentment at being ridden over roughshod by Jim. However, through concurrent critique the blockage to understanding was quickly identified. We can anticipate that Jim and Phil came to an understanding of one another that resulted in an improvement in the quality of the ultimate decisions reached.

These concurrent critiques help identify problems and difficulties and introduce corrective actions before disabling problems block productivity.

Informal, spontaneous, even off-the-cuff commentary on what is occurring is likely to have some value principally by virtue of its spontaneity. However, when spontaneity is replaced by impulsiveness, the remarks made are usually neither well thought out nor readily accepted by others. For example, if Tom says to Bill, "You are being dogmatic. You keep repeating your opinion and don't listen to a thing I say," Tom's statement that he isn't being heard may be valid. However, it is not likely to make Bill listen better. Rather, Bill probably feels more inclined to deny or to justify his behavior. Such interventions often produce injured feelings and defensiveness. Had Tom said to Bill, "I feel that the idea I was putting forward was not heard . . . ," Bill is more likely to say, "Then repeat it and see if I understand."

This approach to learning works best when those engaged in it can give and receive feedback (see Chapter 7) and are committed to using critique as needed. Then false starts are avoided, wrong choices eliminated, and a whole activity can be reviewed to determine how to strengthen performance in the next cycle of experience.

Post Critique. When critique is introduced at the end of an activity, it permits participants to review and reconstruct the entire experience and to figure out why the results were less than they could have accomplished. It enables them to trace interpersonal influences, to identify and to evaluate critical choice points, and to verify recurring patterns. Such insights are significant for deciding what is and what is not the best way to carry out a comparable activity in the future.

These post critiques can range from a casual attempt to determine what happened, usually after obtaining bad results, to a standardized set of procedures to evaluate designated events, such as a quarterly budget review, conducted on a more or less regular basis.

As participants think about a completed activity, they reach conclusions regarding performance on certain critical aspects of it. These relate particularly to procedures used and to people factors that blocked effectiveness. Sometimes a post critique is able to piece together interactions between participants and the effect these had on performance and results.

Using a questionnaire or some other information-gathering device as a starting point for a critique can be particularly useful. The following, for example, is one of several questions answered by participants in a Grid Seminar following a problem-solving team discussion. First, individual members, working separately, allocate 100 points among the five alternatives to indicate their observations about the way critique did or did not occur, as shown on the left.

Next, members reveal their point allocations and use them as the basis for a discussion of similarities and differences in their observations, reaching and recording team agreement as shown on the right.

Individual		Team
A___	Little or no attention was given to analyzing team action.	A___
B___	Compliments were given, and faults were not examined.	B___
C___	Suggestions of how to do differently or a little better kept the meeting moving at an acceptable pace.	C___
D___	Fault-finding; unconstructive criticism.	D___
E___	Concurrent critique of teamwork was present and used for improving action and for learning from it.	E___

If a post critique is delayed too long after an activity is completed, recollections of what happened may be incomplete or fragmentary. The possibility of making real use of the lessons learned is remote, i.e., changes needed, even though identified, are less likely to be put into action.

Maximum benefit is possible when critique follows immediately on completion of the activity.

Many companies lose much of the real benefit of post critique because managers rush headlong into the next activity, glad to be through with the last one. Another reason is the attitude, "Let's not look backward. That's history. You can't do anything about it. Look forward and get on to the next project." This attitude rejects the notion that learning from experience is even a possibility.

The Role of Feedback in Critique

Sometimes critique is relied upon to discover what occurred to prevent it from occurring again, but the facts and data that have to be marshaled for the study have no human content. They are facts based upon the breakdown of machinery or equipment or a power failure, or any number of mechanical things; but people are not a significant component in the performance.

The primary use of critique from the standpoint of 9,9 versatility is where the human factor is the critical ingredient and equipment and physical factors reflect human decisions rather than problems independent of them. When these conditions prevail, the primary means of data gathering relies upon the direct experience of the participants themselves. This means that the critique is likely to be successful only when those who are participating can feed back their observations, experiences, and feelings to one another in an open, problem-solving way.

Feedback that is motivated by or is seen as unconstructive criticism promotes defensiveness. In turn, that can generate counterattack, leading those who started out to be helpful to one another into mutual recrimination, antipathy, etc. Thus, it is essential for those who are involved in a critique to be committed to carrying it out in a constructive way.

There are certain mechanical "rules" that can maximize the benefits from critique.

Feedback is received most appreciatively when it is descriptive, nonevaluative, and nonjudgmental. Nonevaluative feedback is descriptive.It pictures, in an accurate and reconstructible way, what happened in the situation and what consequences occurred as a result of what did happen. This feedback is most valuable and is less likely to generate defensiveness and counterattack, and less likely to hurt, and/or cause subjective feelings of rejection. It is also less likely to be seen as a threat of expulsion, or as a communication that suggests that a person is losing popularity.

The closer the feedback to the event it describes, the better it is. When an event and the critique of it occur in close connection with one another, it is easier for the person whose behavior is being described to reconstruct the actual event and the thoughts, feelings, and emotions surrounding it. This greater capacity for reconstruction enables the person to learn more fully because of being able to "identify" with it and so understand one's own role in it.

Small units of feedback, but not trivia, should be offered. Feedback can be specific, concrete, and limited enough in magnitude to enable it to be thoroughly understood. This is better than a general assessment that is so lacking in specific detail that it is difficult to understand fully what it is attempting to convey.

On the other hand, trivia, or things of minor or no importance, have little bearing on the important aspects of personal effectiveness and so contribute very little to personal learning.

Concentrate on things a person can change. Those things a person has a reasonable prospect of doing something about are far more worthy topics of feedback than are things a person is highly unlikely to be able to change. Since feedback is expected to form a basis for change, the more it relates to things that can be changed, the more useful the feedback will be. It might be more comfortable to concentrate on characteristics and conditions not in need of change, but this is not desirable in the context of learning to be more effective.

Be aware of the personal motivations for giving feedback. An individual is most helpful to others when he or she knows the underlying motivations that stimulate feedback. One motivation is often a 9,9 orientation of concern for contributing to others through a caring attitude toward them. However, feedback opportunities can be used, for example, to score a point or to reap vengeance, and this characterizes what might be the extreme motivation of a 9,1-oriented person. By comparison, a 1,9-oriented person might give positive feedback to be endeared to the recipient. A 1,1-oriented person might do so to indicate a sense of being "with it," and to move things along even though the underlying attitude is "I couldn't care less." A 5,5-oriented person provides feedback to communicate that the recipient is a valued person, and in this way gains some popularity for him or herself.

In comparison with these, the 9,9-oriented person is motivated by the desire to make a contribution through caring for the effectiveness of others and to gain results.

When Is Critique Useful?

Critique may be used when

☐ Work is bogged down and people are unclear of the causes of their lack of progress.
☐ Work practices have been relatively formal and there is a readiness to move toward informality and more spontaneous collaboration.
☐ A new procedure is being introduced.
☐ A group is embarking on an innovative activity.
☐ A group's membership is changed, particularly by the introduction of a new boss.
☐ 9,9 teamwork values are understood by team members who are motivated to learn how to increase their effectiveness.
☐ Results are less than what they can and should be.

Critique is not likely to be useful when

☐ Two or more participants are overtly antagonistic to one another and would use the opportunity for destructive criticism.
☐ There is a crisis and the time needed for deliberation is unavailable.
☐ Activities are so mechanical and routine that few benefits are gained by examining them.
☐ Participants are inexperienced in face-to-face feedback methods, or fearful of open communication.

Strengths and Limitations of Critique

The various forms of critique ensure that those whose participation is under study become their own students and teachers. Then it is most likely that the conclusions reached will be implemented because the implications of what has been learned are well understood.

One limitation lies in the difficulty many people experience in being objective and in making sound observations when they are deeply involved in an activity itself. They are called on to observe as they are participating, that is, to participate in the problem solving but to study the progress simultaneously. Their reactions to the activity itself, as well as to the people in it, may influence what they think and feel, and therefore, how they react. This is a strength as well as a limitation because the more points of view about an activity, the more likely people can learn from it.

Observation and feedback require effective and skillful communication. Participants must develop such skills if the full benefits of critique are to be realized.

Generalizations

When team members identify and discuss in advance the purpose, goals, or objectives of an activity and how it can best be accomplished, they are using one version of critique. This can ensure agreement as to what should happen and set the stage for effective performance. Concurrent critique is interrupting the activity as it is being carried out so that team members can analyze and give feedback regarding procedures, processes, or people's reactions. Then whatever is contributing to or hindering performance can be identified. Post critique, applied when the activity has been completed, is utilized to determine whether the accomplishment was satisfactory, and if so, why, and if not, why not. When these questions are answered, the participants have both evaluated the task just finished and improved their understanding of how to go about undertaking future activities to get better results.

The major limitation to using critique is that it is premised on 9,9 values of candor, conflict confrontation, and reliance on an experimental attitude. If these values are lacking, team members may go through the motions, but it is unlikely that the activity will be worth the effort. It may be necessary to shift values before the benefits of critique can be realized.

Summary

When tactics of 9,9 teamwork are applied to problem solving, there are numerous issues of how interaction takes place in a constructive way. One consideration is that those involved in problem solving often are not the "right" ones. There may be too many, too few, or the wrong people involved. Some problems are best solved 1/0, some 1/1, some 1/some, and still other problems on a 1/all basis. Some may not be solved even on a 1/all basis because outsiders are essential to finding and implementing a sound solution. Trying to solve a problem without mobilizing the necessary human resources is to risk failure.

Another issue is the recognition that the felt problem often is not the real problem and that a diagnostic strategy is preferable to a commonsense definition of the problem.

Developing criteria for an elegant solution is a desirable step because it focuses thought and attention on the properties a best solution could contain. Commitment to one solution over another comes later, after Alternative A has been compared with Alternative B, A and B with C, and so on, all in the light of criteria.

Evaluation of the alternatives appears to be a rational step, but here, too, human elements intrude in the form of vested interests, hidden agenda, and so on, to distort solution selection. This is so, even though criteria of a sound solution may previously have been developed. The 9,9 approach is to aid participants to explain reservations and doubts and to confront conflict directly, so that any person resisting can explore and evaluate reasons for resistance. If the resistance is real it can benefit problem solving; when unreal it can be eliminated from consideration.

The planning step for implementation often is ignored, with the result that other organization pressures act on those who are responsible for implementation, thus making it impossible to bring an effective solution into use. Furthermore, the resources essential for effective implementation may not have been anticipated in the planning stage and may be unavailable to permit implementation.

Critique of problem solving both for operational results and for learning is stepping away from the entire cycle and exploring strengths and weaknesses of decisions made at each step from beginning to end. In this way the members involved gain insight as to what should be retained and repeated—or identified and eliminated—in future problem-solving cycles.

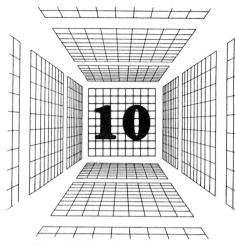

A 9,9-Oriented Approach to Management-by-Objectives and a Reward System to Motivate Productivity

Sound 9,9-oriented management provides a basis for satisfying a person's need to contribute to the organization's success. One important application is in utilizing management-by-objectives as the basis for personal involvement in advancing the business. Another connects the reward system to contribution.

Management-by-Objectives Through Goal Setting

More significant and greater contributions are possible when managers are committed to challenging goals that contribute to achieving organizational purpose than when their efforts are limited to completing daily activities on a more or less stimulus-response basis. Aiding a subordinate to set goals for attainment that are within his or her power requires 9,9 skills.

Conventional Approaches to Management-by-Objectives

A management-by-objectives program is often implemented when top management accepts the validity of the approach and authorizes its use. First, managers are taught a series of procedural steps, beginning with discussing objectives with a subordinate. Thereafter, objectives are recorded and forwarded to a central office where they are accumulated and summarized. This approach is mechanical and tactical. It involves providing how-to-do-it instructions, forms, and other written support materials. Support may be provided by a facilitator who aids groups to complete the steps.

Motivational Dynamics of Goals

This tactical approach can be compared with a principled approach to management-by-objectives that does not begin with *setting* goals but rather with the *dynamics* of setting goals. There are many properties of goals that stimulate people to commit their energies to attaining them. Only when these properties arouse the involvement of those who must achieve them are there likely to be meaningful results from a program involving management-by-objectives.

Personal "Ownership." The concept of ownership is of primary importance. People are motivated most to reach a goal when it "belongs" to them. Then they are involved and become committed to reaching it.

Ownership does *not* come from being told:

"Do it!"
"Would you please?"
"Do it or not if you want."
"Why not take a shot at it?"

The 9,9 alternative is for a person to consider all aspects of a goal and, in doing so, become involved in the possibility of really reaching it. The final aspect is when a person gives his or her personal commitment to the challenge. Then the individual has taken it inside; the individual now "owns" it. The following also influence ownership.

Clarity. It is essential for the goal to be clear to the person responsible for reaching it. A goal may be well understood by a boss who believes adequate directions for accomplishing it have been given, but the goal may be unclear to the subordinate. In such case, the subordinate is unable to decide what action he or she has to take to accomplish the goal in a meaningful way. Yet when a subordinate is clear about the goal and what is entailed in achieving it, effort can be put into reaching it.

Meaningfulness. Sometimes an activity is a meaningful, coherent unit. All components fit together to make a sensible whole. At other times, the same activity is fragmented into "mechanical" pieces, and the pieces do not have any inherent meaning to the person responsible for performing the activity. The pieces by themselves may not make sense. Whether or not the activity is a meaningful whole in itself is an important factor in a successful effort. If the goal is an arbitrary fragment of something larger, it is less likely to be motivating than if it is a unit unto itself. This latter kind of goal gives the person responsible for achieving it a sense of completeness when the goal is reached.

Significance. A goal may be clear and it may be a meaningful whole, and yet it may not be regarded as important. It may be so trivial as to produce an attitude of "So what?" A goal is only likely to be motivating if it is of a significant nature. Possessing significance, then, is an important property of a goal, even though any isolated part of it may not be "important." An example is the spare tire. If never used, it is not important to have one. However, being miles from a telephone when a blowout occurs makes the spare tire highly relevant. There are many such examples in daily living.

Difficulty (Remoteness). A goal that can be accomplished with little effort is not likely to be motivating. Stacking a dishwasher with two place settings a day is unlikely to be challenging. Although necessary, it presents a person with little excitement. At the other extreme, a goal so difficult as to create a probability of failure is also unlikely to be motivating.

One way to create this motivation is to set goals within the framework of what can be achieved under ideal conditions. With a full understanding of why conditions are not ideal, it is possible to remove a sense of failure associated with conditions beyond control. Thus it becomes important to set goals that are difficult to achieve, yet realistic with accurate assessment of the effort needed to reach them.

Sometimes a goal that is very difficult can become motivating when its components can be dealt with as subgoals, so that the main goal is achievable a step at a time. Getting a college degree can be seen as a very difficult or remote goal to a freshman, but completing the freshman year as a subgoal can be challenging.

The Time Between Goal Setting and Goal Reaching. A goal can be too remote, in the sense of being projected so far into the future that it is unrealistic for an individual to feel urgency, immediateness, or relevance in efforts to achieve it. As a result, goals that can only be reached in the longer term are unlikely to be very motivating, unless they, too, can be divided into a series of subgoals, each of which is meaningful and attainable within a foreseeable period of time.

A goal that can be attained almost immediately or in the near term is unlikely to be challenging. Even though value might come from achieving it, it does not stimulate the kind of involvement and effort that a more difficult goal might promote. From a time perspective, an ideal goal is one that is located far enough in the future to make reaching the goal feasible, yet not be so far away that the sense of urgency is lost.

Zeigarnik Effect. Another characteristic of a goal is called the Zeigarnik or "completion" effect, named after the German scientist who studied it. Once a person feels personal commitment, efforts to reach the goal create internal tensions that push for a successful outcome. If barriers are encountered that block goal achievement, the person is unlikely to say, "I am blocked." Rather, the individual increases efforts to remove the barrier. These internal tensions constitute an aspect of motivation. This motivation means that committed people do not quit simply because difficulties are encountered.

Feedback. Measurements furnish the necessary information for knowing whether performance is on track and on time for reaching a goal. Without feedback a person is "flying blind," and the motivation to continue is much lower than if feedback is available. As an example, many companies assess progress through a financial year in terms of quarters, months, or weeks. In this way, information is always at hand about whether the objectives for a given financial period are being met. If they are not, changes can be introduced.

Operational goals can be stated in many different ways. Some involve financial statements. Yet operational statements often are better because they fit reality more closely. For example, an on-time airline is one that satisfies customers' needs better than one which has poor on-time performance. The airline can set a goal of, for example, 90% on-time departures and arrivals to be reached over a three- or six-month period. It can then continuously study actual performance to see if it is moving in the direction required to meet the objective as established. With knowledge of progress, it becomes possible to evaluate whether additional steps are needed. If they are, what is required to implement these steps can be determined. Without the use of feedback on actual performance, less progress toward the objective is to be expected than when accurate and frequent feedback is available.

Some kinds of work cannot provide direct feedback, yet it is possible to go one step removed for a measure of impact. For example, a pharmaceuticals detailer does not take orders, even though he or she brings various drugs to the attention of physicians. The detailer demonstrates the availability of these pharmaceuticals and then outlines their effects and value. Since no order is taken from the doctor, there is no immediate or direct way of knowing whether the effort expended is moving toward the goal of increasing company sales. In this case indirect feedback is needed and can be obtained by monitoring orders placed by pharmacists and hospitals, these being the "sales outlets" when the doctor is viewed as an extension of the drug company's marketing arm.

The Goal Gradient. An interesting property of a goal involves what is known as the goal gradient. One becomes more and more involved in achieving a goal the closer one gets to its completion. While understandable, this property of a goal can produce undesirable side effects.

An example of the goal gradient at work is when attempts to escape from prison become more frequent the closer the prisoner comes to completing the prison term and being released. The goal of freedom becomes so compelling that the prisoner "can't wait," and therefore does the very thing that prolongs imprisonment.

Another example is referred to as the Stackhanoff effect, named after a Russian. It identifies a behavior characteristic first observed in Soviet factories. An objective that is expressed as a quota is established for how much of a product is to be produced in a month. At the beginning of the month work is slow and carried out in a leisurely way. Productivity remains low, and this may continue through the first twenty or more days of the month. Then everyone realizes that the quota will not be reached unless a "total" effort is put forth. In the last few days of the month, stupendous effort is expended and the quota reached. Needless to say, at the beginning of the next month people are exhausted from the effort. Work slows down to a leisurely pace, until the same dilemma is faced at the end of the next month.

The obvious solution is to understand the dynamic involved. By getting true involvement in the objective it becomes possible to manage the pace of activities, ensuring that work is not so hard as to be exhausting at any point along the road to the goal. When effort is maintained at the highest attainable level the finding is that total output is increased, even exceeding the quota.

The Stackhanoff effect is more widespread than might be realized. For example, taking a leisurely attitude toward study in the beginning of a college term and then cramming at the end to get a "B" in the final exam is the same phenomenon. Christmas shopping on December 24 and completing and mailing one's tax return at midnight on the last day are other examples. This phenomenon explains why labor-management negotiations sometimes break down just before contract signing. If either union or management becomes overeager for success, last-minute demands may be made that are unacceptable. Similar examples can be found in commercial negotiations.

Priority of Goals. Two or more goals may be established, but without awareness that they are mutually incompatible. An example is two positive objectives, both of which are equally attractive. One involves funding R&D. Another is to launch a new product that will add to the product line. Funds are insufficient to do both, and a splitting of funds may mean that neither is done well enough.

Managers often face goals of equal value that are incompatible with one another, with no criteria to resolve the impasse. The solution is that issues of priority be dealt with and resolved in the process of goal setting with a "hierarchy of goals." Once the hierarchy of goals becomes clear, then managers can take the initiative to assign priorities to goals and create the conditions under which those that are agreed to can be achieved.

In the case just mentioned a manager at some level takes responsibility for establishing a hierarchy of goals between the long-term R&D goals and the short-term product line enlargement goal.

Involvement, Participation, and Commitment: The Goal-Setting Ingredients of 9,9 Versatility

Management-by-objectives through goal setting relies on the involvement of those engaged in supervising and implementing the goals. The benefits of shared participation include the following:

☐ Thinking through goals provides a basis of personal understanding and insight and, therefore, of improved self-direction.
☐ Thinking through goals stimulates involvement in the real issues, arousing commitment to success.
☐ By open and shared participation, which recognizes that both boss and subordinate have a mutually interdependent role in doing the things needed to achieve a goal, it becomes possible to bring achievement motivation to a high level.
☐ A 9,9-oriented boss values the participation of subordinates, is alert to their reservations and doubts, deals with them through insight-based resolution, and is likely to earn their commitment to achieving goals.

When these conditions prevail, management-by-objectives through a goal-setting program can make significant contributions to organization success, operationally and through real development of its people.

How to Set Goals

Several steps are involved in using goal setting as a 9,9 versatility skill. *Start by identifying goals, not by dealing with current problems.* One place to start is at the other end from the "here-and-now." The "other end" is defined by what might be achieved. Identifying possibilities is the initial step in the formulation of goals.

The best beginning is to think through the soundest outcomes, as contrasted with what might at the moment appear practical and realistic. By thinking about the soundest possibilities and imagining what the situation will be when goals are achieved, opportunities are spotted that might otherwise go unrecognized.

Several sources of data can stimulate thinking about the soundest possibilities:

☐ Conclusions about desirable outcomes from a previously completed performance appraisal and review.

☐ The boss's perceptions of the areas where a subordinate's performance needs improvement and of opportunities the subordinate may not recognize.

☐ Comparison of the individual job description with present performance may point to needed goals.

☐ Team building, as part of organizational development, often results in specific improvement goals.

Obviously not all of the soundest formulations are achievable. Sometimes, after a "soundest" goal has been identified and the specific steps necessary to reach it have been evaluated, it no longer appears realistic. Then it may be necessary to abandon the goal or to pare it down to some lesser objective that can be accomplished. Absence of testing against reality causes "soundest" thinking to become and to be seen as *idealistic* and to cease having influence on behavior.

Walking backwards into the here-and-now. The next step is to walk backwards from the goal and to identify the steps necessary to realize it. Those engaged in the activity can test their specific steps prior to finalizing them. The activity results in designing an operational plan that becomes a working blueprint for future action. The advantage of making this evaluation is that barriers that might otherwise loom unexpectedly and insurmountably can be anticipated and dealt with in a problem-solving manner.

Characterizing the here-and-now. The last step is to specify in an objective way what the prevailing here-and-now conditions are. Does the here and now contain obstacles that will block goal achievement? If so, these must be resolved. Analyzing the actual situation in detail provides a realistic picture of the starting situation. Then the situation is set up for managing by objectives through goal setting.

Implementing the management-by-objectives action plan. Once identified and established, the activity shifts into an agreed-on management-by-objectives action program. Managing the implementation of these objectives, through a sound mix of supervision, consultation, resourcing, and self-direction, is the final step. This is facilitated by drawing up a written plan of action through which the objectives are to be achieved. Specific steps to be taken are scheduled against time requirements. Critique points are designated for review of progress against objectives and replanning sequences are built in to provide for unforeseen circumstances and changes in conditions.

The "paper" program of mechanics. Once managers expend this kind of effort in setting sound goals, a paper program for control of the process is no longer essential. The paper, desirable for keeping the overall effort in focus, comes to be seen as a support for the activity rather than as a burden that is resented and resisted. The motivational underpinnings of a sound goal-setting activity make the difference.

Goals based on excellence are no more difficult and far more rewarding than are those based on convention or mediocrity. The difference is in their quality, which, in itself, is an important source of motivation for extra effort.

Summary of 9,9-Oriented Management-by-Objectives

There is a widespread need for goals that give direction, stimulate effort, and give work a meaningful character. Goal setting is a way of identifying and getting involved in reaching some objective. Being able to identify a goal makes it possible to set a sequence for the steps necessary to reach the goal in an orderly, economical way. The likelihood of getting there is increased when steps are identified, agreed to in advance, and set in a way so they can be changed to fit changes in the situation. The route to achieving a goal should be thoroughly outlined, with specific steps formulated by the persons responsible for taking them to gain the advantages of involvement and commitment to their implementation.

A management-by-objectives approach is doomed to failure if it disregards these properties of goals and proceeds in a mechanical, paper-controlled manner. The reason is that the motivating value of involvement is absent and managerial behavior is influenced very little. The potential rewards possible when people are committed to sound goals and objectives are lost both to the individual and to the organization.

Using Organizational Rewards to Motivate Productivity

Fulfillment through contribution is the 9,9 motivation for changing things to make them better or more productive. Management-by-objectives offers a way to establish direction to individual effort in the interests of achieving organizational goals. How would a company that desires to stimulate managers to attain such objectives use the reward system for doing so? The underlying rationale is that managers tend to do the things they are rewarded for and to avoid doing things for which they are ignored or punished.

When an organization rewards employees for bringing about needed changes, efforts toward corporate excellence are stimulated and individuals are likely to feel personal fulfillment resulting from their contributions.

Organization Rewards

From an organizational point of view, wide agreement exists on the just basis of rewarding performance. The idea is that people who contribute more than their colleagues to achieving organizational purposes are moving the organization toward greater success. Because they are doing so, greater benefits in the form of organizational rewards should come their way. This is reward based on merit. Merit implies that what people do can be weighed and evaluated and compared along a continuum, as a yardstick. The weighing scale includes immediate results achieved and other positive organizational benefits.

There are many examples of how contribution to the organization's future effectiveness is acknowledged. In science, merit is evaluated by basic discoveries, their consequences for new discoveries, and their implications for the future of science and the human race. The Nobel prize is an example of rewarding merit for outstanding contributions to science, literature, medicine, and peace. Contributions to film making and acting are recognized by the highly prized Oscars. The same is true in sports. Players judged to have made the greatest impact on success of the team and teamwork are singled out for public recognition. These are, of course, cases involving contributions that are highly visible and truly exceptional. In many spheres of activity, personal merit based on contribution is acknowledged through rewards that are both symbolic and financial.

Can we expect the same respect for merit in business and industry, where people are engaged in less visible and more interrelated sets of activities and in government and service institutions, such as health delivery systems? From a motivational point of view, it is a valid premise to offer the greatest reward for the most outstanding contribution, and so on, down to the other end of the scale, where those who have blocked or hampered results are dismissed or penalized. This means that through applying talent, the person rewarded most is adding most to the products or services an organization makes available to society in its pursuit of achievement, comfort, satisfaction, and happiness.

The first proposition is: The larger the personal contribution and the greater the promise of further improvement the larger the reward offered.

The second proposition is: Financial rewards are personally motivating to those who do most to advance corporate success. Because of the greater responsibility they shoulder and, therefore, the greater contribution they can make, those who lead the most financially successful corporations generally receive the greatest reward. This is not to say that all rewards are financial in character, and a tax system may result in perquisites that are more valuable than their equivalent in money. The tactics change but not the principle.

Motivation of Individuals

Now we turn the question around and ask, "How does motivation look from the viewpoint of the person whose performance is under evaluation by the system?"

Research is a basic necessity for answering this. The most significant source of satisfaction is doing a challenging job well and being rewarded for it. Unfortunately, work that is inherently stimulating may not be the same work that an organization needs to have done. When an individual must perform unstimulating but necessary work, individual and organizational goals are far apart. But when employees are committed to the organization's success, uninteresting work may serve to motivate. Jobs that contain no genuine emotional appeal may stimulate ingenuity to find ways to automate or eliminate them.

Thus, while the aim may be for all work to be meaningful and for an organization to need no other kind of work, the possibility of achieving this aim is likely unreal. Nevertheless, the importance of rewarding contribution based on merit remains undiminished.

Achieving Organization Purpose Through Rewarding Performance

Organizations might seek to shift the attitudes and emotions of their employees toward the 9,9 orientation by ensuring that the system rewards most those who contribute most to the corporation's success, both short and long term. The question then is, "What should be avoided in a reward system and how is it done?"

What to Avoid in a Reward System. First and foremost to be avoided are across-the-board raises. This treats everyone alike, and the justification usually is "no one is treated unfairly." Actually the opposite is true. Those who have made the greatest contributions are brought to the same level as those who have contributed the least, and thus they are receiving far less benefit from their contributions than the least contributors.

Another erroneous practice is to make small differences in adjustment that distinguish one individual's contribution from another, even though the person's relative position in the pay scale remains the same. What people judge is the amount of change relative to their colleagues. If X gets a salary change of $500 and Y of $550, it is the $50 difference not the $500 increase that is the basis of comparison. Such a difference will be resented if it can be justified only by seniority, friendship, popularity, or devotion, rather than by contribution.

A final factor to be avoided is secrecy. Silence in most compensation programs is broken at only two points. One is principal officers' compensation reported publicly in corporate annual reports. The other is union contracts, often specifying pay level by job classification and spelling out overtime payment. These two exceptions are brought about by legal considerations rather than corporate commitment to an open payment system. All other aspects of payment are most likely to be silent or secret.

The most obvious reason that not much is said about salary treatment is that perceived inequities often result when employees can compare earnings. There are likely to be discrepancies between an individual's judgment of his or her relative worth to the corporation and the judgment of the boss. The rationale is that by keeping these differences private, it is possible to avoid adverse emotional attitudes, feelings of antagonism, jealousy, and envy which disrupt smooth performance.

Is it true that subordinates' seniors can evaluate contribution more objectively than the contributors themselves? Probably in part because self-evaluation of contribution is subject to self-deception. Comparisons are affected by vested interests. Yet, on the other hand, many factors, such as like or dislike, influence evaluation by seniors. Subjective factors, although present, are not related to contribution.

The most equitable system is for seniors to make judgments that are open and therefore subject to correction when inequities are demonstrated. Such a system puts a premium on high-quality performance appraisals that aid a person to be objective and to identify factors that can be changed which would result in revised estimates of the individual's worth in the organization.

How to Operate a Reward System. Objective criteria that relate personal reward to profit contribution should be used whenever possible. This means dividing the overall business structure into functional subunits, each of which can be evaluated in a relatively independent way. The division allows measurable expenses and incomes to be weighed against contributions from each unit compared against one another. This is a positive approach, particularly when compensation decisions also include recognition of cooperation between subunits in those areas where overlap is inevitable or desirable, except when it results in disregard of cutting corners on quality, management, development, etc. These shortcuts may not adversely affect long-term results for some time, but when they do, the losses, monetary and otherwise, can be substantial.

Another involves opening the reward system to public review. This step is strongly resisted, as previously discussed. Nevertheless, an open reward system is valuable because it clearly focuses on the need to confront and resolve inequities.

A third is to ensure that differential treatment is based on two criteria: (1) the worth of a person's efforts in furthering corporate effectiveness, and (2) comparative judgments of contributions by those who perform in the same area under comparable opportunities. This person-to-person comparison is basic. It should be made explicit because those who are judged also compare themselves with one another in this way. Only by such comparison is it possible for those who evaluate contribution to do so against a standard of "more or less."

Still another consideration is evaluation of a person's potential relative to current performance. This can be seen by asking the question, "Of two runners both doing the 100-yard dash, should the greatest encouragement and coaching go to the one who is at his maximum time of 10 seconds or the one potentially capable of getting to 9 seconds?"

The same question can be posed in management. Of two employees contributing equally at a given point in time, greater opportunity should be afforded the one with the greatest potential. Otherwise, this employee is likely to disregard the importance of developing potential and may seek employment elsewhere where his or her potential is more appreciated.

Summary of Using Rewards to Motivate Productivity

Since people tend to do the things for which they are rewarded and to avoid what is not rewarded, it is important to gear the organization's reward system to the 9,9 fulfillment of the organization's real needs through contribution.

When organizations treat contribution as a primary and essential need, it is unnecessary to resort to seniority as the basis of reward, prestige as the basis of promotion, across-the board raises, and keeping people in the same position relative to one another. Merit-based contribution is best utilized as the basis of a reward system when effort is subject to objective measurement through profit, cost, or contribution criteria; when an "open" system of payment is maintained; when judgments involve person-to-person comparisons; and when potential is assessed, understood, and acknowledged.

Implications

In many organizations, management-by-objectives is treated independently of the reward system, and performance appraisal through critique is related to neither of them. As a result each separate system is likely to be based on its own narrow assumptions and contradictions come to exist between the motivations that are linked to objective setting, performance appraisal, and pay and promotion.

The goal of sound management is to recognize that these are not independent but interdependent systems. An integrated approach to human resource management in support of organization performance is possible when this interdependence is recognized through designing each on a common set of principles.

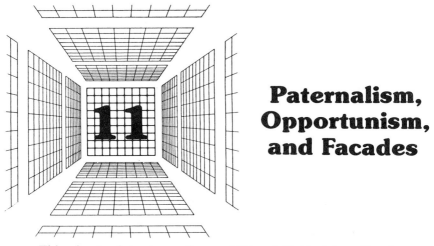

Paternalism, Opportunism, and Facades

This chapter introduces three additional Grid styles. One is paternalism/maternalism, another is opportunism, and a third is facades. All are different ways of combining the underlying assumptions of two or more Grid styles at the same time.

Paternalism/Maternalism (9 + 9)

If paternalism/maternalism were shown graphically on the Grid, it would be indicated by an arc connecting the 1,9 and 9,1 corners. This approach is a combination of a high concern for production with high concern for people added to it. It is not an *integration* of the two concerns as in a 9,9 orientation but rather an additive combination of the two and is denoted 9 + 9. The basic assumption of the boss toward a subordinate is, "I own [or am responsible for] you and want to help your career [as if the other person were a son or daughter]. That's why I expect your loyalty as a matter of course." The reference word used in this chapter is paternalism, and maternalism differs from it only by the gender of the manager exercising it. There are many terms for a manager who operates in this manner, and benevolent autocrat is one of them.

Motivations

The positive motivation is to gain admiration and adulation through giving chosen subordinates the benefits of one's experience, counsel, and guidance. Gratification comes from demonstrating that one is the source of wisdom and knowledge for others to utilize. When subordinates comply with what the paternalist expects from them by way of production, subordinates are rewarded by the boss and they in turn are expected to appreciate the help and guidance provided and reward given to them.

The negative pole is fear of not trying hard enough and losing control through subordinates substituting their own wills in disregard of what they have been told. When subordinates accept directions and guidance, the boss feels warm toward them for their loyalty; but when they resist directions and guidance, this resistance is viewed as disloyalty and may deem them unworthy of further help. The phrase, "You work your heart out and they [subordinates] don't appreciate it," shows the repudiation of a subordinate who does not appreciate the paternalist's sacrifice and becomes noncompliant. Since there is a tendency for subordinates to remain dependent by yielding to the boss's wishes, subordinates are stunted and prevented from growing and developing toward independence of thought, judgment, and convictions.

Managing Conflict

The successful paternalist is one who has succeeded in creating clones. Subordinates have learned to think as the boss thinks, to do as the boss does, to enjoy the same outside activities as the boss enjoys, even to dress in the same manner. At some point along the road, subordinates may resist this parent-child syndrome as too constraining and begin doing things independently of the boss. This is difficult for the paternalist to tolerate and paternalistic bosses have their own distinctive ways of dealing with conflict.

Avoiding Conflict. Conflict is avoided by reinforcement of compliance through praises and compliments. Once the subordinate has come to expect and feel secure with praise and compliments, the paternalist can withhold praise and compliments as an indication of displeasure. If the subordinate continues to resist or withhold compliance, the boss may reprimand, letting the subordinate know that bad behavior has been exhibited. The boss then repeats what is wanted from the subordinate and praise is offered in anticipation that compliance will be forthcoming.

Handling Conflict When It Appears. One way to reduce conflict is to divert attention from disagreement by changing the subject or placing the problem in an alternative context. Then the subordinate can yield without being made to feel guilty for disagreeing.

Another solution when the conflict involves two or more parties in disagreement with one another, but on issues that are of critical significance for the boss, is for the boss to say, "You two get in a room and solve it, otherwise there could be repercussions." This solution is premised on the importance of eliminating the conflict; furthermore it conveys the notion that those who are in conflict can lift themselves by their own bootstraps and by an act of will resolve their disagreement.

Control is again fully restored when the subordinate expresses appreciation and gratitude for all the boss has done. Controlling subordinates through reward and punishment is the model of paternalistic child-rearing extended into the company.

When Conflict Persists. When conflict persists and control cannot be reestablished, the subordinate is "disowned" and repudiated. This is evident when the boss says, "I can't believe it. Think of all I've done for her . . ." Rejection, however, may not be as explicit. The boss may express public appreciation for the subordinate for whom an undesirable transfer or bad shiftwork schedule has just been worked out. Vengeance and retribution may be sought when "genuinely" volunteered help has been rejected by the subordinate. Once a break occurs, it is likely to be permanent, with little the subordinate can do to get back in the boss's good graces.

Paternalism is dealt with further in the appendix, where it is compared with the 9,9 orientation. The differences are vast and they promote significantly distinctive consequences for corporate success.

Behavioral Elements

Initiative. The boss exercises strong initiative up to the point where subordinates can be trusted to do what is wanted without their being told again. At that point direction can be relaxed on the assumption that subordinates have learned to obey and will follow through in a correct manner. When anything out of the ordinary arises, however, the boss insists that subordinates check back rather than acting on their own. This may be interpreted as a degree of delegation but in fact it is pseudo-delegation. The subordinate is not free to exercise independence of thought and judgment or to define the solution to a problem but only to carry out extensions of the boss's direction. Subordinates may misinterpret this, however, to mean they are acting on their own initiative. They may also interpret total compliance as freedom for initiative because they have come to accept what they have been told as though they have discovered it themselves. This reaction of subordinates explains why some prefer to follow and be told what to do. Having been so indoctrinated in doing what the boss tells them to do, they have lost the capacity for thinking for themselves.

Inquiry. Since the paternalistic boss is in charge in the sense of telling people what to do, guiding their actions, and counseling, much inquiry is focused on ensuring everything is going according to expectations. It may not be direct in the sense of asking for reports, but the questions asked are intended to let subordinates know what is wanted of them. The paternalist relies on questions as a primary teaching tool to determine if the subordinate can respond correctly. This indicates that the lesson has been learned; if not, further instruction is needed. Much inquiry is also indirect through listening and observing to establish that things are being done as they should be.

There is a high degree of need to know because the paternalistic manager cannot afford to be wrong or to learn from subordinates. Thus, written information may be heavily relied on to keep informed. The information may be concerned with technical matters if they are pertinent, rules and regulations if they are relevant, machinery and equipment that play a role in supervision, etc. Thus the paternalistic boss is likely to be known as a person who reads a lot and is well-informed. No detail is so small that it can be skipped over because the paternalist feels compelled to "know everything."

Advocacy. The paternalistic boss has strong beliefs and advocates them intensely, often with an overtone of moralism as in "shoulds" and "should nots," in "oughts" and "must nots." Adulation comes when subordinates admire and respect the convictions the paternalist embraces. They realize the boss is wise and profound and therefore worthy of being followed.

Decisions. The paternalistic manager is the sole decision maker until subordinates have learned compliance, but decisions are not made and barked out as commands. Rather, once having decided what a subordinate should do, teaching, coaching, counseling, and guidance are used to determine that what is desired is fully understood and accepted. Thus, the manager does not appear abrasive and harsh, but rather kind, warm, and helpful, even though the subordinate is learning in an imitative or rote way to do whatever has been taught. This may create the need to check back rather than to operate on personal initiative. Thus, the subordinate is carrying out what the boss expects and in this sense may never become an independent thinker based on individual analysis and judgment.

Critique. The boss cannot afford to be open to feedback from subordinates because anything of a negative character would suggest a weakness, and the paternalistic boss takes pride in what is thought to be infallibility. Thus, personal feedback is one-way, from the boss down. Subordinates understand this and limit their reactions to weaker or stronger applause. However, if "father knows best," there is little or nothing to learn from children; therefore they take a "be seen and not heard" orientation whenever criticism might be applied.

The paternalist feels little or no reluctance to give feedback to subordinates through discussion of their performance. It is the boss's obligation to pass on to them whatever subordinates need to know for their own good. Then they can benefit from the boss's wisdom and guidance offered them.

This approach to feedback sometimes has been referred to as stroke-and-strike leadership. The subordinate is instructed and then, upon compliance, is rewarded by compliment. If compliance is expected but not forthcoming, then the subordinate is reprimanded. Then compliments are resumed, telling the subordinate that, "You're really OK, so let's move on."

Management Practices

A paternalistic manager treats subordinates as part of the organizational family, by telling them how to perform any new activity and rewarding or reprimanding as needed and desirable. Subordinates are encouraged to be responsible, but they are likely to be slow in taking initiative. Subordinates soon learn their manager is only happy with them when they are handling problems the manager's way.

Planning: "I think out in advance what it is that needs to be achieved and then seek to involve others in independently coming to the same conclusion I have drawn."

Organizing: "I arrange conditions of work so that everyone feels I appreciate their efforts."

Directing: "I rarely give direct orders or make unreasonable demands. Rather, I discuss what needs to be done to the point where they come to see it my way."

Controlling: "I reward those who see things the way I do and withhold rewards or reprimand those who do not cooperate. When people balk I hold out the promise of reward for renewed effort to do it right."

Staffing: "I rely on and utilize those on whose loyalty I can depend."

Management-by-Objectives: "I identify and review the goals I think important for each subordinate to meet and point out the advantages of accomplishing them."

Performance Appraisal: "I acknowledge what people are doing well and let them know what they are doing wrong for their own good."

One result of this way of managing becomes clear when the boss is heard to say, "My subordinates are reluctant to accept responsibility. They are bright and capable, with plenty of know-how, but they check with me first even when they don't need to. They won't take the ball and run. It is difficult to see how they will ever succeed." What the manager fails to realize is that subordinates want to please and feel the need to double-check because the manager may undercut their confidence if they act autonomously.

Consequences

Impact on Productivity. Moderate to high productivity is to be expected as a result of paternalistic supervision. Subordinates are motivated to reach norms established by the boss. It is unlikely subordinates will go beyond what is expected of them, though the potential for productivity may be far above the level set.

If the manager emphasizes quality, subordinates will be concerned to eliminate mistakes and errors. If the manager has little concern with quality, subordinates can be expected to have the same attitude. In other words, over the longer term subordinates come to model whatever it is that is expected of them and to avoid engaging in activities not advocated by the boss or ones that might draw a frown.

Impact on Creativity. Since the paternalistic boss does the thinking for subordinates, there is little or no likelihood that subordinates will be creative or innovative. They will not trust themselves to do anything that appears expedient or appropriate. The dependency created in the subordinate stifles creativity.

Mentoring: The Special Case. It is clearly desirable to use the experience and wisdom of senior personnel as one basis for strengthening the management development of juniors, and the mentor-protegé model can serve this purpose. To be fully successful, however, it must avoid the pitfalls of paternalism, such as producing dependency in the protegé and resentment/envy among his or her peers. These consequences can undermine this model of management development.

The most important factors in making the mentor-protegé model work are to ensure that the mentor is not satisfying personal needs for adulation; that the protegés are among the best qualified to benefit from this approach of accelerated learning; and that opportunities are not exploited for or by the protegé, which result in career benefits based on unfair advantage.

Impact on Satisfaction. With consistent application, paternalism can create a highly stable organization, with minimum turnover. Organization members tend to become compliantly obedient to requirements placed on them. The reward for compliance is economic and personal security; thus, subordinates prefer being dependent to acting on their own. Employees who buckle under are given many fine things—good pay, excellent benefits, recreational facilities, retirement programs; even low-cost housing, to say nothing of personal acceptance. Even though these contributions to welfare are not directly connected to output or productivity, they tend to increase the sense of well-being. Once a person has become so locked in there is no escape. "I owe my soul to the company store" describes feelings about paternalism.

However, some of the worst upheavals and disruptions have occurred where paternalism has been extensively practiced. Against a background of what appeared to be a stable and long-enduring organization, waves of resentment and retaliation have broken out against the management that had for so long treated its people so "well." Such a shift from compliant acceptance to defiant retaliation appears contradictory and warrants explanation.

Management that discourages and when necessary rejects the thinking and capabilities of people generates frustration, resistance, and alienation. These feelings are difficult to express directly toward an employer who, at the same time, offers economic, social, and personal security to those who comply with such unilateral demands. Reactions to felt indignities, as a result, may be swallowed and bottled up for a time, but they are there. Masking seething resentment and unrest produces the appearance of docility and devotion. Under these circumstances, even a minor irritation can trigger an eruption of vitriolic reactions. *The formula for concocting hate consists of arousing frustrations under conditions of dependency.* One feels antagonized and aggressive but cannot fight back because of fear of losing acceptance and security. Although paternalism has failed repeatedly to solve problems of getting production through people, it remains a widespread attitude underlying much managerial thinking.

Impact on Career. Superiors see the paternalistic boss as being able to supervise without disagreement and disruptive conflicts, and therefore such a manager will probably advance steadily though not rapidly up the managerial ladder.

Recognizing Paternalistic Behavior

The following words and phrases give indications of managerial leadership in the paternalistic mode:

- Benevolent dictator
- Condescending
- Constantly gives advice
- Discharges obligations
- Expects blind loyalty
- Father (Mother) knows best
- Graciously demanding
- Jealously guards prerogatives
- Leads by inspirational zeal
- Leads the flock
- Makes those who disagree feel guilty
- Martyr
- Moralistic
- Patronizing
- Perfectionist
- Preachy
- Prescriptive
- Self-righteous
- Stands for the "virtues"
- Tolerates private disagreement but resents public challenge

Suggestions for Change

The underlying motivation of a paternalist is domination, mastery, and control exercised to gain adulation. This means those with and through whom leadership has been exercised have become dependent on the boss to call the shots. When they have done what has been wanted of them, they may endear themselves to the paternalist who may as a result become even more highly motivated to "steer" people. Thus, the key problem a paternalist needs to concentrate on to change toward a 9,9 orientation involves becoming aware that others are remaining dependent. This kind of "helping" weakens their ability to exercise initiative and to contribute. Readiness to steer others is not likely to enable subordinates to develop autonomy and self-reliance. Leading for results by stimulating more open participation earns the respect of subordinates and stimulates their development of problem-solving skills.

Opportunism

Opportunism is present when all Grid styles are relied on in an unprincipled way. The basic assumption of the opportunist is to "get there first, and then you can clean up your act and project whatever image will make you look like a statesman, hero, or strong leader." This is situationalism in its purest form. Every action is for "tactical" reasons; a means to the end of personal advancement.

Motivations

The opportunist's positive motivation is to be preeminent, number one—a person wants to be on top because the top is in the limelight. It is the position that gets attention and adulation.

The opportunist seeks to avoid any actions that might result in being unnoticed, just one of the crowd, or even being dropped into a number two position.

The motivations are quite different from the domination, mastery, and control of the 9,1 orientation, or the popularity and "being in" motivation found beneath the 5,5 orientation. Equally, the *contribution* motivation observed in the 9,9 orientation is absent because the goal is not to make a difference or to make things better—the aim is to be number one.

Because there is such a variety of Grid-like ways of responding to situations, it might be expected that the opportunist behavior is unpredictable. This is the case for some few; however, they are the exception rather than the rule.

Most opportunists, while appearing to be all things to all people, behave in a predictable manner, no less than do persons managing under any Grid style. The notion is that everyone has a selfish interest that can be appealed to or a vulnerability that can be threatened. The person who elicits cooperation in exchange for helping someone satisfy a vested interest, who honors a vulnerability, or threatens to expose a raw nerve is said to be able to "manipulate people," each in a different way. However, in order to predict their behavior, one has to know the *importance* accorded by the opportunist to those with whom he or she is dealing. For example, if the person is of higher rank, greater social prominence, more wealthy, or held higher in public esteem, an opportunist adulates them in order to gain their favorable attention or tries to be ingratiating to them in order to gain their affection. The reason for this, of course, is that those of higher rank can help a person move up more than can anyone else.

A paternalist-as-boss is particularly vulnerable to the attentions of an opportunist. From the boss perspective, there is positive motivation to help a subordinate learn the ropes, bringing the favorable attention of others to bear on his (or her) "up and coming" protegé. When the subordinate is an opportunist the paternalistic boss may become the captive of his or her "creation." The former subordinate may outshine or abandon the boss once these "services" are no longer needed.

The opportunist is alert to possibilities of doing helpful things for persons of equal rank. These have a string attached and put the other person under implicit obligation to return the favor. In other words, equals are treated in a manner similar to how one might think about a bank account. By making a deposit now, a withdrawal can be made later, with interest. An opportunist may also play the other side of the street when dealing with equals. The opportunist can create "leverage" by being alert to signs of weakness. This is done in a quiet manner, and the opportunist takes care to ensure that others are unaware of what he or she knows about them. Nonetheless, this knowledge can be used, should it prove advantageous, to apply pressure in the interest of enhancing one's position at some future time.

The opportunist is likely to deal with subordinates in a heavy-handed manner, pressing them for whatever is necessary in order to move up the ladder. Subordinates are eliminated when they no longer can serve or when they get in the way.

These different ways of relating to people create a clear pattern as the opportunist seeks to get on top: adulate or ingratiate, obligate, subjugate, or eliminate—all depending on "who."

Managing Conflict

The opportunist prefers to avoid conflict if at all possible, but does not shrink from it when it appears. The reason for this is that when people's emotions are aroused, it is difficult to control or to predict what they may or may not do, and therefore it is risky to try to "use" them. For this reason, the opportunist relies on dealing with disagreement without confronting it or polarizing it.

Preventing Conflict. An opportunist is an "expert" on people. By learning their likes and dislikes, preferences and prejudices, their needs and wants, and their blind spots, it is possible to maneuver in the interest of moving their reactions into a yes or an okay while avoiding abrasiveness. When dealing with those above, the opportunist is solicitous, supportive, and agreeable. Their convictions may be reinforced even though the opportunist's personal convictions are in a different direction. When dealing with people of equal rank, the opportunist is likely to be a hail-fellow-well-met, a soft-soaper, and to play the angles in currying their favor. With subordinates, conflict is unlikely to arise because compliance is demanded and suppression is immediate should resistance be encountered. Elimination is the consequence of continued resistance.

Handling Conflict When It Appears. If conflict arises with a person of higher rank, the opportunist backs off and makes an effort to land feet first. With equals, the opportunist is a smooth operator and attempts to depolarize an issue saying, "Let us reason together." An effort is made to find an accommodation that shows reasonableness, even though on deeper examination the opportunist turns out to be a cagey horse trader in making deals that create future obligations. Much is promised but delivery occurs only when there is a personal payout.

The attitude is to either capitulate or leave when conflicts occur with subordinates. However, the leaving is not brought about in a sharp and decisive way—that would reflect adversely on the opportunist. Rather, the subordinate's job may be narrowed, needed information withheld, or assignments given others. The subordinate's departure is brought about, not as a result of a *direct* firing but as a matter of resignation.

Behavioral Elements

Initiative. An opportunist exercises initiative on a calculated risk basis, particularly to satisfy what superiors seem to want. These are initiatives that are self-serving in the long run even though they may appear opposite from a short-term point of view. Do a favor, lend a helping hand, wink at a faux pas, take whatever action advances one in a stepping stone way from one position up to another.

With subordinates initiative is exercised through close supervision, which ensures that they are acting to advance projects from which the opportunist stands the possibility of gain. The boss takes the credit as if it were a one-person show even when subordinates deliver. He or she is the egotistical star, often reinforcing personal importance by boasting of accomplishments.

The opportunist can usually avoid getting caught in the cross-winds of his or her own creation by thinking ahead and always having contingency plans in mind to grapple with whatever may happen. When uncertainty arises or indecision on the part of others occurs, whether boss or colleagues, the opportunist takes the initiative and rivets their attention on his or her prefabricated answers as to "what to do." The opportunist offers a positive alternative and thus diverts attention from inconsistencies or contradictions in his or her own past behavior. This use of planning ahead with contingency plans is part of the opportunist's path to the top. It has little or nothing to do with thinking ahead as in the 9,9 orientation.

Inquiry. An opportunist lives in a state of alertness, with attention concentrated on "What's in it for me?" Inquiry is not undertaken out of curiosity or interest, but rather it serves to maintain vigilance about who is saying what to whom, who is on the fast track, with whom it is good to be seen, or who has the inside advantage. This premeditated inventory of knowledge about people and their relationships allows opportunists to take advantage of their strengths and to avoid being entrapped by them.

Advocacy. An opportunistic manager may be accused of lacking in credibility. Rhetoric is unrelated to personal convictions, since the opportunist advocates whatever values or convictions appeal to others. Thus, advocacy is likely to be intensive but positions taken are dictated by the politics of the situation rather than by principles or values known to govern sound and productive human relationships. When it becomes expedient to advocate a point of view that is opposite to what had been advocated previously, this is readily accomplished by making it known that the situation has shifted. "I've thought about it and here's how I see it (now)." Beyond that an opportunist may advocate for opposite points of view with different audiences. Explanations are readily provided that diminish the discrepancy if caught in a contradiction.

Advocacy, in other words, is a means to the end of personal advancement rather than a way of advancing thinking as to what constitutes sound solutions to corporate success.

Decisions. Decision making is approached in a similar manner. A thought or an idea might be planted, letting the other person "make" the decision, particularly with persons of higher rank. Then the opportunist compliments that person on the wisdom of the decision.

An opportunist invites openness and candor from equals without being open or candid in return. In this way, decisions that gain agreement are accelerated without committing to a position first.

Decisons that involve subordinates are made unilaterally. The opportunist announces them by specifying who, what, when, and how the activities are to be undertaken.

The opportunist may appoint "weak" subordinates and then exercise close supervision as a way of exercising control over an activity without appearing to do so. The subordinate is a figurehead acting in one's own name but, in effect, carrying out detailed boss-based decisions. The opportunist needs a larger and larger cheering section to move toward the top and may appoint the subordinates the second and third layer down. Opportunists seek approval, and by applauding the person who appointed them, they can stay in favor. This can have a disastrous effect on teamwork, however, because subordinates the second and third level below give their loyalty to the big boss rather than to their intermediate supervisors who may feel undermined even though responsibilities for supervision have been assigned to them.

Critique. The opportunist is ready with compliments and indications of respect and affection for those of higher or equal rank; with self-serving remarks to reinforce whatever they most admire about themselves; courage if hard decisions have to be made; brilliance if intelligence is held at a premium; and compassion when the person shows human feelings. Critique to subordinates is likely to be limited to the negative or critical.

The opportunist solicits critique only when the feedback is likely to be favorable. Feedback that might identify weaknesses, limitations, or mistakes is avoided.

Management Practices

It is unnecessary to review management practices related to supervising subordinates because an opportunist is likely to rely on strategies in dealing with subordinates already discussed in the chapter on the 9,1 orientation.

Consequences

Impact on Productivity. Actions relevant to corporate success are undertaken as a means for advancing one's own position rather than contributing to organizational success. Thus, an opportunist is interested in productivity only if it stands out as an activity through which other ends can be achieved.

Impact on Creativity. Creativity is likely to be high in finding ways to be in the right place at the right time or finding what others want to hear and telling it to them. This is not creative problem solving.

Impact on Satisfaction. Persons in a position to assist an opportunist's upward organizational movement are likely to feel "satisfied" because of lending a helping hand or because they think the opportunist is creating a favorable climate for them as well. Those under control, such as subordinates or colleagues who are obligated, are likely to feel resentful and bitter.

When the opportunist reacts more and less favorably at different times to the same person, the person receives a double message of sometimes being okay and sometimes not okay. This person becomes insecure and over-dependent on the boss for guidance, and thus loses personal initiative. In addition, the opportunist treats different people in different ways. Those who feel less well-treated are likely to be jealous of those treated in a better manner. Then people may pull against one another rather than being harnessed toward common objectives. The under-appreciated person feels that helping one who is seen more favorably is forwarding the career of that other person at personal expense and thus is unlikely to give needed support.

Impact on Career. An opportunist may score striking achievements in the short term, but the outlook is different when viewed from a longer perspective, because it is a self-serving approach that "uses" the corporation and its people to get on top. If actions contribute to the corporation, fine, but if they are only self-serving, the attitude is, "so what." "Double-guessing" and "playing it close to the chest" become the defenses against being "taken in" and this means reduced candor as well as reduced spontaneous cooperation.

Another risk is that as others catch on they are likely to counteract the opportunist by blocking such tactics. This may also mean bringing the opportunist to his or her knees by putting one's foot in the aisle. Sooner or later the opportunist is likely to sacrifice credibility. "Being all things to all people," he or she becomes suspect and this appears to others as inconsistent, contradictory, and untrustworthy. Thus, the approach may be successful in the short term but is self-defeating in the long run.

Questionable integrity often prevents the opportunist from actually arriving at the top. People who manage in an opportunistic manner are likely to be characterized by job-jumping. In each case they make progress by moving up a new progression ladder and standing on the shoulders of others, jumping forward until those in the next organizational setting have come to experience a credibility gap that undermines trustworthiness.

Recognizing Opportunistic Behavior

- All things to all people
- Aloof to those below
- Attention-seeking
- Basks in the limelight
- Builds reputation by boasting
- Cagey
- Curries favor
- Favors given with a string attached
- Hard to pin down
- Ingratiating
- Knows people's blind spots and how to exploit them
- Loyalty to people shifts with their utility
- Name-dropping for effect
- Personal rhetoric is unrelated to convictions
- Premeditates every action
- Promises anything but delivers only when there is personal payout
- Self-promoting
- Smooth operator
- Stepping-stone philosophy
- Sweet-talks those above but pushes those below
- Takes credit for whatever he or she can get by with
- Takes only the initiatives that make him or her look good
- Takes the initiative to give what superiors seem to want
- Thinks it important to be number one
- What's in it for me?

Suggestions for Change

An opportunist faces two kinds of key problems in trying to shift toward 9,9-oriented effectiveness. One is a shift in fundamental values regarding production. The shift is from seeing production as a means to personal gain to seeing it as an end in itself, because what is produced meets the needs of consumers for goods and services and of the corporation for profitable operations. Furthermore, it can be a gratifying activity in the sense that solving problems that impede productivity is itself a potentially rewarding experience; problem solving challenges one's ability.

The same barrier to shifting applies to values associated with people. Achieving results with and through others with everyone—the leader included—involved and committed to the *success of the enterprise* is far different than seeing the shoulders of others as steps to one's own advancement.

When productivity is placed in proper perspective and bosses, colleagues, and subordinates are regarded as capable of involvement and commitment to corporate success, then a shift from opportunism to a 9,9 orientation is feasible.

Facades

The concept of facade is useful to distinguish manipulative managerial practices from ones presented earlier that have a more authentic quality. As used in architecture, the word *facade* refers to the face or front of a building as distinguished from the parts lying behind it. Sometimes the front is *false*—it obscures what actually exists behind.

A managerial facade is similar. It refers to a front, a cover, for the real approach lying behind. The face obscures the true intentions. They remain undercover. Hence, a managerial facade is deceptive.

Motivations

The pure theories—9,9, 1,9, 9,1, 5,5, 1,1 and paternalism—all share a basic attribute in common. They are well intended in the sense of not taking advantage of others or deliberately hurting them.

In creating a facade, the goal is to achieve by indirect or by roundabout ways something that otherwise is unavailable or believed to be unattainable, hence the thrill of risk and gamble. Thus the approach is manipulative with the negative side being fear of getting caught.

The general feature of all facades is that the person avoids revealing the contents of his or her own mind yet gives the impression of doing so.

At a deeper level, then, this person is closed and hidden but gives the appearance of being open and aboveboard. Why? If one were, in reality, open and aboveboard, others would understand true intentions and the deceptive facade would be apparent. Neither can the "facadist" afford to be seen as closed and hidden because that raises suspicions and doubts, or at least it alerts curiosity.

One factor that makes it difficult to recognize a facadist is that the facadist qualities may not be present in all aspects of leadership. Sometimes a sound action can be expected to gain the endorsement of those who must implement it and there is no need for manipulation, deception, or hiding of true intentions. Facadist actions come into play when what the facadist wants cannot be accomplished through open leadership.

The facade maintained by a given individual may or may not be internally consistent. Strategems may shift from time to time depending on what is workable or legitimate in the context of organizational requirements. The surface often appears as 9,9 or 5,5 and less frequently as 1,9, or 1,1, and almost never as 9,1.

The underlying aim beneath a facade is to cover up the drive for control, mastery, and domination. The authentic 9,1-oriented manager is interested in task mastery and achievement—proving through work the validity of his or her position as outstanding and worthy of respect. Striving for power and the opportunity to exercise it rather than contributing to the organization is what distinguishes the facadist from a 9,1-oriented manager. Drawing valid distinctions between straightforward, hard-driving 9,1 and 9,1-oriented facade strategies is important. An individual who wishes to avoid the consequences of becoming a pawn in the facadist games must be aware of the difference between coercion and manipulation.

In a similar way there is a distinction between the opportunist's motivation and the facadist's. The opportunist wants to be seen on top and basks in reflected glory, whereas the facadist derives gratification from calling the shots or pulling the strings without others being aware of the source of devious influence. The facadist may seek to control the boss from a number two position, then a different set of manipulative practices may appear: slipping up on the boss's blind side, pouring on compliments about cleverness, soundness, depth, and whatever else the boss wants to hear. It's not that the facadist wants to become number one, it's just that the facadist wants to control number one in comparison with the opportunist, who may do some of the same things in the interest of getting on top.

Avoiding Self-Exposure. The facadist's negative motivation is to avoid self-exposure by hiding one's true aims, to screen spontaneous responses, and not reveal his or her inner experience and motivations. The facadist does not respond from intuition or conviction, but uses analysis, examination, and diagnosis to calculate what others expect as the basis of response in order to gain personally.

There are many simple ways of throwing a cloak over intentions. One is that the facade builder simply avoids revealing intentions by not initiating discussions that invite others to inquire. Then there is no reason to be questioned regarding motives. Another is to withhold the reactions to a problem by seeming not to notice it. The difference between a 1,1 orientation and this attitude of indifference is that the facadist does notice problems and seeks to ignore them rather than remaining truly uninvolved as is true of the 1,1-oriented person.

A third way is speaking so as to reflect others' opinions back to them without their noticing. In this way, personal opinions or attitudes of the facadist are not revealed. In a similar fashion, reacting to a question with a counter-query may serve to deflect a problem.

A fourth way involves a reaction of half-truths which invite favorable interpretations. Then motivations appear quite legitimate. Still another is through outright lies. However, the most acceptable facade-like lie is the kind that cannot be checked. One might refer to a promise made by a dead associate but not by a live one who can put the matter straight, or to a handwritten document known not to have been copied and no longer available because it has been shredded.

Building and Maintaining a Reputation. The facade builder not only avoids revealing intentions but also builds a positive reputation to aid in maintaining deception. The reputation serves the purpose of actively causing intentions to appear quite different than they are. By throwing up a smokescreen, the likelihood is increased that true ambitions will not be recognized, and the appearance of integrity is maintained.

Pursuing a Good Cause. Writers since Machiavelli have suggested how a *reputation may be used to control, master, and dominate.* Reputation is built around virtue of good deeds and subscribing to popular causes. Toward this end, for example, a person works to bestow honor on those who excel and thus one is identified with excellence. Another cover-up is to express lofty convictions and to embrace socially-valued ideals. Working for social movements and institutions that are admired because they contribute to human dignity and to the reduction of human suffering may in fact be a facade. Whether or not depends on intent.

Front organizations have been aptly described, because their intent is to hide the real purpose for which the organization exists. A cover is deemed necessary because if the true intent were revealed, organizational purpose might be thwarted. Using the names and activities of well-respected persons to bolster one's own actions is a similar technique. If the facade builder can name-drop or enlist the support of an opinion setter, this can serve to further personal ambitions.

Showing Concern. Showing concern for the other person's needs and opinions is a subtle form of exerting influence. The significance of demonstrating an interest in people can hardly be over-estimated, even to the point of learning and using a first name. Ways in which this is done vary from being a good listener, encouraging others to talk about themselves, to never telling a person he or she is wrong, to avoiding arguments all together. As one person said, "I make it a point to find out what a person is most interested in so that I can ask questions and get him to talk. In this way he is put in a positive frame of mind and it also helps him to feel important. Because he is friendly toward me, he is more likely to buy what I want him to later on."

When these actions are well-founded, the behavior can appropriately be assessed as a 9,9 orientation or as a 1,9 orientation. When the intent is that of gaining a private point of view or to achieve a personal advantage that is unknown or misperceived, the facade-like characteristics are present.

Bluffing. Another facade involves projecting a false image of power and authority. The strategy is to appear stronger than one's adversaries when real strength to back up the image may be lacking. Bluffing or intimidation can be valuable to a facadist in achieving success. Though it may be unnecessary, a manager using this strategy flies to meet a business associate to close a deal rather than doing so through the mail or by telephone. For image projection, a personal jet is more impressive than commercial flights. Having the business associate come aboard to close the deal in the plane is better than meeting in a downtown hotel or office. Bringing along an assistant or secretary to whom details can be entrusted conveys the impression that the person in question is concerned with the proper management of detail but that one's own efforts are concentrated on the main game. Having legal or other experts readily available adds to the facadist's demonstration of importance. Outer trappings such as these are increasingly common at higher executive levels and are relied on to add that additional degree of "persuasion."

There are at least two reasons for building and maintaining a managerial facade. Mutual trust is not valued in its own right. Yet the appearance of trustfulness is important. Through creating the impression of trust, confidence, and respect as the basis for interpersonal reactions, personal goals are achieved more easily. On the plane of social ethics, in consequence, shortcuts are taken to achieve an end. They are not governed by commonly accepted rules for maintaining social morality.

Another factor is when one strives to achieve a goal that is beyond his or her capability and skill. By employing a facade to hide trickery and deceit, objectives can be gained that cannot be achieved through honest, ability-based performance. The end sought justifies the means for getting to it. Both of these disregard commonly accepted rules of social morality. The disregard is in a calculated and knowing way.

Facade-type behavior appears when the underlying motivation is hidden, even from the person employing the facade. Psychiatry and clinical psychology have described tricks of the mind. These are tricks by which persons' motivations are unclear to themselves; they can't be identified by them or described to others. If directly confronted with their own self-deceptions, they would deny them. Rationalization, projection, justification, and compensation are examples.

Facade-type behavior may be related to any of these factors or by some mixture of them. To further complicate matters, the behavior may contain components of the pure theories as well. When the latter also are present, it only adds to the subtlety of the deception (self and others) involved.

Managing Conflict

Dealing with conflict is a critical area for orienting personal behavior. *The facadist does not avoid conflict.* However, the goal is not to resolve it as in a 9,9-oriented approach nor to suppress it as in 9,1. Rather, conflict is used to gain one's own purposes. Many ways in which this can be done are utilized by the skillful manipulator.

One avoids getting involved in direct conflict where one might be vulnerable. Also, one wages only limited offensive battles. As one manager said, "It's better to ask for a smaller change and go one step at a time than to try to go the whole way at once and stir up resistance, resentment, and open conflict." Even with reservations, the facadist feels no reluctance to compromise. A 5,5-oriented manager believes the problem has been dealt with realistically when compromise is utilized. The facadist recognizes that compromise is a maneuver, a tactical accommodation to undercut resistance because it presents the appearance of reasonableness. As one skillful manager says, "I compromise at the time in order to be able to go underground with my real purpose. Then at a later time I come up again and usually the second or third time around I win."

When resolving a disagreement, "principles" may be cited when in fact none are involved. This is another way of maintaining a win-lose as contrasted with a problem-solving orientation, and making it appear important because "a matter of principle is involved." On deeper examination, the facade-oriented manager's "principle" often turns out to be dogma converted into an "absolute" fueled by self-righteousness such as "Stick with it. Be patient. Talent is always recognized. Nothing to worry about." All of the above may be spoken while the facadist knows full well that the person to whom it is spoken is about to be given an unpleasant assignment.

Advantage is gained by using conflict existing between others. A neutral position is retained until factions in the conflict have become clear. *Once the issue is drawn, the conflict is entered and weight thrown to the stronger faction. If win-lose conflict between one's peers develops, the facadist does not stand aside.* The reasons for avoiding neutrality are clear. They are based on, "What happens afterwards?" What happens if one remains neutral while others fight it out? After the fight is over, the victor well knows the support that might have been given during the fray was not forthcoming. With the victor, then, one's stature is in jeopardy. Furthermore, if one has supported the victor, the victor in turn is obligated for the help received. If neutrality is maintained, the vanquished is equally well aware that withheld support might have made the difference. There is no reason to be obligated to those who fail to offer support.

In building a successful facade, the significance of conflict and fighting to win one's position is kept clearly in mind, while on the surface the clever manager avoids the appearance of relishing a fight. In addition, one strives to avoid impatience, anger, and temper while remaining calm and rational. It is winning in the long run that counts and then being able to persuade the loser to become an ally. In this respect, it is important to maintain and live by the rules of competition and to give the appearance of conformity so as not to attract undue attention.

Attitudes toward conflict are different when conflict is between subordinates. Then those in conflict are given the opportunity of direct accusation and confrontation of one another. In such disputes the supervisor serves as the unbiased mediator, the fountainhead of justice, and is then considered by subordinates to be a fair administrator, a person to be respected.

Behavioral Elements

Although other Grid styles may appear to be evidenced in managerial leadership, when the underlying motivational assumptions are ones of deception then clearly the behavior indicates a facadist at work. Many times it is difficult to know whether one is seeing the "pure" behavior or whether what is under the surface is different. Some indications of clues to look for in detecting a facadist are indicated in the description of the elements that follow.

Initiative. Characteristic of the facade builder is that he or she acts with initiative and continues until success is ensured. Although it might not appear on the surface, this is a tough-minded approach. Action is taken quickly when an advantage is to be gained. Even though interest is feigned, the facadist does not become sentimentally involved with people. Rather, people are used and alliances that are easily made are quickly set aside as the occasion demands. Obstacles are not a deterrent. If one action does not succeed, another tack is taken until one's objective is assured.

In a like manner, the facadist is not daunted by difficulty of execution or external stress and is responsive to new facets and new opportunities that might provide additional leverage. Thus, authority and tradition are set aside or challenged as these present obstacles. However, when it is to one's advantage, the status quo is upheld.

Inquiry. A facadist is likely to be well-informed because of the benefits from knowing in detail what is going on, where different people stand on issues, and so on.

When the topic of study is neutral in character, inquiry is carried out in a forthright manner. There is nothing to be lost or gained by revealing one's level of understanding and then getting the facts.

If the situation is different, then inquiry can be "used" to build one's reputation. This happens with people who pride themselves on their knowledge of the subject and are eager to pass on what they know. Then the facadist may listen with apparent interest, thanking them for useful information even though already familiar with it. Even here, though, a sharp distinction is drawn by the facadist between information and advice and counsel. Advice and counsel are seen primarily in the perspective of personal gain or loss and influence over or acceptance by others.

While the aim of a facadist is for others to feel important, asking unneeded advice from those above or below is avoided. To do so gives the appearance of being weak. In addition, unsolicited advice is undesirable because when received it creates an obligation to the person who provided it.

Observations about the inquiry of a facadist point in a different direction when the topic is loaded with emotions or touching on the vested interests of others. Now the facadist's inquiry is anything but open because what is really needed by the facadist would alert others to his or her true intentions. Furthermore, the information gleaned in an indirect way is likely to be more accurate because the information-giver can be kept uninformed of the purpose for which the information is to be used.

When these conditions exist, inquiry is indirect and circumspect. It may be carried out by asking oblique questions or even by making remarks others feel compelled to correct. But if they do, they are telling the facadist the desired information. Alternatively, inquiry may be carried out by a third party, someone who is not known by those whose information is sought to have any special interest in the situation or is not known to be reporting on what is learned to the facadist.

Advocacy. In building a facade, a person expresses convictions but convictions are expressed in a special way. They are set forth to maintain maneuverability. One may use anonymous authorities or public opinion as sources. In this way beliefs can be relinquished without having to back down personally. Convictions are never presented so strongly that one can be proven wrong or stood by so firmly as to be seen as obstinate or defiant. By expressing convictions while keeping other alternatives open, one is not demonstrated to be wrong if the course must be shifted. While gains (and contributions) from being right may not be fully achieved, the losses from being wrong are avoided. On the surface, then, there is the appearance of a 5,5 orientation when flexibility in expressing convictions is confused with maneuverability in pushing one's hidden positions.

Another possibility, though, is to express strongly lofty convictions and to embrace socially-valued ideals. These are positions that no one can be "against" but give the appearance of strength when expressed in a convincing manner.

Giving advice and counsel can be fraught with danger if the facadist counsels action that fails. For example, the frustration associated with failure invites criticism. Furthermore, his or her judgment is proven unreliable. On the other hand, if one counsels action that ends in success, one may receive commendation. The reward for counseling success, according to Machiavelli, rarely reaches the magnitude of the punishment associated with counseling an action that fails. Over the long-term then, the facadist builder is wary of giving advice. The goal is to act with moderation and to avoid acting out of zeal. Advice should be given commonly and modestly. If advice is given, the person who uses it should feel he or she is accepting it out of personal judgment and free will.

One way to elicit the favorable notice of a boss is to support the boss's convictions, hiding the fact that one's own personal position may differ. The payoff comes when the boss is considering promotions or a replacement and remembers and rewards those who think "correctly." The "yessir, yes-ma'am" is not motivated by need for approval as might be the case were a straightforward 1,9 orientation involved. It is a devious strategy for getting ahead that bypasses considerations of merit but that comes through to the boss as genuine agreement.

Counseling caution through fear-provoking remarks is one of the most subtle as well as effective ways of using advocacy to immobilize a person or team. The idea is to create anxiety about a projected course or to prevent an action from being taken by blocking action before testing the consequences. Such remarks as "The boss wouldn't buy it," "It costs too much," and "It didn't work in plant X" are examples of anxiety-provoking advice that may prevent *logical* problem solving. Characteristically, such remarks are not documented with reasons or evidence, yet they give the impression of avoiding risks associated with probable failure.

Such fear-provoking remarks set off the personal anxiety of an individual relative to an action being considered. From the perspective of the person who hears it, it may appear realistic when in fact it is a false assessment of the consequences of some proposed action.

Decisions. Anyone operating under a facade needs to maintain intimate knowledge of what is going on and to retain responsibility for key decisions. Indeed, the making of the key decisions—1/0—is indispensable in achieving mastery and domination with no regard for organization purpose as such.

Incomplete delegation is ideal for making it possible for the facade strategist to maintain control while appearing to release subordinates to be independent. On the one hand, the goal is to be known as one who delegates authority—who uses people well. But for protection the delegation, though apparently full, is incomplete. Leaving jurisdictional boundaries fuzzy is one way to ensure uncertainty as to who is free to act under authority. Another tactic is to arrange overlapping responsibilities. In both cases, subordinates act as counterweights on one another; no one has sufficient authority to decide an action alone. Thirdly, information that would permit decisions to be made is not fully communicated, but enough is given so that people feel informed. Fuzzy boundaries, overlapping responsibilities, and partial information all lead in the same direction as far as decision making is concerned—upward. Then subordinates have to ask for help. In this way, control is increased and retained by the supervisor as the final decision maker.

If these strategems are to be skillfully applied, the troubles people have in arriving at decisions should appear to be due to the system—not to the administration of it.

Another significant way to retain control is to operate on a one-by-one basis with one's subordinates or peers and to avoid situations of interaction where there is a free exchange of ideas and information. Two advantages can be gained. One is that information needed by subordinates to coordinate activities can only be had by their coming to the supervisor, who thus retains control. The other is that it becomes more difficult for peers or subordinates to track one's own actions.

Proper weight, however, is given by the facadist to cliques and other features of the informal organization. By having a thorough knowledge of cliques and their membership, one can tap into the grapevine at strategic points and keep a finger on the pulse of the organization. Exerting influence on key members of cliques can usually result in a saving of effort as others follow their lead. Consulting key clique members, before decisions that affect them are made, frequently can result in reducing or eliminating resistance points. Finally, by manipulating clique action, sanctions can be brought to bear on members who are running counter to his or her purposes.

Teamwork. Work teams, information groups, and cliques, rather than individuals considered singly, are the building blocks of modern organizations. To a facadist, a group is a significant unit to understand and to utilize for personal benefit. From one point of view, meetings are a means to exert influence on more than one person at a time. In this respect, then, a group is a convenient unit for advancing individual interests. Knowledge of power tactics and group dynamics is an indispensable tool for using group action for personal interests.

Committee action places responsibilities for high-risk major changes or innovations on the group. The facadist sponsors the more minor changes that can be construed as tests of ability and are most likely to succeed.

Tapping the resources of others can be facilitated through brainstorming, and other similar techniques in which ideas are elicited but not evaluated. This makes it relatively easy to take credit for others' ideas without either being forced to negatively discard a person's ideas or being committed to action by group problem solving. By clever hitchhiking onto another's work or thoughts, they can be presented as if they are one's own.

These points demonstrate how the facade strategist can manipulate and maneuver in a more forceful way through group situations. On the other hand, team action in the sense of involvement of others in problem solving, interdependence of action, confrontation and working through of issues, etc. are fraught with pitfalls.

Interaction for the purpose of problem solving is viewed with distrust. In situations where team action is seen to be organizationally appropriate, the goal again is to give the appearance of team action. One way to avoid real interaction is to feel out positions and achieve commitment from those concerned prior to assembling them. In this way, influence can be more easily exerted and uniformity of opinion quickly achieved without the necessity for open debate and deliberation. Composing the unit from among one's allies, rather than convening those from whom divergent points of view are likely, is another. By intensely debating minor issues that make no real difference, the big ones can be reserved for unilateral decision making.

A useful way to keep control and to make certain that one's own direction eventually is taken, under the guise of team action, has been described by one manager in this way: "In order to keep one part of the organization from achieving more influence than other parts (and thus to reduce my own power), I find it necessary to keep problems in a fluid state far beyond when a decision could be made. This can be done easily by keeping the situation open under the guise of not making a premature unworkable decision or by testing all possible alternatives before a step is taken. In this way, the stronger faction is weakened, the weaker faction is not hurt, and when I finally make a decision, everyone is relieved and ready to move my way in order to get some action." Because skills of team action are not highly developed by many persons, a group is an easy match for a clever facadist.

Critique. Critique as a double-loop opportunity of mutual learning between boss and subordinate is unknown and unwelcome to a facadist, who utilizes feedback as a method of control primarily through the use of praise and punishment. The paternalist who also utilizes praise and punishment does so for the "subordinate's own good" while the facadist does so to further personal interests.

One way of creating a positive reputation for oneself is to build up the other person. The clever use of praise is a way to do this. Concern for another person may be read into the recognition and emphasis given to the good points of people. The person with a 1,9 orientation in truth is interested in people and wants to like and be liked by them. The facadist wants to use them. The uniform recommendation, from Machiavelli to Carnegie, has been to "be lavish with praise and approbation, even when there is no indication that the praise has been earned or merited." Praise and compliments make a person feel important and build up pride. When given, the one who has been made to feel personally praiseworthy also comes to like and to admire the individual from whom the praise originated. As a result, the praise can buy influence and liking. However, the danger of flattery is to be avoided because flattery is praise that can boomerang. The facadist is also careful not to be led astray by the flattery of others.

Direct use of negative feedback or criticism carries danger. As Carnegie says, ". . . even though one feels critical, and criticism is, in fact, justified, it should be avoided." The reason is explained in the following quotation:

> "When dealing with people, let us remember that we are not dealing with creatures of logic. We are dealing with creatures of emotions, creatures bristling with prejudice, and motivated by pride and vanity . . . And criticism is a dangerous spark, a spark that is likely to cause an explosion in the powder keg of pride."

Carnegie's suggestion, then, is that direct criticism is much too dangerous for an individual to play with if one wants to win friends and influence others. By avoiding criticism, the negative reactions associated with it are avoided. The act of deception itself is thought to be of no consequence. The manipulative feature is that negative information is withheld. In doing so, the person to whom the negative information might prove instructive is misled.

When it comes to punishment, another somewhat different aspect can be seen. If possible, the facadist never is seen as a direct agent of punishment. This is in contrast to the authentic 9,1 approach where punishment is meted out directly. One way to indirectly punish is to delegate the responsibility for dispensing it. If delegation isolates one from knowing of either the decision to punish or its severity, then the facadist is most successful. Henry Ford, for example, is said to have been lavish in his praise of performance, but relied on a "hatchet man" to handle punishments.

Management Practices

Because praise and punishment are so central as a means of establishing and maintaining control over subordinates, the managerial practices employed in supervision are similar to those characteristic of a paternalist and therefore not repeated here. The reader may wish to reexamine that section.

Consequences

Corporate. In the final analysis, self-interests not corporate interests are served by the facadist. As a result, it can be expected that productivity may be emphasized as a means to get ahead but sacrificed when self-interests diverge from organization objectives.

Creativity tends to be stifled because the kind of open confrontation of issues essential for seeing original solutions is seen by the facadist as risky in the sense of threatening the basis of control. The likelihood of resentment to resistance or rebellion—all of which are stimulated by a 9,1 orientation—is also lessened because there are few or no sharp win-lose confrontations in which the facadist is seen visibly to gain or others to visibly experience defeat.

Satisfaction with this kind of leadership varies directly with the facadist's success in deceiving subordinates. Satisfaction may be high when the facadist is successful in doing so, but it falls dramatically once the facadist is found out. Trust is eroded when people sense a contradiction between the two "levels" of the facadist's behavior. Subordinates come to realize that the boss has no regard for their best interests; they are little more than puppets with their actions controlled by the facadist's strings. Then they have little or no basis for judging where they truly stand. Security is at a low level when such anchorages have been lost.

Personal. As long as the maneuvers of a facadist are carefully contrived, the facadist is likely to make continued progress in the organization. The major risk is that the complexity of maneuvers may increase as success is achieved. The facadist may become so impressed with personal capacity for manipulating others that larger and larger maneuvers are attempted up to the point where someone finally punctures the front, discovers what's going on, and blows the whistle. Then the game is over.

More often than not, however, those who work with the facadist come to realize that the approach does not ring true. Small discrepancies may appear that raise doubts and alert observers to be increasingly doubtful of the facadist's integrity, which, ultimately limits the facadist's accomplishments.

The facadist's self-esteem soars with each indication that a clever manipulation has proven successful. Gain is in deceiving and hoodwinking others, and that's where the fun is. Self-esteem may plummet when in the face of evidence that can't be denied, the facadist is caught in the effort to put something over and loses control, mastery, and domination as a result.

Recognizing Facadist Behavior

The following kinds of words have been used to characterize a known facadist.

- Blind ambition
- Calculating
- Circuitous
- Confidence (con) man
- Constantly role-playing for effect
- Cunning
- Double-dealing
- End justifies the means
- Enjoys power behind the throne
- False front
- Hides true colors
- Hypocrite
- Indirect
- Manipulative
- Open to praise but not criticism
- Over-developed sense of personal power
- Shrewd
- Tends to bluff
- Values own positive reputation
- Violates the rules but wants to be known as a statesman
- Vulnerable to exposure

Suggestions for Change

A facadist's underlying motivation is to gain domination, mastery, and control through disguise and deception. The problem to be solved in moving toward a 9,9 orientation is related to the facadist's willingness to allow his or her motivations to become more transparent to associates. Since a facadist is always wary that someone will see through the disguise, it may be found that in achieving such a shiftover through greater candor, the manager is more relaxed and capable of greater spontaneity. These make collaborative problem solving easier.

****

Paternalism, Opportunism, and Facades are the major theories in use beyond the Grid styles already introduced. There are three other theories of lesser importance that need to be mentioned in order to complete the picture.

Wide-Arc Pendulum

Under the wide-arc pendulum approach, either 9,1 or 1,9 may be operating but not at the same time. One follows the other.

The wide-arc pendulum swing can be seen when a manager drives for production in a 9,1-oriented way and in doing so arouses resentments and antagonisms. He or she recognizes these negative attitudes and then overcorrects by removing all pressures and becoming exaggeratedly interested in the thoughts, feelings, and attitudes of subordinates. Production falls, but relationships are restored to a smooth basis. Once again the manager becomes careless and reverts to a 9,1 manner of managing, only to back off again as tensions peak.

At least two circumstances can result in the swings of this kind of wide-arc pendulum. One is before and after a representation vote or a certification election in companies that want to remain nonunion or keep an independent union that has been challenged by an international one. Supervisors say, "The signal is out. Management wants to be sure they win the election that's coming up. For the next few months let up on the tough stuff. Ease up on applying wash-up time and the coveralls and gloves policies. Show an interest in people. Find out what's annoying them. Take whatever action is required to show employees that management is interested in them."

When the election is over and it went the way the management wanted it to, the same supervisors are told, "Get production back on line. Cut out the soft stuff."

The other circumstance is related to cyclical movements of the economy from troughs of recession to peaks of prosperity. When hard times hit, there are feverish activities to tighten up for increased output at reduced expense. Included are such efforts as cost control, waste control, and terminating employees. Cracking down to get efficiency, then easing off to get back in the good graces of subordinates, then pushing for increased production again, etc. is the pendulum swinging from hard to soft to hard. To those whom they affect, these actions seem cold and impersonal because they result in an increase in pressure. Sometimes the kind of production improvement decisions that are made do, in fact, result in an improved P/L position. But relationships become so disturbed that trouble can be seen brewing. As soon as health has been restored to the economy and company conditions improve, attention turns away from the kinds of efficiency moves previously taken. Management feels compelled to ease off and to show increased concern for the thoughts, feelings, and attitudes of people, thus shifting to a 1,9 approach to restore confidence that management cherishes human values. Control programs tend to fade out while uneconomical practices creep back in. Without the goad associated with economic threat, practices that are in fact "soft" are likely to be overlooked or accepted. After a degree of confidence and peace has been restored, another period of hard times leads to a new tightening up to regain the losses in production and efficiency suffered during the previous swing.

As people catch on to what is buffeting them, these kinds of swings sow the seeds of their own destruction. People cease to trust management's word, and the union becomes progressively more attractive as a bulwark against these kinds of ups and downs. These kinds of pendulum swings are most likely to occur when managers see people and production needs as two ends of a seesaw, where one is "up" and the other is "down." An alternative formulation that they are two sides of a single coin could lead to a 9,9 solution to such problems.

Counterbalancing

This is a third way of applying 9,1 and 1,9. The line organization operates on a 9,1 orientation, producing the usual negative reactions of frustration and aggression. As a safeguard against such feelings festering and breaking out with disastrous effects, a staff organization has the responsibility of keeping its finger on the pulse of the organization and providing disgruntled people the opportunity to ventilate their feelings. Thus, the staff becomes a safety valve to prevent the entire system from rupturing under high pressure. This kind of a staff department is seen in places that have people who are called "field representatives," "personnel representatives," or "employee relations coordinators." Their responsibilities are to keep in touch with what is going on and counsel with those who are antagonistic. In some settings, staff services have taken an even more elegant form. Psychiatrists, psychologists, ministers, and other professionals skilled in listening are employed for relieving pent-up feelings. The World War II management response to gripes—"Here's your card, take it to the chaplain and have it punched"—exemplifies the concept of counterbalancing. This "solution" has been strengthened and refined since then through the more extensive training of chaplains as counselors.

An example of the counterbalancing concept comes from the Hawthorne plant of Western Electric where nondirective counseling at the work site originated in the following way. While interviewing employees in an experiment on the relationship between lighting and productivity, the experimenters came to understand the benefits of the interviews for the people working in the experiment who were able to get feelings off their chests and who thereafter began to produce more. Recognizing this, management took another step by making the interview *a part* of the management approach to the maintenance of morale. The idea was to have counselors, paid by management, available to all employees but not reporting to management except to keep them apprised of trends that suggested adverse attitudes were building up toward management. Employees could feel free to talk out their problems because when they "spilled their troubles," they would not need to worry about being reported.

There are other forms of counterbalancing in addition to balancing a "hard" 9,1-oriented line with a "soft" 1,9-oriented staff department. For example, in some organizations the line organization has become fixed into a 1,9 orientation, and is unwilling to make harsh personnel judgments. Then evaluation of managers for promotion becomes the responsibility of the "tough" 9,1-oriented staff department, which exercises competency judgments and controls promotions. This is a reverse swing where the personnel staff serve to buck up the weak line.

The critical feature in counterbalancing is that responsibility for production and for people is not seen as a single integrated aspect of managing that rests on the shoulders of those who manage. The responsibility is divided and separated into two aspects, production responsibility on the one hand and people responsibility on the other.

Whether in industry, the military, or elsewhere, the serious disadvantage of this kind of ventilation of feelings and hostility is that it treats symptoms rather than causes. While tensions are reduced for the moment, the 9,1-oriented management responsible for generating the tensions remains unchanged.

The Two-Hat Approach

The two-hat theory is applied by managers who separate their concern for production from concern for people while making the same persons responsible for both. Using the two-hat approach, a manager who practices 9,1-oriented management in daily work removes the production hat at six-month or yearly intervals and puts on the people hat to counsel with subordinates in ways that deal mainly with attitudes-at-large and only incidentally as they relate to work. Job counseling is not part and parcel of work activity and individual development. Rather, it is a scheduled activity and is concentrated on when the people hat is worn. Line managers are likely to view this kind of counseling as an activity they must engage in, not because it contributes to improved work but because the personnel department has placed them under obligation to conduct these sessions as a matter of company policy.

Two-hat can be seen as an organizational practice. For example, on one day, the top team considers P/L problems and inefficient operations. Then on another day, the same group meets again, this time to discuss people problems. The actions taken on one day solve production problems. They are considered mainly in terms of technical production aspects. Even though they may be tied in with personnel problems, they are not likely to be considered in light of their effects on people. The same is true on another day. The people problems considered at that time may bear significantly on production, but they are viewed mainly in the light of human needs. On Monday, problems concerning people are set aside until Wednesday. On Wednesday, production problems are delayed for discussion until the next Monday.

The two concerns are separate but equal in importance. The basic assumption again is that there are two sets of problems with the inherent connections between them frequently inadequately recognized.

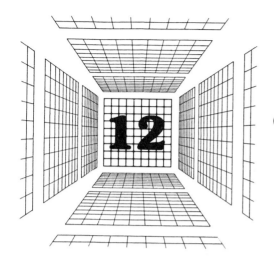

Organizational Change

Each of the Grid chapters ended with suggestions for how a person might experiment with leading in stronger and more effective ways. Now we shift the focus to examine how change in the organization may be brought about. The purpose of presenting 9,9-oriented principles was to enable you to assess practices that prevail in your organization as matters of tradition, precedent, or long-established practice. You probably have seen many gaps and discrepancies between what occurs in your organization's work life and what could be expected if these principles were in daily use. Productivity and quality suffer when such gaps and discrepancies prevail, as do satisfaction and creativity.

The issue is how to go about shifting from current practices of management rooted in the organization's history and culture to stronger and more effective practices based on principles. To speak about change is well and good. In fact, though, organizational change is something far more difficult to accomplish than personal change. You can do the latter without getting the OK from anyone. The former involves a high degree of cooperation with others.

Bringing about the kind of changes based on principles on a widespread basis is far more complex and subtle. Therefore, in this chapter we want to deal with some considerations related to change that must be understood and dealt with if efforts to change the organization are to be successful.

The first question is who you are relative to others in your organization; that is, "Who's in charge?" If you are in charge, your ability to effect change is far different than if you are not in charge. This chapter concerns how to go about the introduction of organizational change under both sets of conditions.

Are You the Person in Charge?

There is a straightforward answer to this question. If you are the top person, you are in charge. This means that there is no one in a position above you from whom you have to get approval or authorization. There may be others associated with you to whom you go for counsel or guidance, but you shoulder the ultimate responsibility for decisions.

The likelihood is very great that you are the person in charge if you are the chief executive officer or the director of an agency. As a chief executive you may have a board of directors, and for certain special problems it may be necessary or desirable to gain its approval. But you are the person ultimately in charge of utilizing the organization's resources in a profitable manner. If you decide to take the steps necessary to bring sound principles of behavior into everyday use, you can do this under your own responsibilities.

An important distinction needs to be made between the top person and the person in charge because they are not one and the same.

The situation is not quite so clear if you are the head of a subsidiary or if you are the manager of a plant, a district, or a region. Under these conditions, you may or may not be the person in charge, even though your job description says you are the responsible person. The key test of whether you are the person in charge is whether you have line authority for expending funds. If you do not have such authority, the likelihood is that you are not the person in charge. There may be exceptions, the most important of which is this. You tell them what you want to do, they review it, probe your reasoning, but more or less routinely give their approval. For all practical purposes you are in charge.

If you are not the top person, then you are not the person in charge because you do not have authority to approve organizational change.

The introduction of change is a different problem if you are not the person in charge. This by no means implies that your influence is limited, because your ideas may generate keen interest among others. It may not be within your authority to initiate development, yet you may see the importance of sound development. For purposes of illustration, make the assumption that neither *you* nor *your boss* is the person in charge. This means you have no direct relationship to the person who is in charge.

Word of mouth is a significant approach to get others interested in development. Other possibilities include passing around literature, visiting companies that are engaged in development, and so on. Another approach is for you to attend a public Grid Seminar in order to evaluate it for yourself. Then you are in a position to use word of mouth to recommend that your boss do the same; his direct experience of possibilities can serve as a foundation to interest others up the line until the person in charge is reached.

We can now consider how you can bring change about assuming that you are the person in charge.

Nine fundamental principles were identified earlier. You will recognize that these principles of human relationships are difficult to practice if they are being violated by others. Therefore the issue is to change underlying behavior that characterizes the human system of organization, not just an individual or a team.

This awareness has led to the concept of organizational development, which means seeing the organization as the unit of change. Individuals may change on a one-by-one basis, but organizational change can facilitate and strengthen this when it is a fully integrated approach that can result in a rethinking of how to optimize the operation of the entire system.

Three Approaches to Organizational Development (OD)

There are three broadly different approaches to the introduction of organizational change. The sketches below will convey the underlying assumptions about change on which each is based.

Technique-Centered OD

Technique-centered OD is attempting to bring about change by introducing a new technique. One of the best examples of technique-centered OD is management-by-objectives. Unlike a 9,9-oriented approach, management-by-objectives in many locations has become a mechanical system that involves discussions between bosses and subordinates to set objectives, with the subordinates then being held accountable for achieving them. The mechanics of technique-centered management-by-objectives are complex and the paperwork may be extensive.

Other examples of technique-centered OD include job enrichment, flexi-time scheduling, quality circles, and survey research. All of these approaches are technique-centered when they involve introducing managers to a different way of managing on a piecemeal or segmented basis. Little or no effort is expended to enable managers to investigate their own management styles and to learn to distinguish sound and unsound principles as the basis for using these techniques.

A 9,1-oriented manager is likely to embrace the mechanics of management-by-objectives in a wholehearted way but not because he or she sees it as a way of aiding subordinates to strengthen their contributions.

Rather, it is a technique of managing that enables the 9,1-oriented manager to strengthen control over subordinates by forcing agreement with goals and then holding them accountable for reaching them.

In a comparable manner, a 1,9-oriented manager may embrace management-by-objectives and then invite subordinates to set their own objectives at whatever level of excellence or output they may be prepared to accept. The boss does not help subordinates think through which goals are important for them to accomplish. A 1,9-oriented manager would see this as an intrusion that is likely to produce resistance. In fact, it might lead to disagreement, and a 1,9-oriented manager risks personal rejection when faced with conflict.

Comparable distortions of management-by-objectives are evident when a manager's basic orientation is 1,1, 5,5, paternalistic, opportunistic, etc. The point is that any technique-centered approach to change tends to be distorted in the direction of the Grid style of the person who is implementing the technique; the more so when techniques are introduced in a piecemeal way. As a result, many potentially sound ways of strengthening operational effectiveness are weakened by the manner in which they are brought into being. Technique-centered OD has been found to be unsatisfactory time and time again but, being unaware of the impact of Grid style on the utilization of an otherwise neutral technique, managers persist in repeating the approach.

Process-Centered OD

A second approach to increasing the effectiveness of behavior in organizations is process-centered OD. This approach, which involves managers in studying their own behavior, is basically sound. However, the manner in which this learning occurs causes it to be weak and, for the most part, ineffective.

The basic approach to process-centered OD is for groups to study behavior of each member and to give feedback that may aid the person to be more effective. Such sensitivity or T-group training, role playing or even psychodrama is done by relying on an outside expert who meets with the group to facilitate its study.

The catalyst, or facilitator, goes about doing this in any one of several ways. One is to interview or collect data from group members to find out how they see their own group. The catalyst then summarizes the conclusions and reports, which are discussed by the group. Alternatively, the catalyst may meet with the group without prior interviews for face-to-face discussion, aiding members to bring forward facts and feelings about the group and its individual members.

In either of these approaches, the catalytic way of learning about group process suffers from three major weaknesses. One has its roots in the intermediary role played by the catalyst or facilitator. Participants have not learned how to open up communication based on their own skills; the catalyst provides a crutch that enables them to do so. The catalyst is present and is the one who provides the assurance that everything is okay. Therefore, group members never learn how to communicate openly.

The second major weakness is the same as was introduced in the context of technique-centered OD. Learning about theory and principles of behavior has been bypassed and reliance placed on the manager's conventional wisdom, the source of guidance that resulted in difficulties in the first place.

A third limitation is that this approach also segments the organization, drawing a line between behavior and performance on the assumption that personal insight is sufficient to promote strengthened practices at the operational level, better long-range planning, financial analysis, etc. The approach, in other words, does not take the next step and produce a fully integrated approach.

Experience with process-centered OD can be interpreted in the following way. Participants find it a useful procedure and are encouraged that it will enable them to solve their problems. This is the early reaction. A later reaction is that while what was studied was relevant to increasing their effectiveness, they are unable to make significant use of what was learned in the absence of the catalyst or facilitator. This is the problem of catalyst-in versus catalyst-out. When the catalyst is in the situation, participants can use his or her model and rely upon it to increase the effectiveness of their discussion. When the catalyst is absent, they seem unable to transfer what has been learned.

Theory-Centered OD

Theory-centered organizational development is based on a different set of premises regarding how managerial effectiveness may be acquired. The fundamental notion is that people are behaving about as well as they know how; therefore, it is essential that people first learn more about what constitutes effective behavior. When this learning is coupled with direct experience, particularly in terms of one's own exercise of initiative, inquiry, advocacy, etc., then a person can relate with others in ways that are sound according to the model or to stop conventional ways of behaving that are now recognized as unsound.

The Grid is a major approach to organizational development in which the change strategies are premised upon learning to think more systematically about how to behave effectively, and then to gain personal insight into concrete actions that enhance one's own effectiveness. This approach avoids the mechanical presentation of technique without insight into the human assumptions underlying technique. It also avoids problems of experiencing interaction processes in a subjective way and in the absence of an objective framework for evaluating it.

When change is viewed in this manner, it becomes self-evident that the culture of one's own company is also made up of operational habits, many of which have come into use in an unthinking or unsystematic way. These continue to be employed not because they are necessarily sound but because they typify the way things have been done in the past. Thus, the Grid approach to OD rests upon (1) aiding *all* managers of an organization to learn Grid theories first in personal terms that clarify to each the current ways in which he or she is trying to achieve production with and through people, and (2) helping them learn the skills necessary for applying sound principles of behavior to solving the major problems of organization.

Grid OD is a fully integrated approach to corporate achievement because it provides the basis for bringing all aspects of the business into one manageable, coherent whole.

Phases of Grid OD

Before describing the six stages or phases of development in detail, it is important to consider how Grid OD is introduced into an organization. This is a major factor in its success.

Steps for Getting into Organization-Wide Grid Development

A critical dilemma is in finding a way to achieve awareness among all members about the importance of Grid OD without demanding participation. Ordering members to take part in development is close to a 9,1 way and violates the underlying principles of a 9,9 approach. A sound approach lies in a series of exploratory steps designed to orient members to possibilities. These steps permit the organization to test the implications of Grid OD without the obligation to become deeply involved in it. When these steps are taken in a planned way, organization members have the opportunity to develop their own commitments through a series of self-convincing experiences. Orientation without obligation creates the opportunity to test the temperature before plunging in, it produces awareness of possibilities from which a conviction-based decision can be made. Some of these steps and activities include the following:

☐ *Background reading*—Explains how applied behavioral science is used to strengthen organizations.

☐ *Seeding*—Provides a few organization members deep insight into Phase 1 and the Grid without the organization's being committed to doing more.

☐ *Pilot Grid Seminar*—Provides a test-tube trial of what would be involved were the organization to engage in Phase 1.

☐ *Grid OD Seminar*—Gives a few managers insight into the whole of Grid OD as the basis for evaluation and possible recommendations for next steps.

☐ *Pilot Teamwork Development*—Affords the top team direct understanding and benefit from applying the Grid to strengthening its team effectiveness and the effectiveness of individuals. Then, based on their own experience participants can assess the probable impact of Phase 2 if it were to be applied on an organization-wide basis.

☐ *OD Steering Committee*—After these steps have been completed an OD steering committee is appointed to consider strategies and tactics for long-term OD. It is a diagonal committee with heavy top-level line involvement. Its purpose is to oversee the entire effort. Leadership is centered in line personnel, but it is important that the steering committee also include pertinent staff who are in a position to provide significant support for the entire effort.

Once a decision has been made to move forward, the first activity is Grid Seminars, Phase 1.

Grid Seminar

In the initial phase of organizational development everyone in the organization is involved in learning the Grid and using it to evaluate personal styles of managing. This is made possible through attending a five-day seminar.

Maximum impact is possible when all employees participate. Included are persons who manage others, though some companies extend participation to include technical, wage-earning, and other salaried personnel. The decision on extending Grid learning to other than managerial levels can be made at this or at a later time.

Grid Seminar Goals. The seminar has four major goals:

☐ Increase self-understanding by—
- learning the Grid as a framework of thought, analysis, and comparison,
- gaining insight into how others describe one's own Grid style,
- increasing personal objectivity in self-critique of work behavior,
- reexamining managerial values, and
- developing a common language for communicating about behavior.

☐ Experience problem-solving effectiveness in teams by—
- experimenting with and revising ways to increase effectiveness,
- studying the use of critique,
- developing standards for openness and candor, and
- examining the need for active listening.

☐ Learn about managing interface conflict by—
- studying barriers between teams,
- examining conflict within teams, and the origins of distrust and suspicion of other teams, and
- exploring ways of reducing or eliminating such conflicts between groups.

☐ Comprehend organization implications by—
- understanding impact of work culture on behavior and
- gaining appreciation of Grid OD and how it can be used.

These seminars involve hard work. The program requires thirty or more hours of self-directed study before the seminar week itself, which usually begins Sunday evening and runs through the following Friday. Participants are actively involved in learning teams that solve projects and study how they did and what to do to improve.

A high point of seminar learning is when participants receive critique of their managerial performance from other members of the team. Another is when managers critique the dominant style of their organization's culture. A third is when participants consider steps for increasing the effectiveness of the whole organization.

Grid Seminars aid managers to increase their effectiveness in many different ways. Two approaches are useful in assessing actual impact. One is quantitative and involves field research and statistical analysis. The other is qualitative and includes subjective reports.

Quantitative Studies. The following summarize typical kinds of changes found in field research:

☐ *Changes in promotion* practices following Grid OD favor merit over seniority.
  • those promoted are three years younger on the average.
  • time of service to promotion is reduced 2.8 years.
  • promotion rate to higher positions in same company but outside plant is up 31%.

☐ *Behavior changes* are toward sounder relationships.
  • 62% better communication between bosses and subordinates
  • 61% improvement in working with other groups
  • 55% better relationships with colleagues
  • 48% more leveling in one study, 21.8% in another
  • 22% improvement in goal setting
  • 20% more openness to influence
  • 14% increase in delegation

These kinds of changes all are in the direction of a 9,9 orientation. They suggest that significant changes occur through Grid Seminar participation.

Qualitative Reports. The following are typical participant reactions:

Theories increase understanding and insight—"Now I see a means of improving in a total way rather than a piecemeal way. A sound theoretical framework."

Grid Seminars offer growth-giving personal experiences—"Much greater insight into my managerial style will provide guidelines into how I can improve my effectiveness."

Critique is central to valid problem solving—"Best personal learning experience ever, particularly since individuals and teams learn through experience with continuous critique and positive reinforcements."

Openness is basic to sound relationships—"The frankness and openness created by the Seminar experience is a significant factor in enabling useful discussions to be carried out in depth with team members."

Better teamwork is one of the rewarding outcomes—"I saw synergistic action and understand now that when a group works well together, its end product is superior to the sum of the products of the same group members working individually."

Perspective for seeing one's own performance in more objective terms—"It forced me to take a critical look at myself and also, through practical Grid experience in a team setting, showed me how some of my beliefs can actually be detrimental to the company."

Deception in Self-Assessment

A major barrier to change is found in self-deception. It can be seen in the following way. Before attending the Grid Seminar managers describe themselves by choosing Grid paragraphs that they believe reflect their personal managerial style. During the Seminar each participant receives written feedback from colleagues concerning the dominant and backup Grid styles they observed in the participant's problem-solving and decision-making behavior during the week's discussions. The feedback is in the form of paragraphs written around the elements of initiative, inquiry, advocacy, etc. Yet, it is a tailor-made description of specific and concrete behavior. Then the participant reexamines personal behavior by reranking the Grid paragraphs again to describe what is thought to be dominant and backup Grid styles.

As can be seen in Table 12-1, a large shift in self-assessment, particularly with respect to the 9,9 Grid style, occurs between the first self-assessment and the second. Prior to the Seminar 67.9% saw themselves as having a 9,9 orientation. After the Grid Seminar 16.5% saw themselves as being 9,9.

Table 12-1
Self-Ranking of Dominant Grid Styles
Pre and Post Seminar Attendance

Grid Styles	% Self-Rankings of Dominant Grid Style	
	Pre	Post
9,9	67.9	16.5
9,1	10.7	36.8
5,5	18.9	41.5
1,9	2.2	4.2
1,1	0.3	1.0

How can we account for this reduction of 51.4%? There are several explanations:

☐ *Better understanding.* A more thorough comprehension of the concepts makes it possible to be more objective.
☐ *Self-deception.* A person who looks inside is likely to misjudge what is viewed. One looks at one's intentions. Most people have good intentions that correspond generally with a 9,9 orientation, but the individual is unlikely to see personal behavior that may be, and often is, contradictory to good intentions.
☐ *New data.* When people receive feedback as to how others see their behavior, they may learn things about themselves that they previously had not recognized. With this new information, they can see themselves more objectively and thus are motivated to change in the direction of more effective behavior.

Seminar Composition. Although 100% of a firm's managers engage in organizational development, it is rare that all can participate in seminars at the same time. Members participate in a particular Grid study team composed of a *diagonal* slice of the membership.

A diagonal slice Grid team is not composed of a boss and his or her direct subordinates. A boss and a subordinate may be present in the same seminar but they do not engage in learning in the same study team. It is six to ten line and staff managers, technical and professional personnel, and supervisors who study together. The same is true for different ages and organization functions. The only basis for grouping is that, insofar as possible, each Grid team is composed to be a miniature replica of the organization. This basis of grouping makes possible exchange of perspective not only among persons from different functions but among those from different levels as well.

A question raised is whether lower level members are able to participate effectively with persons from higher levels. The implication is that lower level members, because they are more likely to be persons with practical experience only, may not be able to learn as fast as persons with college backgrounds. This is not the case, however. Lower level persons often have a depth of practical human experience as rich as any. When those who have risen from the ranks have opportunities to study and learn with college-educated managers, they gain a better understanding of the other's thinking—how he or she goes about analyzing problems, formulating alternatives, weighing advantages and disadvantages, and deciding on a course of action. For a person from the ranks, this in itself can be a useful educational experience.

Nonsupervisory personnel are often included, particularly in high tech, knowledge-oriented organizations. This means that those who engage together in study teams are upper-level management, professionals, and hourly personnel. This is desirable because participants gain insight into cleavages between management and operating levels. Participants have often pointed to this as one of the important contributors to strengthening organization integration.

Another related question is, "What is the minimum formal education a person needs to benefit from a Grid Seminar?" Formal education is less important than the ability to comprehend concepts. Anyone with sixth-grade-level reading comprehension usually has the learning skills essential for benefiting from a Grid Seminar.

One disadvantage of diagonal slice participation stems from the number of levels represented rather than the method itself. When levels are too far apart within the hierarchy—vice-president and front-line supervisor in a large company, for example—participants may find it difficult to talk back and forth in an easy and understanding way. While the diagonal slice method is most desirable, a sound number of levels in any one team should probably be limited to three or four.

Sometimes the question is, "What about those who are nearing retirement? Should they be included in the development effort?" A person nearing retirement may not see value in further involvement with the organization within the time remaining. On the other hand, many managers near retirement find gratifying personal reward in the learning itself and in the opportunity to study and be with others. Managers preparing to retire certainly should be invited to participate.

There are some ground rules but there are no hard and fast answers regarding how many should participate in any one seminar. Achieving speed and getting many through must be balanced against ensuring that organizational performance does not falter because too many people are absent from work at the same time. Most companies find that under the diagonal slice concept about 10% of the organization can be away from the job without undesirable effects on organization performance. Furthermore, the diagonal slice approach ensures that no work unit is seriously depleted.

In large organizations the 10% figure is limited by the numbers that can be accommodated in a single seminar. The question is, "How many people is too many for a seminar?" The maximum number is around seventy-five for two seminar administrators for an in-company seminar. The optimum is forty to sixty and large companies might consider several seminars run concurrently or consecutively.

A Special Case of 1A

1A projects are activities that managers can implement as soon as they return to the job after Phase 1 Grid Seminar learning. They may be launched as a part of the final seminar learning activity but they also may occur in a spontaneous way.

Some examples are described below.

"For the first time in a year, I walked over to the maintenance department and sat down to talk about some of our problems. They were surprised and pleased to see me as I am the one who always picked up the phone and complained whenever something went wrong."

"It was now obvious to me that I had been avoiding Jim, who seemed to complain a lot. I decided to have a conference with him together with the marketing people on the schedule slippage problem. It took us very little time to develop a checklist and tickler system. We are routinely relying on it now to keep work flowing in an orderly way."

"I had a performance review coming up and in the past these had been perfunctory. I decided to use my boss as a resource and to open up with him on some of the areas where I needed more help. He saw this as a 180-degree shift but seemed to welcome the opportunity to get down to brass tacks. We both made some commitments and if we keep them we'll have a more productive relationship."

"It became apparent to me that I had been creating problems by being away too much. My rationalization to myself was that by traveling I am able to learn more about what's going on in the field firsthand. I hadn't realized that was over-delegating the solutions to some tough problems. This has been effectively solved simply by cutting back on my travel schedule. The slack has been taken up by my subordinates traveling more, which was the correct solution in the first place."

These are illustrations of 1A projects. They all seem to involve shifts in the exercise of initiative, either doing more or less than in the past but, in any event, bringing the exercise of initiative into alignment with organization needs. Other illustrations include better inquiry and more effective critique. It appears to be more difficult to shift advocacy, conflict solving, and organized teamwork and decision making without moving into Team Building, as described below.

Team Building

Chapter 9 pointed out the value of teamwork for increasing organization effectiveness. Phase 2 Team Building comes after Grid Seminar participation. It is addressed to diagnosing specific barriers to sound teamwork and identifying opportunities for improvement within actual work teams of boss and subordinates.

Team Building Goals

☐ Replace outmoded traditions, precedents, and past practices with a sound team culture.
☐ Increase personal objectivity in on-the-job behavior.
☐ Use critique for learning and for improving operational results.
☐ Set standards of excellence.
☐ Establish objectives for team and individual achievement.

Issues of problem solving and decision making are central, such as when 1/0, 1/1/1 and 1/all teamwork are needed. However, many more facets of teamwork are explored in depth. These include each team member's reactions to the contributions of others, assumptions about what constitutes effective teamwork, identification of particular problems existing within the team that are barriers to effectiveness coupled with specific plans to remedy them. Setting team objectives for future achievement is the final assembled activity. Later follow-up in three or four months is a useful additional step.

Team building can begin when all members of any management team have completed a Grid Seminar and are ready to apply Grid concepts to their own team culture. It is initiated by the person in charge and those who report to him or her and it moves downward. Each manager then meets with subordinates to repeat the activity as a team, studying their barriers to effectiveness and planning ways to overcome them.

Grid team building typically is a five-day activity usually implemented on the job during working hours. The activities can be segmented into parts and conducted over a longer period if this is necessary or desirable.

Impact. The following quotation indicates that team building can have a major impact on team effectiveness.

"Phase 1 is like getting a check; Phase 2 is when you cash it. . . . The period of Phase 2's implementation in the automotive division coincided with a 300% increase in divisional profits—a significantly better profit improvement than that of the rest of the domestic organization—even though we concede that market conditions, expanded plant capacity, the state of the economy, etc. may have contributed to the improvement in profits. Top management believed that Phase 2 and the striking turnaround in the automotive division were more than a coincidence, that Phase 2 made a substantial contribution to the performance, even though it was impossible to measure precisely."

Taken together, Phase 1 and 2 unlock communication barriers.

"In the past, when we would set budgets, I would calculate what each department would get. . . . Then they would yell and complain, 'Why did you give me this?' I would say, 'This is the way it is, boys, I'm the boss.' Now, since we went to Grid last year, there's no such happening. Perhaps we've got to reduce our margin in meat. We know we've got to make it up somewhere else. The group comes to a decision. This year it took us an hour-and-a-half to set our budget. Before Grid, we were in there for eight solid hours table-pounding. But now we were committed . . ."

One marketing manager put it this way,

"I never realized our department could really work as a team. Phase 1 of the Grid was great, but it really took Phase 2 to bring it all out. Sure, I was apprehensive at first, all the guys were, but when it came right down to it, we were able to work together, solve problems, open up and really communicate with each other. It wasn't what you would call an easy experience, but it was certainly worthwhile."

Interface Development

The third step is to achieve better problem solving at interfaces between groups through a closer integration among those that have working interrelationships. The need for Phase 3 development activities comes about when a department or unit or division concentrates on its own assigned responsibilities, without considering the effect on total company performance or its relations with other units. People may act and react in the interests of their department and neglect the interests of the entire organization. This is viewed from inside the department as selflessly serving the corporation but such preoccupation may mean less attention is paid to other departments than is needed to produce cooperation and coordination. The second department may ask, "Why are they dragging their feet? Why are they unable to provide the service we need, which is the only reason for their existence in the first place? They are deliberately ignoring our requirements."

The importance of an integrated approach to development is made evident when the extent to which the industrial world is segmented into artificial divisions is recognized. The splits are manufacturing and marketing, personnel and operations, central engineering and the plants, operations and maintenance, etc. Each of these separations is intended to make possible a better utilization of personnel and the assignment of specialists who have competence to deal with the problems in the segmented components. However, there is a need to integrate with the other side of the split, and yet no particular understanding of issues that have been "put" on the other side of the split can be presumed. As a result, a heavy expense is paid in misunderstandings, distrust, suspicion with resultant lack of coordination, empire building, etc.

The situation is particularly evident when the problem is examined on a splits-within-a-split basis. Often, for example, different people in personnel are involved in designing performance appraisal as though it were separated and isolated from promotion and reward policy. Both of these may be treated in a separate manner from selection and all of these may only indirectly be connected to training and development. Furthermore, the specialists in each of these domains may at best be casually or mechanically connected with the line personnel, who in many respects should carry ultimate responsibility not only for implementing but also designing the subsystems under which they exercise leadership.

If the artificiality of this multiplicity of splits were understood, those who make these decisions would know that training and performance appraisal are so intimately interconnected that they cannot truly be separated and compartmentalized, that the reward system and operational performance are so closely connected as to be interdependent. All these separations produce subsystems that at the worst may effectively contradict one another and even under the best of conditions may not provide the needed coordination.

An integrated approach makes it possible to redesign subsystems so that a coherent basis of organization is available for strengthening overall performance, and this is one purpose of interface development as the central activity of Phase 3.

Interface attitudes of frustration can quickly turn into feelings of mutual hostility, rooted in mistrust and suspicion. These are easily provoked and, once formed, become win-lose power struggles. When this happens, needed cooperation is sacrificed, information is withheld, requests are perceived as unreasonable demands, etc. When members are asked what their problems are, they tend to answer, "Poor communication." However, the underlying problems of distrust and suspicion at the interface must be resolved before fundamental changes in effectiveness of communication can be brought about.

Interface Development Goals

☐ Use a systematic framework for analyzing barriers to interface co-operation and coordination.
☐ Apply problem-solving and decision-making skills for
  • depolarizing antagonisms,
  • confronting relationships based on surface harmony or neutrality that hide problem-solving difficulties, and
  • resisting compromise when differences cannot be solved in this manner.
☐ Utilize confrontation to identify focal issues needing resolution.
☐ Plan steps for achieving improved cooperation and coordination between units with scheduled follow-up.

Phase 3 is engaged in only by those groups where actual barriers to effective cooperation and coordination exist. It is not a universal phase in which all groups automatically take part. Locally, interface development usually is undertaken after Phase 2 Grid Team Building has been completed, but some interface problems may be so acute that earlier attention is warranted.

Impact. How Phase 3 resolves union-management chronic difficulties is described in the following:

"The union-management Phase 3 has been completed for eighteen months and it has been very successful. The time since then has been spent systematically analyzing all the important aspects of the union-management relationships. The outcome has been a mutually agreed ideal on each of these aspects plus a whole series of action steps designed to move towards this ideal. Some of the areas covered were overtime, job performance, grievances, seniority, job ownership, the Agreement, work fluctuations, job evaluation, communications, compensation, the pension plan, and objectives.

"Overall, these Phase 3 activities have served to develop trust and respect between union and management participants and have provided an excellent forum for the candid discussion of problems. Many traditions have been broken down and a new culture has emerged. There are two particularly striking features to this new atmosphere. The greatest improvement has come in the area of listening and trying to understand the other side's viewpoint. Secondly, this and the very nature of the Phase 3 design (management presenting how it sees itself and how it sees the union on various elements, and the union presenting how it sees itself and management) have tended to make both sides more objective. As a consequence, many of the flare-ups that occurred in the early stages are no longer happening.

"That is not to say that both sides agree on everything by any means. However, where disagreement arises, it is approached rationally and there is a basic trust between the two groups that each is committed to finding a sound and acceptable solution."

The first three phases of OD deal with strengthening behavior to allow members to become more effective. The last three phases can then be undertaken with greater likelihood of success. These last phases are concerned with the *fundamental business logic* on which the firm is based by testing its soundness and strengthening it whenever needed. This step is prior to *planning,* since planning can be no better than the assumptions on which it is based.

Phases 1 through 3 make important contributions to corporate excellence, but none are sufficient for reaching the degree of excellence potentially available to corporations based on the systematic development of the business logic. The key to exploiting organizational potentials is in the organization having a business model of what it wishes to become in comparison with what it currently is or historically has been.

Designing an Ideal Strategic Organizational Model: Phase 4

The top team of a corporation is situated to carry out such a fundamental approach by examining and rejecting whatever in its current business logic is outmoded and unprofitable and by formulating a replacement model. The model is based on the organization's defining its future business activity to be geared to the needs of society for products and services; to the corporation's need for profitability; to the employees' needs for security and satisfaction with work based upon involvement, participation, and commitment; and to the stockholders' needs for a meaningful return on invested funds.

Goals of Designing an Ideal Strategic Organizational Model

☐ Specify minimum and optimum corporate financial objectives.
☐ Describe the nature and character of business activities to be pursued in the future.
☐ Define the scope, character, and depth of markets to be penetrated.

☐ Create a structure for organizing and integrating business operations.

☐ Identify development requirements for maintaining thrust and avoiding drag.

☐ Delineate policies to guide future business decision making.

The top team studies, diagnoses, and designs an ideal corporate model for what the organization should become in a step-by-step examination of business logic. The study is an intellectual investigation of the most basic concepts of business logic currently available. These are drawn from the writings of managers who pioneered in the development of a systematic discipline of business logic.

Using concepts of "pure" business logic with which the team is in agreement, the second step is for the top team to specify the operational blueprint for the redesign of the corporation. Phase 4 is completed when this strategic corporate model has been evaluated and agreed to by the next layer up and approved by the board of directors.

Impact. The kinds of changes brought about through Phase 4 are described as follows:

"Other important outcomes of the OD effort that must be evaluated are in the area of strategy. There is a widespread conviction that the strategic insights that occurred during Phase 4 have been beneficial and have served to start the corporation moving in the right direction.

"The Phase 4 team at . . . first reached agreement on details of what actually exists in the present organization. That is, the team developed a clear picture of . . . management, with no rationalizations, excuses or apologies; they developed simple, concise statements that picture the actual model today. Then, using the same format, they developed statements as to how a hypothetical, ideal . . . would operate. This ideal model served to focus attention on needed changes in policy.

"All participants committed themselves to action based on statements of concepts and principles that were agreed upon. In support of these concepts and principles, policies were drafted that are to serve as the specific basis to guide management action."

Implementing Development: Phase 5

Phase 5 is designed to implement the model developed in Phase 4. It is unnecessary to tear down the whole company and start from scratch to build a new company to meet the requirements of the model. What is done is more like remodeling a building according to a blueprint of what it is to become. Architects and engineers study the existing structure to identify what is already strong, sound, and consistent with the blueprint and should be retained, what is antiquated and inappropriate and must be replaced, and what is usable but needs modification or strengthening to bring it into line with the blueprint. Phase 4 develops the blueprint; Phase 5 identifies and implements what must be done concretely to shift from the old to the new.

Goals in Phase 5

☐ Examine existing activities to identify gaps between how it is now being operated and the way it is expected to operate according to the ideal strategic model.

☐ Specify which activities are sound, which can be changed and retained, which are unsound and need to be replaced or abandoned, and what new or additional activities are needed to meet the requirements of the ideal model.

☐ Design specific actions necessary to change to the ideal model.

☐ Continue to run the business while simultaneously changing it toward the ideal model.

A series of steps provides the basis for changing the organization from what it is to what it should become. They begin with analyzing and subdividing the company into its components. A component is a smallest grouping of interrelated activities that are tied together because they all are essential in producing a recognizable source of earnings and an identifiable cost or expense, with as little dependence on sources within the company but outside itself as possible.

Another step is to compute the investment related to these activities tied up in plant and equipment, and personnel. Once these steps have been taken, it becomes possible to evaluate whether the business activity identified by that component meets or can be changed to meet the specifications of the model. Test questions such as the following are answered with regard to each identified component. Is the return currently realized on this investment consistent with the strategic model? If not, are there controllable expenses or pricing factors that could be altered to bring it within specified return on investment standards? Is this area of business activity consistent with market areas identified within the strategic model as areas for sound future growth? These questions are typical of the many employed to decide whether each segregated activity should be expanded, shortened, changed, or eliminated in pursuing corporate development.

Implementing Phase 5 often contributes a quantum leap in productivity because of the depth of change involved. The results shown in Figure 12-1 demonstrate the character of improvement possible. It illustrates the profitability of two autonomous corporations operating nationwide on opposite sides of the United States-Canadian border. Corporation A engaged in Grid Organization Development. Corporation B did not. They are owned by the same parent, located in a third country. They engage in similar businesses and face the same character of competition in comparable markets.

Figure 12-1. Typical impact of Grid organization development.

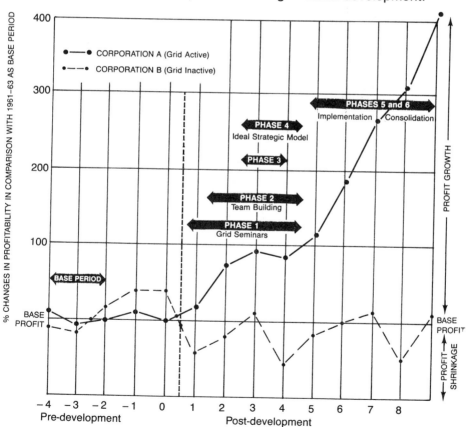

The starting comparisons show that for five years prior to the introduction of Grid development, the control corporation, B, appeared to be obtaining somewhat better economic performance, but the results were well within the range of chance fluctuations. Then, after introduction of Grid Organization Development, Corporation A experienced a continuous and rising curve of profitability during the next nine years. By the end of the study, profitability in the Grid company was 400% greater than in Corporation B, which had not engaged in Grid Organization Development. Corporation B had just managed to hold its own over the fourteen-year period.

The following remarks by the president of Corporation A at a time when his company had been engaged in Grid OD for six years offers his evaluation of the change.

> "There is no doubt that OD has had a significant and positive effect on profits. . . . A major objective of the Grid was to change behavior and values within the organization in the direction of showing a high concern for both task accomplishment and human motivation, and then to sustain these changes and institutionalize them. . . . There has undoubtedly been a substantial transformation in this area, with positive effects accruing through improved communication, the use of critique, profit or cost consciousness, some aspects of planning, the handling of conflict, meaningful participation in a group, and commitment among key managers . . . there is one other most important benefit that has accrued from the OD program and that is a substantial improvement in the working relationships between management and union officials.
>
> "Much of the work involving the union can be considered as a breakthrough in the application of OD principles and there is little doubt as to its success."

Impact. An organization member who was directly involved in his company's implementation project summarized his reactions.

> "Once we could specify how we needed to change to meet the Ideal Strategic Model, we were in the management-by-objectives business in a way that wasn't limited by blind acceptance of the status quo. Some of the specific things we learned included:
>
> 1. How to approach the business in a scientific way to analyze and evaluate variables selectively.
> 2. Taking corporate perspective as opposed to previous functional or departmental view.

3. Looking at existing business more critically, growing more and more displeased with current efforts.
4. Gaining a new perspective on the role of planning in effective management.
5. Focusing on results expected by using return on assets as the basis for business decisions in comparison with conventional profit and loss and share of market thinking.
6. Grasping the deeper implications of effective teamwork for increasing the soundness of any implementation plan.
7. Developing more basic insight into the dynamics of change."

Consolidation: Phase 6

Phase 6 is used to stabilize and consolidate progress achieved during Phases 1-5 before recycling into another period of change.

Goals of Phase 6

☐ Critique the change effort to ensure that activities that have been implemented are being continued as planned.
☐ Identify weaknesses that could not have been anticipated throughout the implementation and take corrective action to rectify them.
☐ Monitor changes in the business environment (competition, price of raw materials, wage differentials, and so on) that may indicate that fundamental shifts in the model are necessary.

Three features of business life suggest the importance of a consolidating phase in organization development. Managing change is the opposite of managing the tried and true. People tend to repeat the tried and true, but they may lose interest, convictions, or courage about something novel and unpredictable, and reduced effort in making the novel work as it was intended may cause it to fail. A second reason to consolidate progress is that by continuing the study of what is new, additional improvement opportunities may be identified that add to organizational thrust. A third is that significant alterations in the outer environment may occur to cause changes specified in the model and implemented in Phase 5 to be more or less favorable than had been anticipated. The monitoring activities of Phase 6 provide a basis for specifying needs for additional change.

Phase 6 strategies and instruments enable an organization to assess its current strengths and to consolidate its gains.

The significant aspect of Phase 6 is that the consolidation effort must be managed rather than left to its own momentum.

Impact. The following is a quote which relates the importance of Phase 6 activities.

> "It's important to keep in mind that the Grid is not a fad that is 'in' for a few years and then phases 'out.' The program is designed so that the last step is never-ending. The company will always be monitoring what is being done, judging how far that is from the ideal, and taking the necessary steps to reach the ideal."

Summary

Change is important because principles of behavior only come into use when the values on which they rest are understood and appreciated.

It is easiest for the person in charge to introduce change. There are two reasons for this: (1) There is no need to consult superiors for approval, and (2) the financial resources for supporting the change process can be authorized directly.

Two ways of introducing change include technique-centered OD and process-centered OD.

The third approach is centered on learning theory and principles and then bringing leadership into line with them. Grid OD was presented by describing a series of six phases of change as a fully integrated approach.

From a behavioral point of view it brings individual effort into more effective teamwork and promotes the development of more effective interfaces between organization teams. From a business point of view it enables organization members to design and implement a system of business logic that is supportive of operational results and profit.

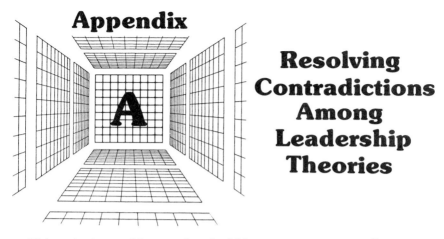

Appendix

Resolving Contradictions Among Leadership Theories

Things in the world around and within us are not necessarily as we say they are because they "are" that way, but they appear as they do because of the way we think about them. What we have learned about how to think about them may be far different than if we were thinking in a truly sound or objective manner. Social activities involving leadership, power, and authority are based on our personally created "*conceptual* structures" (formulations) that many times are deeply-embedded, silent, and invisible. When such formulations do not square with outside facts, human affairs are conducted in unsound and unhealthy ways. When they are congruent, human activities can be carried out in a sound, productive, creative, satisfying, and healthy manner. This generalization appears true for all human experience activities, but in this context it is particularly pertinent in comprehending what constitutes the sound basis for exercising leadership whether in business, finance, education, industry, medicine, military activities, etc.

This appendix presents a general semantics-based foundation for a theory of face-to-face leadership. Whenever two or more people are engaged in an activity, leadership involves determining a course of action while achieving coordination. The importance of leadership in our daily lives is difficult to overestimate. Its influence is reflected in such words as "god," "king," "tribal chief," "president," "father," "boss," "high priest," "ayatollah," "parent," "general," and "teacher." The term "leadership" points to something of apparent significance to people over many centuries.

---

* Part 1 of Korzybski Memorial Lecture, "Foundations for Strengthening Leadership" presented before the Institute of General Semantics by the authors in 1982 and published in the General Semantics Bulletin, #50, 1983, pg. 93–128, and reproduced with permission.

The important question here is not "What 'is' leadership?" A recent conversation is representative of the difficulty in trying to identify "it."

"What is the mission of your institution?" we asked an instructor at one of our military teaching centers; it might have been Annapolis or West Point.

"In the final analysis," he responded, "to train young people to lead."

"But," we continued, "what does it mean to teach people to lead?"

"It means leaders lead through the exercise of command," he observed.

"Can you explain that?" we asked.

"That's all there is to it," he replied. "You can't take it any further than that. Leaders exercise command by leading."

This circular conversation portrays the conviction that "Leadership *is* a mystical, indescribable thing." We know better. Our goal is not to define what leadership "is," but to develop a meaningful set of operational definitions which can be used to produce a "map" that serves as a valid representation of what happens in actual relationships between people who are engaged in a shared activity.

Processes of leadership are involved in achieving results with and through others. Whether it is called management, supervision, or administration, the underlying processes establish direction and permit coordination. Experiencing these processes in everyday settings may generate a range of emotional responses (semantic reactions): enthusiasm, apathy, anger, commitment, complacency, indifference, involvement, and so on. These different reactions, which include so-called "emotional" and "intellectual" aspects, tell us that leadership is exercised in many different ways. Leadership behavior may be characterized as persuasive, punitive, strong, "inspirational," "charismatic," or comforting, again telling us that it is a very complex human activity.

A thorough analysis of leadership requires that we deal with the structure of language and "thought" embedded within Aristotelian and non-Aristotelian orientations. By examining various ways of formulating the analysis of leadership, we demonstrate, through experimental research, the implications of relying on Aristotelian logic in conceiving leadership theory and prescribing leadership practices. By comparison, a non-Aristotelian formulation of effective leadership processes yielding significantly different conclusions will be explored. Let's take an example—the airliner cockpit.

The captain as a leader in the modern jetliner can utilize cockpit resources in an Aristotelian or a non-Aristotelian way. The basis of resource utilization employed makes an important difference in terms of safety and on-time performance. We will clarify this conclusion later by describing an experiment which has significant implications for understanding the exercise of effective leadership and its relationship to flight safety. The key role of non-Aristotelian logic in the successful outcome of this experiment will become clear as we proceed.

We wish to emphasize Korzybski's diagram of the process of abstracting from a non-Aristotelian point of view because it has become so central to understanding leadership. (See Figure A-1.)

The "happenings" on the left side of this figure are events or occurrences that are taking place "out there." "Out there" may be physically separate from the observer or within his or her own skin. In either case, the unspeakable happening sets off a chain of reactions beginning with physico-chemical electro-colloidal nervous impact from I. Activation of

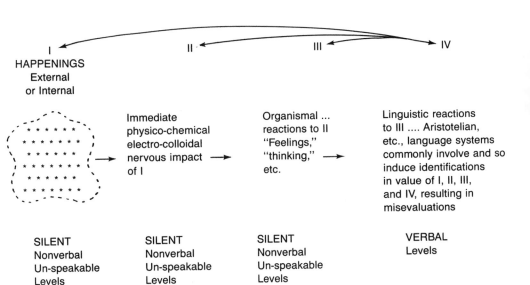

Figure A-1. The process of abstracting from an electro-colloidal non-Aristotelian point of view. Source: Korzybski, A. "The Role of Language in the Perceptual Processes." Blake, R. R. and Ramsey, G. V. (eds.), *Perception: An Approach to Personality.* NY: Ronald Press, 1951, pp. 170–205. Slightly revised by Blake and Mouton.

the retina, cochlea, or other sensory mechanisms occurs at silent Level II, but this reaction is still nonverbal and unspeakable. Organismal reactions to Level II sensory stimuli occur at silent Level III in the form of "feelings" and "thinking," probably including visual images, still at prespeakable levels. At the fourth level, language systems are employed by the observer to express and verbalize the Level I happening.

When this natural order of the abstracting process is reversed, Level IV formulations about the happening may reshape the observer's perception of it in ways that may be very different from the happening itself. If the Level IV language structure has Aristotelian-type logic embedded within it, the interpretation of the happening is likely to contain misperceptions and inappropriate evaluations which lead to faulty assumptions, generalizations, and actions. Let us now examine a number of studies which derived their conclusions about effective leadership from an Aristotelian, elementalistic research base, i.e. starting at the right end of Figure A-1 and "imposing" preconceptions on what was "there" at the left end.

Aristotelian Logic Applied in Empirical Studies of Leadership

Following World War II the United States military services remained deeply interested in leadership and commissioned well-financed research to study it further.

One research center was located at Ohio State University where Professor Edwin Fleishman conducted investigations which have become widely known as the Ohio State Leadership Studies. We will characterize this research in schematic outline to clarify the Aristotelian logic on which it was premised and to demonstrate its reversal of the natural sequence in the order of abstraction, i.e., starting at the "wrong" end.

These researchers started by collecting more than 1800 statements characterizing Level IV abstractions about aspects of leadership *behavior.* The information was collected as an empirical, seat-of-the-pants undertaking with little or no guidance from theory or systematic thinking and little apparent awareness of the sequence of abstraction. The many items were winnowed to 150 and assembled into a questionnaire. Typical questionnaire items were: "he emphasizes meeting of deadlines," "he treats people under him without considering their feelings," "he insists that he be informed on decisions made by people under him " (Fleishman, 1960 and 1973).

Subordinates of military officers and industrial personnel responded to the Fleishman instruments by indicating the extent to which each of these items characterized his or her supervisor's exercise of leadership.

Elementalism

The next question posed by Fleishman, Hemphill, and colleagues was something like, "Could there be clusters of items which seem to group together but are different from other items which also may be grouped together? If we identify these, we may discover the common elements underlying the practice of leadership."

They used the statistical methodology called for in a factor analytic approach to identify several common elements. The use of a factor analytic approach presumes that a process such as leadership is created from elements that can be separated from one another. We will concentrate on the two elements considered most important, understanding that additional factors present were evaluated as lacking sufficient statistical significance to be useful in characterizing leadership. These elements were thought to be present in different amounts in different leaders, and so scales were constructed that were thought to measure how much of "it," i.e. a given element, was present.

Labeling

Once committed to the blunder of isolating leadership "elements" consistent with Aristotelian logic, the next step was to "label" them. One was entitled "Initiating Structure," calling attention to whatever the leader tells the subordinate "to do." The Structure dimension is represented in Figure A-2. At the high end, a leader tells a subordinate what to do, where to do it, when to do it, how to do it, and so on. He or she rarely goes into "why," because explaining rationale is not consistent with the other kinds of behavior found within this activity.

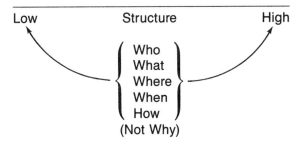

Figure A-2. Structure dimension of leadership.

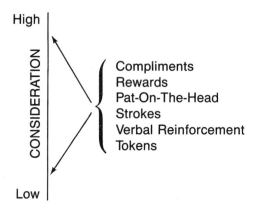

Figure A-3. Consideration dimension of leadership.

The second element, shown in Figure A-3, was labeled "Consideration," referring to the extent to which a leader gives subordinates social-emotional support. Consideration is present to a high degree when the leader treats subordinates in a warm or emotionally-supportive way, as demonstrated through compliments, rewards, pats on the head, strokes, etc.

Now the groundwork has been set for comprehending the Aristotelian logic inherent in this approach. Clusters became independent elements representing the two discrete or independent "activities" to be found in leadership. Since Initiating Structure and Consideration are viewed as two separate, uncorrelated actions, a leader can apply any magnitude of one in combination with any amount of the other. The Ohio State studies seem to have concluded that "it," something "out there," had been described. The presence of elementalistic "thinking" (formulating) was apparently unrecognized.

Fleishman's reversal of the natural order of abstracting, as shown in Figure A-4, is deeply embedded in the Ohio State approach. Clearly, Fleishman's collection of 1800 leadership behavior items is a Level IV rather than a Level I beginning. The resultant "theory" is superimposed on the "happening" rather than derived directly from it, constituting a reversal of the natural sequence of abstracting. Conclusions about the happening itself, i.e., the exercise of leadership, are drawn at verbal Level IV without apparent regard for the silent Levels I, II and III.

The logic of elementalism led to the conclusion that "Leadership *is* Initiating Structure and Consideration."

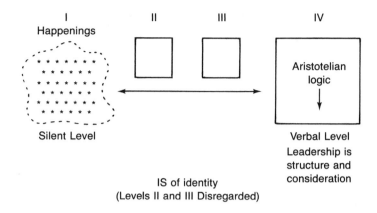

Figure A-4. Fleishman's reversal of the natural order of abstracting.

Combining Elements by Adding Them

Fleishman now saw the need to recombine the two leadership activities to gain a view of any specific individual's leadership behavior. The manner of recombining is of signal importance for comprehending the consistency with which Aristotelian logic was relied upon in this important research.

Fleishman said, in effect, "We'll create *two* questionnaires, one for measuring behaviors called for by Initiating Structure, and the other for behaviors resulting from Consideration. We will then employ a system of coordinates and combine scores of varying magnitudes for each of the two activities to picture variations in exercising leadership.

"To display individual scores on a graph," Fleishman might have continued, "we will place Initiating Structure and Consideration at right angles to one another. If a leader's score is high on one activity and high on the other, we represent that person's approach to leadership in the upper right quadrant of the graph (Figure A-5) and so on for other combinations of scores, e.g., low + low, high + low, and low + high.

What is high + high when translated into actual leadership behavior? We think that the terms Paternalism/Maternalism accurately describe the exercise of high + high leadership. A paternalist exercises a high degree of control through giving directions and instructions but is considerate, warm, affectionate, and supportive in exchange for compliance (Levinson, 1968).

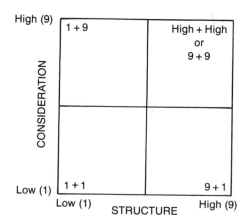

Figure A-5. Fleishman's representation of consideration vs. structure.

Items selected from the two Fleishman questionnaires indicate the character of paternalism. In Figure A-6, items from the Structure test on the left side are aligned with Consideration items which appear on the right side. Controlling others with an iron hand and also doing personal favors for them is the formula for rewarding subordinates with consideration in exchange for compliance. Expecting after hours work and then helping those who comply to solve personal problems is another example of high+high behavior.

The following illustrative dialogue provides an operational view of paternalistic leadership in action. Joe is the subordinate, and *Smith el* is his boss. (Smith el is a boss who exercises leadership according to elementalistic assumptions.)

Initiating Structure		Consideration
Always rule with an iron hand	(but)	Often do favors for persons under me
Encourage after duty work by persons of my unit a great deal	(but)	Often help persons under me with their personal problems

Figure A-6. Sample of how items based on the Ohio State Leadership Model are answered by those who earn a high-high (9 + 9) score.

Smith el

Boss: You've read the shift book. It's pretty full, but you need to get it all done.

Subordinate: I'll do my best.

Boss: Here's how I want you to do it. Instead of making the seven adjustments on each of the three machines, a machine at a time, I want you to make the same adjustment on each machine, one at a time in sequence. Start with balancing the rotes on all three. Then come back to the first machine and replace the belt. Repeat that on machines 2 and 3, and so forth.

Subordinate: But boss, that's inefficient. It's really better to deal with all seven adjustments on machine 1 and then work on machine 2.

Boss: I appreciate your suggestion, Joe, but this way I will have your guarantee that each one of the adjustments was completed.

Subordinate: Okay, if that's the way you want it. It's wasteful, but if that's the way you want it . . . okay.

Boss: That's great, Joe. I can always count on you. Give me a ring 30 minutes before quitting time to let me know your progress.

Subordinate: Okay.

Boss (answering phone hours later): Yeah, yeah, Joe. What . . . ?

Subordinate: I've almost got it done except for the seventh adjustment on 2 and 3. I'll get through by quitting time.

Boss: That's really wonderful, Joe. You've given me a great day's work. If you have any extra time before quitting, knock off and go to the smoke pen. Have yourself a break on me.

Subordinate: Okay, boss. Thanks a lot. Glad I did what you wanted.

The boss structures how Joe is to make the adjustments and, against his better judgment, Joe gives the boss what he wants. The boss demonstrates his consideration by giving Joe high support, not because he did good work, but because he obeyed and did the work the way the boss directed. This addition of two independent elements results in paternalism. The paternalistic relationship becomes even more vivid in the remark in which the boss confuses himself with the company and says, "You've given *me* a great day's work . . ." He also identifies himself as the company when he uses company time as though he personally owned it, giving it as a reward to the subordinate for compliant behavior.

Fleishman expected that leaders scoring in the high + high quadrant would be more effective than other leaders since their test scores reflect the maximum presence of both of the elements. A series of studies designed and conducted over 30 years to empirically test this prediction have failed to demonstrate that it is a "useful" map for characterizing the territory of leadership (Korman, 1966; Larson, Hunt, and Osborn, 1976; Nystrom, 1978).

We have focused here on the Fleishman leadership model, because Fleishman's work continues to have influence. In spite of its faulty formulation and lack of demonstrated validity, Fleishman and others including Fiedler (1964), Reddin (1970), House (1971), Hersey and Blanchard (1982), Blanchard (1982), Lefton (1980), Vroom and Yetton (1973), Kipnis, Schmidt, Swaffin-Smith and Wilkinson (1984), et al, have extended or emphasized variations of this leadership theory.

An illustration of this is provided through an examination of the validity of these two fundamentally different formulations by evaluating the test produced for measurement of leadership of Hersey and Blanchard. The prediction that the 9,9 test items will not be represented in a test constructed according to 9+9 concept formation is confirmed. When 9,9 kinds of items are inserted into the 9+9 based test, it is found through empirical research that managers overwhelmingly choose the 9,9 statements over the 9+9 statements as descriptions of the most effective leadership approach (Blake and Mouton, 1982). Maccoby advanced the notion in 1976 that opportunism (see Chapter 11) is the coming leadership theory, but more recently he revised this view and replaced it with a 9,9-like leadership orientation (1981). Shutz, relying on a different definition of elements regards them in an elementalistic way and combines them additively, again reflecting a theory of leadership resting on Aristotelian logic (1984). By way of summary, Korzybski might observe, "The Aristotelian language [applied to leadership theory] perpetuated what I call 'elementalism,' or splitting verbally what cannot be split empirically" (Korzybski and Kendig, 1942).

Differential Analysis Applied to the Exercise of Leadership

A next major step in establishing a more valid formulation base for describing the exercise of effective leadership was taken by Professor Rensis Likert in Navy-supported research conducted at the University of Michigan. Likert might have formulated his hypothesis as follows.

"The way to understand effective leadership is to identify two kinds of groups which differ from one another in terms of production effectiveness. Subordinates of leaders in the more effective groups should then be asked to describe their leader's behavior. Subordinates of less effective leaders will be asked to describe their leader's behavior as well. This will permit a comparison of leadership behavior at the high end of the effectiveness continuum with that at the low end." (Likert, 1961)

Likert also concentrated on the fourth step in the abstracting sequence, but he added the interesting twist of asking subordinates to characterize two kinds of leaders, not just leaders "in general." By doing so he made a forward step. At least by inference, respondents were asked to think about Level I happenings and he could now contrast what the respondents said of one set of leaders with how the other leaders were described.

More effective leaders were generally described as "employee-centered" and less effective leaders as "job-centered." From these findings, Likert concluded that

> "Supervisors with the best records of performance focus their primary attention on the human aspects of their subordinates' problems and on endeavoring to build effective work groups with high performance goals . . . those supervisors whose units have a relatively poor production record tend to concentrate on keeping their subordinates busily engaged in going through a specified work cycle in a prescribed way and at a satisfactory rate as determined by time standards." (Ibid.)

Likert emphasized "group centeredness" over the idea of individuals as followers by elevating the concept of membership. Effective leadership was characterized by boss-subordinate(s) give-and-take around the job itself reflected in terms such as goal integration, mutual confidence and trust, and mutual support. His research told him that employee-centered *participation* induces *commitment* to results. While Likert's findings empirically described and predicted more and less effective leadership behavior, he was unable to provide a basis for drawing systematic generalizations because the interaction involved in the give-and-take processes for inducing these experiences were not examined.

About this same time, McGregor (1960, 1967) and Argyris (1976) were moving toward non-elementalistic, non-additive formulations of effective leadership. McGregor's Theory X and Theory Y and Argyris' Models I and II are, however, severely limited by the two-valued, either-or character of their formulations. Leadership is not a case of either-or but of infinite variations.

Non-Aristotelian Logic Applied to the Exercise of Leadership

Our own work in establishing conceptual foundations for evaluating leadership started in a different way. Being aware of the contradictions and discrepancies among approaches prevailing at that time, we spent some fifteen years as participant-observers engaged in *in situ,* Level I "happenings" in live groups (i.e., the left side of the Korzybski model, Figure A-2 earlier) as the basis for drawing our conclusions. Our experiences included working in the late 1940s with psychoanalytic therapy

groups at London's Tavistock Clinic under Bion and Ezriel and continued for the next ten years in "T" groups, i.e., sensitivity training, conducted primarily in Bethel, Maine. Significant insights also were derived from working with Moreno in psychodramatic settings over a number of years and from general semantics seminar work with Bois. During this same time, we conducted many experiments in university settings in which we observed the group processes of students interacting as they sought to achieve synergistic results. Along the way we entered industry and gained further insight into Level I happenings by helping leaders mobilize their human resources in order to increase effectiveness in problem solving and decision making.

As participant-observers during this entire period we experienced as "happenings" our own and others' participation as leadership appeared and was strengthened, faltered, shifted, or reappeared. We were particularly attuned to what members did and did not do in seeking to establish direction and coordination. Importance is attached to the key word "we," as our sharing of many of these experiences permitted us to correct one another's perceptions and in this way increase our understanding of leadership phenomena as "happenings."

These experiences led us to focus our attention on processes of interaction rather than on traits or attributes of successful and unsuccessful leaders or on leadership "in general." Our formulations of leadership effectiveness, then, are derived from the 'happenings' themselves and we can picture how we went about describing leadership as a process of interaction.

Leadership cannot be experienced without a task or in a solo situation. Recognizing again that additional dimensions may be needed for a complete description, we identified two primary leadership dimensions, *concern for accomplishing the task* and *concern for one another as participants*. These concerns, as represented in Figure A-7, are not "out there" somewhere. They are *within* the leaders-(and members)-as-coparticipant-observers of the happening and cannot be separated and dealt with without losing the phenomenon they describe.

Concern for production and *concern for people* as dimensions for characterizing the leadership process can be depicted diagramatically. First, degrees of the production concern can be pictured as continual from a minimum amount (1) to a maximum amount (9), with intermediate degrees of concern in between. A cumulative scale from a low amount of 1 to a high amount of 9 can also be used to depict varying degrees of concern for people.

By placing these dimensions on a Grid surface as seen in Figure A-8, the interdependencies between magnitudes of the X and Y variables are represented by the comma between them, as is customary in application

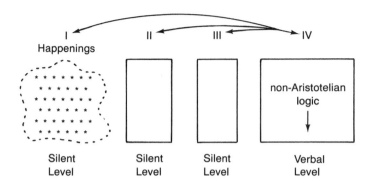

Figure A-7. Process of abstracting as it pertains to the primary leadership dimensions of concern for accomplishing the task and concern for one another as participants.

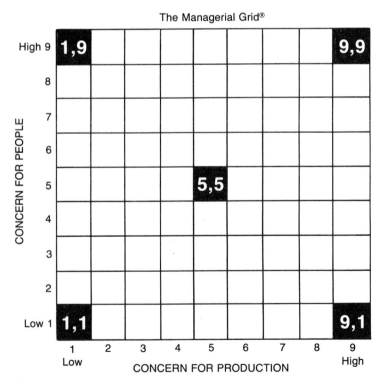

Figure A-8. Use of Grid® to characterize and illustrate concern for production and concern for people.

of the notational system utilizing Cartesian coordinates, and has been used throughout this text.

Because the analysis of leadership happenings begins at this point, reaching a valid description of the happening rests on the notion of interaction between *interdependent* variables (,) as compared with an arithmetic coupling of independent elements (+).

This important difference in formulation is found in many fields. An example from chemistry illustrates the critical distinction between an arithmetic coupling (+) of independent variables and an interaction of interdependent but uncorrelated variables (,). A physical mixture is analogous to the arithmetic combination of variables as exemplified in the Fleishman model. In a physical mixture, such as smog, each element in the combination retains its distinctive features. The particles and gases that compose smog retain their unique "identities" even when combined. (See Figure A-9.)

The mixture analogy depicts how Initiating Structure and Consideration each retains its distinctive character when arithmetically combined. For example, a "9" amount of task behavior is revealed in the supervisor's structuring the subordinate's activities by directing the what, how, when, and where aspects in a "complete" way. A "9" amount of socioemotional support is evidenced in giving rewards, compliments, and strokes. Task direction and consideration are two independent behaviors. "Conceptually", 9 units of "direction" retain the same character whether combined with 1 unit (9+1) or with 9 units (9+9) of support.

By comparison, the interaction brought into definition by the Grid concept of leadership parallels a chemical compound in which variables interact with one another. In the interactive combination of chemical elements, the separate components lose their individual identities in the

Additivity	Interdependence
Mixture	Compound
Smog	Water (H_2O)
Stew	Cake
9 + 9	9,9

Figure A-9. Illustration of the difference between an arithmetic coupling (+) of independent variables and an interaction of interdependent but uncorrelated variables (,).

compound produced. Water, the compound composed of hydrogen and oxygen (H_2O), has a very different character than either of the gaseous elements that make it up. It is not understandable, as in Aristotelian logic (or Fleishman's model) as $H + H + O$ = water.

Similarly, these two interdependent dimensions of the 9,9-oriented leadership process are not treated or measured separately. It is not possible to remain structurally consistent with the happening itself and develop two independent tests which measure behavior on one dimension in isolation from the other.

As a further example, the compound character of this approach can be depicted by examining a test item which attempts to describe the leader's behavior in terms of task accomplishment without simultaneously exploring concern for people. This might be expressed as:

> "I exert vigorous effort   Grid Style Orientation
> and . . . . ?"   ?

This statement reveals nothing of the interaction processes since we do not know how "vigorous effort" on the leader's part is related to the subordinate's efforts, actions, or perceived reactions.

If a test item reads,

> "I exert vigorous effort and   Grid Style Orientation
> pressure others to do the   ?
> same."

the leadership orientation is clarified. Here, the Grid style describes the 9,1 orientation; *force* is used to induce compliance.

If the leader says,

> "I exert vigorous effort and   Grid Style Orientation
> reward compliance of others.   ?

a very different expression of leadership, the paternalistic (9+9) orientation occurs; *reward* is used to induce compliance.

The vigorous effort might be exerted as shown here.

> "I exert vigorous effort and   Grid Style Orientation
> others enthusiastically join   ?
> in."

When others enthusiastically join in, open participation in the interactive process can occur and the commitment of others is heightened. "Openness" in the 9,9 orientation is premised on mutuality. Rather than exercising unilateral control over who will do what and when, an optimal approach to how things will be done emerges from the interaction process.

Very different "compounds" of leadership are produced as a function of what combines with "what" and how the combination is joined.

Thus, from the perspective of non-Aristotelian logic, in mapping the Grid style orientation, we see in Figure A-10 the interdependence between the task and people dimensions is significant for describing a mutual influence process. The sociological terms *boss and subordinate, leader and led,* which refer to one "doing something" to another, are inappropriate when used to describe a 9,9-oriented leadership process. As yet there is no functional language to describe the coparticipants in a relationship when both (or several) engage proactively in accomplishing a task.

What does this mutual influence process mean in the "real world"? Any given task is characterized by its own internal logic. Optimally effective task completion by several is contingent on sound processes which allow technical, material, and human resources to be fully utilized in the soundest way. Effective leadership contributes to sound task completion while ineffective leadership detracts from it. 9,9-oriented leadership processes for achieving coordinated direction involve multi-loop, open communication predicated on finding the best alternative or course of action congruent with the logic inherent in the situation seen in its entirety.

A 9,9-oriented leadership applies the processes of shared participation, superordinate goal orientation, conflict resolution, and double loop learning, all of which are attributes of effective task completion.

When the task involves a problem to be solved, for example, the 9,9-oriented leader seeks input from others before a decision is reached. Potential solutions are examined to clarify underlying differences and to

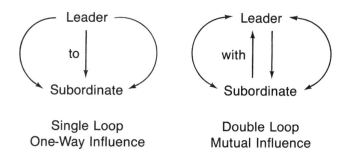

Single Loop
One-Way Influence

Double Loop
Mutual Influence

Figure A-10. The interdependence between the task and people dimensions is significant for describing a mutual influence process.

discover an alternative which best responds to the perceived "logic of the problem." Emphasis is placed on utilizing all available resources to determine the optimum course of action. Synergistic problem solving through the processes of interaction may be superior to the "best" solution which any one individual might have produced working alone.

That we sometimes fail to find these superior synergistic solutions entails no breakdown in "intelligence." "Intelligence" is "there," but something blocks its use. Faulty leadership processes permit the intrusion of hip-pocket solutions, seniority, rank, "old boy" networks, etc. They block coordinated and collaborative effort and prevent "intelligence" from being employed in sound ways.

With this clarification of 9,9-oriented leadership as a problem-solving approach, let us return to Joe, the machinist we encountered in an earlier dialogue, now with his boss, *Smith non-el*. Smith non-el is a boss whose behavior is congruent with non-elementalism or non-Aristotelian logic.

Smith non-el

Boss: You've read the shift book. It's pretty full, but you need to get it all done.

Subordinate: I'll do my best.

Boss: Instead of making the seven adjustments on each of the three machines, a machine at a time, I want you to make the same adjustment on each machine one at a time in sequence. Start with balancing the rotes on all three. Then come back to the first machine and replace the belt. Repeat that on machines 2 and 3 and so forth. Does that make sense?

Subordinate: But boss, that's inefficient. It's really better to deal with all seven adjustments on machine 1 and then to work on machine 2.

Boss: I appreciate your suggestion, Joe. I know they have nothing to complain about, but I can't prove that to the operators. It's one of those trust and confidence problems between two departments. This way I can personally guarantee them that each one of the adjustments was completed.

Subordinate: Well, if there's a problem with guaranteeing them, let's solve it, but in a way that permits me to work in a sound manner.

Boss: Yes, you're right. I suppose we could . . .

Subordinate: We could. It's true that anyone might miss an adjustment or two working down through one machine. You see something that needs fixing and it captures your attention, interrupts an orderly sequence . . . I've a checklist in my mind anyway, but I could put it on paper and check off each item as I complete it. That way you could offer them the same assurance of quality but without my losing efficiency.

Boss: Of course. Give me a ring 30 minutes before quitting time to let me know your progress.

Subordinate: Okay.

Boss (answering phone some hours later): Yeah, yeah, Joe, What . . . ?

Subordinate: I've got it all done, even before quitting time.

Boss: That's good. How'd it work?

Subordinate: The checklist is really a good idea. It permitted me to go faster because I didn't feel the need to circle back and double-check on myself. It's a creative solution to the problem; better for me and I can assure you as to thoroughness.

Here we see the same machine-maintenance situation managed from a 9,9 leadership orientation. The boss acknowledges the subordinate's disagreement but is open to an examination of what Joe had in mind. Joe's proposal seemed to have merit and the addition of a checklist led to action that is jointly agreed upon as sounder. Here we see the result of open participation, candor, and conflict solving based on respect for differences. Mutual exploration of alternatives and possibilities has led to a more productive, efficient approach to the task. The impact of sound leadership processes is reflected in involvement and commitment, mutual problem solving, and so on.

Now leadership joins the ranks of the "unsplittable" phenomena of nature. The 9,9 teamwork orientation has consistently been associated with heightened productivity, improved creativity, and increased satisfaction (Argyris, 1976 and 1957; Argyris and Schön, 1976; Blake and Mouton, 1980; Likert, 1967; Likert and Likert, 1976; Blake and Mouton, 1978) as well as total organismic health (Blake and Mouton, 1980).

Indexing the 9,9 Orientation for Use in Specific Situations

Answers to a new question can now be explored. How can the strategies embedded within the 9,9 orientation be implemented across a wide variety of distinctive situations? Our answer is that the structural properties of a 9,9 orientation remain constant, but are tactically extensionalized when applied with specific subordinates in concrete activities. That is to say that the emerging principles discussed in Chapter 8 of this text represent relatively invariant structural properties that are foundations of a 9,9 orientation.

Extensionalizing is an invaluable tool for more precise analysis of the leadership tactics for any particular situation or set of circumstances. The general proposition is that leadership tactics are a function of the person(s) (P) interacting within his or her environment (E). This relationship can be expressed in the following way:

$LT = f(P,E, \text{etc.})$

Indexing aids us in choosing the soundest tactics for implementing the 9,9-oriented strategy in any given situation. Significant situational factors for indexing which are related to characteristics of subordinates (P) relative to any work activity are experience, age, education, "IQ," socio-economic background, etc.

Applied in a particular case, we can extensionalize an individual subordinate, Mary, as shown in the following relationship:

$$LT = f(Mary_1, {}^{1982,E_1^1,Age\ 18,G12,\text{"IQ"}\ 90,etc.} E, \text{etc.})$$

The relationship indicates Mary 1, in 1982, is an entry level receptionist, age 18. She has completed grade 12, her "IQ" is 90, etc.

Experience level of the subordinate relative to the activity in which he or she is engaged is a significant factor for analyzing leadership behavior in an operating context. It is therefore used to demonstrate the utility of indexing in determining the tactics for implementing a 9,9-oriented strategy. As seen in Figure A-11, experience levels can vary from a maximum of E_4, where the subordinate is knowledgeable, competent, and skilled in carrying out an activity efficiently and effectively, to a minimum of E_1, where prior experience in completing the task is essentially absent.

To concretize this illustration, we can apply E-level indexing to the 9,9-oriented principle of mutual goal setting. Looking at Figure A-12, we see that there is no shift in the underlying principle of mutuality or in adherence to the principles of open participation, subordinate involvement, and shared commitment. Goal-setting tactics vary, however, when indexed to the subordinate's experience level.

In more specific terms, goals set through boss/subordinate interaction at the E_1 level of maturity are short-term and attainable. As displayed in Figure A-13, the pathways to accomplishment are relatively clear and immediate feedback as to progress is provided.

When a task is approached by a subordinate from a higher experience level, i.e., E_4, mutually established goals are likely to be more complex. Generally, progress is described in terms of large, broadly-outlined units

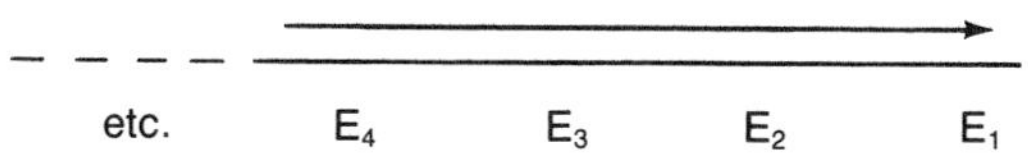

Figure A-11. Experience levels can vary from a maximum of E_4 (or more) to a minimum of E_1.

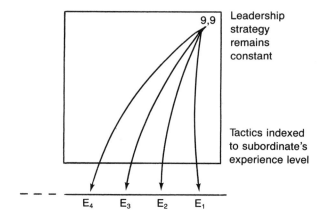

Figure A-12. There is no shift in the underlying principle of mutuality or in adherence to the principles of open participation, subordinate involvement, and shared commitment.

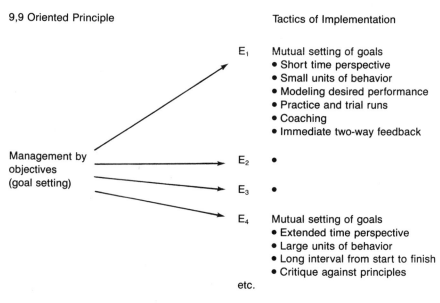

Figure A-13. Goal-setting tactics vary when indexed to the subordinate's experience level, and pathways to accomplishment are relatively clear and immediate feedback of progress is provided.

of behavior. Intermediate critique points along the way from start to finish provide a measure of achievement.

Dialogues beween leader and subordinate can again be used to further illustrate, operationally, the variance of E_1 and E_4 tactics.

Receptionist (E_1)

Boss: This is your first day. It's likely to be a little tough. How do you feel?

Subordinate: I'm all thumbs. I don't know what to do.

Boss: Then that's a good place to begin. That's where we start setting goals. What is your understanding of this job?

Subordinate: Well, I'm to be the receptionist. I've never had any experience with that.

Boss: Let's look at what a receptionist does.

Subordinate: Well, one thing is answer the phone.

Boss: Yes, what else?

Subordinate: Greet visitors, type some.

Boss: Anything else?

Subordinate: I suppose I might be expected to be your person Friday.

Boss: Maybe. That's a good overview of the whole job. Let's talk about those things, one at a time. Telephone answering is our first contact with our clients. Let's talk about goals for answering the phone.

Subordinate: What goals? What's that got to do with answering the telephone?

Boss: Let me ask you a question. How do you feel when the phone rings twenty times and there is no answer?

Subordinate: I don't like it. Either no one is there or people are too busy, or they are visiting . . .

Boss: I don't like to be kept waiting either. Can we set an objective for prompt answering?

Subordinate: Maybe I can answer it within the first several rings. I can experiment with it to see if I can get it down to three.

Boss: That sounds fine. Now, what's the best thing to say?

Subordinate: "Good morning."

Boss: But then the caller doesn't know whether it's the right number.

Subordinate: I could say, "Good morning. This is Strategic Systems, Inc."

Boss: That's it . . . what we've talked about so far covers a lot of detail, but it shows that goals are involved in just answering the phone.

Subordinate: Yes it does . . . but, I'll never remember it all.

Boss: It'll take a little practice. I'll go to a phone and call as though I were a real caller. We can critique how the call went after you deal with me.

Subordinate: That's a good idea. That way I can check myself out.

The readiness for participation and involvement is present even at this lowest experience level. A proactive orientation is released through active two-way, give-and-take participation. Questions are asked, and problems are posed and discussed in the context of empathy, trust, respect, and openness. Goals are set, and an experimental test of how to reach them is introduced—as is the concept of learning from critique through immediate feedback.

The following dialogue between an energy company president and the vice president of exploration exemplifies E_4 goal setting.

President: We've reviewed the facts and created a large data base. We've checked our logic. It's a gamble, but still a gamble worth taking.

Vice President: I think you're right. The potential rewards are too great to pass up.

President: Who do you think should have the overall responsibility for direction and coordination?

Vice President: I'd like to develop and manage the project.

President: Well, you've certainly had more experience than anyone else. What's your best judgment as to what it will take to make north slope oil commercially available in the lower 48?

Vice President: We're talking long-range here, so there are a lot of variables that are difficult to predict. One important consideration is transportation. My people see both the pipeline and tankers as viable possibilities, but we can develop these options as we solve the problems of getting it out of the ground.

President: How long before this project begins to pay off for us and makes a real contribution to the country's oil-related problems?

Vice President: Eight, maybe ten years, but then we'll have a dependable, predictable oil supply for the U.S. market and a substantial source of capital for ourselves.

President: I still have an uneasy feeling about the intensity of the reservations coming from the environmentalists. Do you think a pipeline could have the damaging effects they predict?

Vice President: No, I don't. We've assessed their data and checked it against the results of our own experiments. I think we're being subjected to scare tactics rather than to an objective assessment of risks. However, I've considered their protests in the contingency plan.

President: And you want this assignment?

Vice President: I think, given the special knowledge and experience needed, I'm probably in the best position to take it on. Besides, I'm intrigued by so many complexities and unknowns. It's like a pioneering adventure, a rare and unique opportunity.

President: You're right. If I were younger, it's the type of challenge I'd accept myself. I'll recommend your appointment as project director to

> the Board. I'd like to have your final estimates on costs and time frames before I present the idea.

Vice President: As long as the Board understands we're only making educated guesses, I can have a proposal put together within the week. Most of the pieces are in place from our preliminary work and my staff pretty well anticipated this move.

President: Good, I appreciate your initiative. I'll have retired long before the soundness of this venture is known. I wish you the best and hope I'll be watching from my rocking chair.

Though the same principle has been applied in the sense that mutual goal setting is involved in both examples, the tactics of implementation are conspicuously different between the receptionist illustration (E_1) and the vice president example (E_4). Answering the phone is a fairly simple, straightforward task in comparison with the North Slope oil project.

Goal setting is common to the interaction in both situations, but in one case the goal is set for a day, and in the other, for a decade. In the former case, small units of behavior (i.e., answering the phone within the first few rings) characterize established objectives, whereas objectives in the latter case of oil discovery, recovery, and delivery, expense and environmentalism, etc., are necessarily left open-ended. Leadership practices in both situations are characterized by mutual influence, open participation, shared understanding, and commitment to implementing emergent solutions.

Back Up to 39,000 Feet

Now we can return briefly to the introduction where we made remarks about flying the modern jet in a non-Aristotelian way. In 1979, NASA published a study which revealed the causes of airline industry accidents and near accidents. The gist of their conclusions is contained in the following paraphrase.

> Too many crashes and near misses occur in circumstances where the "ultimate cause" cannot be traced to air-to-ground communications, equipment failure, lack of technical competence, or a time factor. In too many cases, it has been demonstrated that adequate technical resources for solving the problem *were available* in the cockpit, but were not mobilized effectively. (Cooper, White, and Lauber, 1980)

United Airlines had long been interested in the problem of effective cockpit resource management and had significant influence on bringing the NASA study about. United initially placed the problem before us about three years ago. It's one thing to recognize that a problem exists but quite another to understand its underlying dynamics. In order to study the dynamics underlying leadership processes in the airliner cockpit, seven airline officers were placed on temporary duty with our organization at that time. We designated seven of our own key personnel to join with them in a task force which had major responsibility for this priority effort. The task force worked for 18 months, meeting together for a week at a time, then returning to their home bases (Jackson, 1983).

At the beginning of our work, the flying personnel made a major point with regard to the exercise of captain authority. They emphasized the importance of decisiveness as an indispensable element of leadership process. Without decisiveness, uncertainty is communicated; divergent, uncoordinated, individually-centered actions are more likely to be taken by other crew members, and conditions for insubordination may be created. A primary concern as we continued our exploration was that captain authority should be strengthened so that conditions favorable to insubordination are not created.

In any hazardous setting, whether the leader is commanding a submarine, aircraft, control tower, nuclear plant control floor, or fire fight, conditions of crisis can and all too frequently do occur. When an emergency situation develops, the leader's response is a critical factor in determining the likelihood of a desirable and safe outcome. Typically, the paternalistic or 9,1-oriented airline captain or other leader responds to a crisis by dominating, mastering, and controlling the situation, quickly announcing the course of action to be implemented and often extending appreciation for dutiful compliance. While this is certainly a decisive response to the happening, it is not always the best response. In some instances, immediate, unilateral action taken by the captain without provision of the opportunity for other crew members to offer input and alternatives has proven not only ineffective, but deadly.

Now we can examine the 9,9 orientation to leadership in hazardous situations and see that it remains consistent with the principles of openness, involvement, and participation. The leader acts quickly in seeking the soundest possible definition of the problem and proceeds to a solution after utilizing available resources by soliciting others' input, contributions, recommendations, reservations, and doubts.

When viewed from a non-Aristotelian perspective, effective leadership, as shown here, requires the ability to mobilize available resources and bring them to bear on solving the problem at hand. To this point, over 5,000 airline industry captains, first officers, and second officers have learned this effective 9,9-oriented basis of crew leadership and teamwork. Simulator studies reveal that such learning enhances the quality of solutions to programmed crises that are unexpected by the crew, thereby increasing the likelihood that in-flight emergencies will also be resolved safely. Additionally, "United crew members have had a 50 percent lower mistake rate on FAA proficiency checks than they did before the program was started" (Feaver, 1982).

Comparable results have been demonstrated in other settings where 9,9-oriented leadership strategies have been systematically applied. In fact, the positive impact of 9,9-oriented leadership on productivity and creativity has been reported in a wide variety of organizations and from such diverse fields as college and university administrators (Blake, Mouton, and Williams, 1981), social work (Blake, Mouton, Tomaino, and Gutierrez, 1979) and sales (Blake and Mouton, 1980), nursing (Blake, Mouton, and Tapper, 1981) and real estate, secretarial and office support systems (Blake, Mouton, and Stockton, 1983). In our experience, applications of 9,9-oriented leadership have also proven requisite in establishing collaboration and cooperation between union and management groups locked in win-lose conflict, strengthening relationships between organization headquarters and field locations, increasing the success rate of acquisitions and mergers, etc. (Blake and Mouton, 1985).

Future Implications for an Emerging Society

Stepping away from the present for now and looking at the past from a broad culture-centered perspective, it is pertinent to ask whether it is "natural" in preliterate history to reinforce compliance with reward as in the paternalistic orientation or whether the mutuality inherent in 9,9 is the more "natural." Anthropological research leads us to believe that most behavior in preliterate times was regulated by custom. Remaining behavior which was subject to free choice was apparently organized consistent with the 9,9 orientation of involvement and commitment predicated on open, shared decision making. To quote, ". . . Hunter-gatherers have habitually made their decisions as equals, by consensus, and in face-to-face meetings." (Service, 1975)

The 9+9 separation of the inseparable probably developed with the shift from hunting to herding and from picking to planting, possibly beginning somewhere in the 12th–10th centuries B.C. This change of leadership orientations may have been related to the production of "owned" surpluses.

In many respects modern Western society has adopted as sound the 9+9 version of leadership in the supervision of work, conduct of military affairs, rearing of children, educational and penal systems, in much of organized religion, and so on. We may profitably examine the conditions that may have caused its appearance as a central style for exercising leadership.

Modern theories of leadership are rooted in the basic religious model of what was, and often is, presumed to be a sound relationship between God and man. "Not my will but Thine be done . . ." is a paternalistic precept in which the person relinquishes self-responsibility by acting not on what he or she wishes or thinks to be right, but rather on what religious authority says is correct and proper. Consideration or reward for compliance, it is traditionally believed, is withheld until the hereafter.

Paternalism flowered during earlier periods of poverty, hunger, and deprivation. We can believe that its acceptability was not based on its presumed inherent soundness so much as upon the needs of people to earn rewards and to gain other sources of security granted in exchange for compliance.

As materialism and affluence have expanded in the aftermath of World War II, we see that people generally are less dependent on the leader's discretion in providing external (i.e., dollars, etc.) rewards and less fearful of severe financial deprivation for non-compliance with leadership direction than in previous times. The readiness to "tolerate" paternalistic leadership has begun to disappear from all walks of life. Successful resistance of college students in the 1960s to the "in loco parentis" orientation of academic administrations and the rising divorce rate are two examples of such intolerance. Students throughout the school system now seem far less prepared to do what the teacher requires in exchange for grades and promotion to the next level. Husbands and wives seem far less content to maintain a marriage based on reward and compliance rather than on mutual understanding and fulfillment.

Accepting this scenario as essentially correct, it leads to important implications. The main one is that society cannot expect to reestablish voluntary order by moving in the direction of increasing paternalism.

A primary prospect for a sounder social future is in society-wide learning of how to exercise leadership in the non-Aristotelian manner indicated by a 9,9 orientation and to apply 9,9-oriented strategies to societal institutions of education, family, etc. This means opening situations to participation in such a way as to gain the involvement and commitment of people to solving problems and bringing more valid solutions into use. The strategies of a 9,9 orientation are simple enough to describe in "intellectual" terms. Acquiring the behavioral skills requisite to open leadership, conflict resolution, inquiry, advocacy, critique, and so on is another matter, but also within our grasp as discussed in Chapter 12 and Appendix B.

Conclusion

Much of the confusion and many of the apparent contradictions between leadership theorists are removed through systematic examination of the logic on which theoretical explanations are constructed. Aristotelian logic compels one to construe leadership as based upon isolatable elements which are then combined by adding them together. This has been shown to produce faulty theory which does not permit adequate representations of Level I happenings that are the most effective for achieving results with and through others. By comparison, theory derived from non-Aristotelian logic pictures leadership as a double loop interaction process which cannot be divided into components, elements, or fragments. The 9,9 leadership orientation emphasizes participation as an interaction process based on openness and candor, strong initiative, thorough inquiry, effective advocacy, confrontational approach to conflict solving, appropriation delegation, sound teamwork, and two-way critique. It provides a positive alternative to Aristotelian logic as the basis for constructing a valid theory of sound leadership.

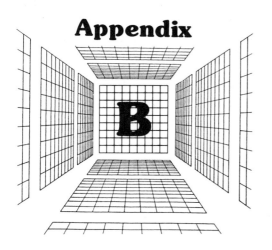

Appendix

Learning
and
Change

The theory and skills involved in gaining effective results with and through others have been tested and refined and in significant ways demonstrated to be an important improvement over past approaches. The 9,9 leadership orientation offers a comprehensive view of the theory and skills essential for operating effectively in managerial situations.

It is one thing to know a theory intellectually and quite a different thing to shift one's own behavior towards greater effectiveness by using it. The depth of the problem is evident when people talk about leadership in one way, but then exercise it in a different manner. "Do as I say, not as I do," catches the contradiction. This leads many to the conclusion that "if you don't have it, you can't learn it."

Yet we know that many leaders learn to lead more effectively as their experiences increase, while resistances to change prevent others from benefiting from experience. Such resistance needs to be understood if new knowledge about leadership is to be effectively applied.

To view resistance to change in general terms, it is useful to look to Korzybski's formulations relative to learning and change. Korzybski might have asked the question, "How can individuals be aided to shift from one basis of leadership logic to another?", i.e., from 9,1 or 1,9 or 5,5 or 1,1 or paternalism or opportunism, etc. to a 9,9 orientation? The key to appreciating his answer is understanding the diagram pictured in Figure B-1.

---

* Part 2 of Korzybski Memorial Lecture, "Foundations for Strengthening Leadership" presented before the Institute of General Semantics by the authors in 1982 and published in the General Semantics Bulletin, #50, 1983, pg. 93–128, and reproduced with permission.

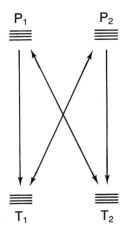

Figure B-1. Schematic answer to the question "How can individuals be aided to shift from one basis of leadership logic to another?" Source: Foreword by A. Korzybski and M. Kendig in General Semantics Monographs III, The International Non-Aristotelian Library Publishing Co., Lakeville, Connecticut, 1942.

By way of explanation,

". . . (P_1) represents a set of conscious or unconscious assumptions, or what we may call axioms, . . . 'self-evident truths,' . . . creeds, beliefs, dogmas, premises, or postulates. (T_1) represents the automatic more elaborate consequences of higher order abstractions, which we may call theories, rationalizations, inferences, opinions, orientations, attitudes, evaluations, etc. These influence our internal reactions on which ultimately our overt actions are based. Similarly from a different set of assumptions, etc., (P_2), also a different set of consequences, etc., (T_2) follows.

"For our practical purposes we may consider (P_1) a set of assumptions [9,1, 1,9, etc.] about the world and ourselves taught to us in infancy and childhood, and aggravated by the implications of the structure of our daily language. The traditional consequences (T_1), based on false 'knowledge,' follow. (P_2) may be considered as revised assumptions [9,9 leadership orientation] based on modern scientific data and methods, from which consequences (T_2) of science and sanity follow." (Korzybski and Kendig, 1942)

An adaptation of this diagrammatic formulation to the leadership context is seen in Figure B-2.

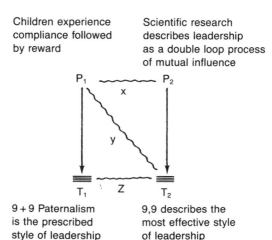

Figure B-2. Adaptation of diagrammatic formulation shown in Figure B-1.

(P_1) of this diagram represents concepts based on conventional wisdom regarding leadership, paternalism, 9,1 or 5,5, or opportunism, etc., as learned in childhood from parents or teachers. (T_1), then, is the operating logic for exercising leadership as it is seen in adult behavior. If (P_2) represents scientifically validated leadership processes characterized by the 9,9-oriented system of logic, (T_2) becomes the operating logic of "how to do it" on an everyday basis.

As we have seen, (P_1) and P_2) are contradictory ways for thinking about leadership. Individual efforts to resolve this contradiction that produce resistance to change might take any one of several directions as shown in Figure B-3. In Korzybski's words,

> "The wavy lines x, y, and z represent our vain struggles to reconcile the irreconcilables. The lines y and z represent our dissatisfactions, feelings of bewilderment, confusion, insecurity, frustration, fears of an incomprehensible unknown world, often despair, etc. . . . The line x represents the vague and uneasy feelings of inadequacy, contradiction, conflict between science and the prevalent notions about life, lack of communication, blocking of intelligence, cultural lag, protest, doubt, disillusionment, cynicism, helplessness, hopelessness, etc." (Ibid)

Though it is common to try, it is virtually impossible when dealing with people who operate from outdated, ineffective (P_1) leadership assumptions to convey a (T_2) 9,9 orientation to leadership in modern life.

For example, to lecture on 9,9-oriented (P_2) assumptions to a person who is listening through 9,1-oriented (P_1) assumptions (wavy line x) pro-

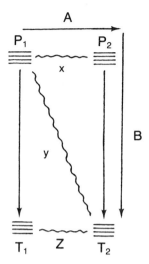

Figure B-3. Individual efforts to resolve P_1 and P_2 ways of thinking about leadership can produce resistance to change that might take any of several directions. Source: Foreword by A. Korzybski and M. Kendig in General Semantics Monographs III, The International Non-Aristotelian Library Publishing Co., Lakeville, Connecticut, 1942.

motes rejection of the lecturer as not knowing what he or she is talking about or as "never having lived in the real world." In a similar way, it is difficult to convey a 9,9 orientation (T_2) to a person operating from (P_1) leadership assumptions. An example is a paternalistic boss (P_1) leading a quality circle (T_2) or conducting an MbO conference, etc. Paternalistic leadership is being poured into the quality circle format which, in terms of (P_2) theory, is intended to be led in a 9,9-oriented manner. As a consequence, subordinates comply with emotions expected of them by the paternalistic boss, but in a most non-reactive and non-innovative manner typical of (T_1) as shown by wavy line y.

A similar situation occurs when behavior modeling or behavior modification techniques are used to reinforce 9,9-oriented (T_2) skills to replace (T_1) behavior which has held them in place by (P_1) or 9,1-oriented assumptions as represented by wavy line z. The learner brushes the (T_2) behavior aside treating it as hypothetical or impractical because it creates a contradiction for the learner whose thinking is consistent with and who embraces values (P_1) and behavior (T_1) of a 9,1 orientation. One aspect of understanding resistance to change is when a contradiction exists between (P_1) and (T_2) with (P_1) controlling the outcome. This involves continued (T_1) kinds of behavior, sometimes obscured through using (T_2) language.

Figure B-3 indicates the essential steps to aid leaders in shifting from $P_1 \leftrightarrow T_1$ to $P_2 \leftrightarrow T_2$.

We deal with students and practitioners in leadership education who are full of $P_1 \leftrightarrow T_1$ while they live in a world desirous of (T_2) derived from (P_2). The processes represented by wavy lines x, y, and z will not reduce resistance to change, but the clear-cut changes represented by arrows A and B will.

To the best of our knowledge, such a revision from Aristotelian to non-Aristotelian assumptions and systems has been formulated for the first time in *Science and Sanity* (Korzybski, 1958). Instead of continuing with the wavy lines x, y, and z of bewilderment and confusion, this process of self-discovery *makes an individual conscious of the errors of (P_1) assumptions* and the assumptions are, therefore, subject to deliberate study and change. Then, as indicated by the arrow A, we are able to replace (P_1) thinking with (P_2) thinking, from which (T_2), the modern world orientations and foundations of leadership, education, and practice, follows. Resistance to change is diminished when this step is inserted into the educational process.

When a person is fully aware of the (P_2) basis of systematic analysis relative to behavior, he or she is then in a situation which permits "happenings" to be designed in order to induce effectiveness through the systematic use of intelligence, rather than simply having to live passively with "happenings" as they occur and take shape out of the everyday give-and-take. The idea of being in a position to *design* happenings is very important to a more constructive future. When "happenings" can be *designed,* then (T_2) behavior dealing with a 9,9 orientation becomes an indispensable behavioral skill for all participants.

These observations explain why the processes of traditional education, rooted in $P_1 \leftrightarrow T_1$ leadership, authority, and discipline are so often ineffective in creating meaningful change. Effective leadership cannot be conveyed by conventional $P_1 \leftrightarrow T_1$ means of pedagogy and andragogy. In our efforts to induce change, we have learned that the processes of leadership education, or "reeducation," are relatively simple, but in practice are not easily applied.

Persistent obstacles to shifting from (T_1) to (T_2) behaviors have been identified in our work. One obstacle comes from some of our deepest assumptions which are called "motivations." Motivations appear to take on the character of a "bipolar" scale with intermediate degrees of intensity in between. The midpoint of this scale, which is the neutral position, is centered on the Grid and the negative end on the near side and the positive end on the far side of the Grid. Thus, it moves from a negative pole through a neutral zone to a positive pole as seen in Figure B-4.

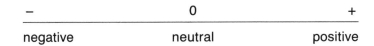

Figure B-4. Motivations appear to take on the character of a "bipolar" scale with intermediate degrees of intensity.

The plus (+) end tells what kinds of achievements "pull" a person, that is, what he or she strives to reach. The minus (−) end is what he or she seeks to avoid. These are not traits an individual possesses. Rather, they are scales in terms of which people perceive pertinent events in the environment, calibrate them, evaluate them for personal significance, and respond to them. One of these scales relates to each Grid style. Behavior modification and other kinds of "response" technique training attempting to aid people to shift from (T_1) to (T_2) disregard the (P_1) motivational assumptions and may therefore only increase a person's internal conflict. When a person thinks one way (P_1) but is "told" to act in another way (T_2), he or she will most likely resist the change and continue the (T_1) behavior or try to escape the situation. The assumption that a change of thinking occurs from response training is open to serious question. Response training can be useful when a consonance can be presumed between what a person is learning to do and how he thinks, but otherwise only a cognitive dissonance is produced.

Another obstacle to change is self-deception. By our findings, approximately 80 percent of any group of American leaders who enter a learning experience initially report that they *are* operating in a 9,9-oriented or (T_2) way. Once their own (P_1) and (T_1) kinds of actual assumptions and behaviors have become explicit through critique, only 16 percent now view their own behavior as 9,9 or (T_2)-oriented (see Chapter 12, p. 182). When self-deception is reduced, the conditions conducive to change are created.

Another source of resistance to change arises from the fact that any individual or team is embedded within an organizational system. The structure and culture of organizations are also obstacles to change when heavily laced with $P_1 \leftrightarrow T_1$ systems of thought and action. They must also be challenged and revised if deep and lasting change is to occur. Time-binding has deepened the expectations of people interacting within such cultures and unsound practices of leadership are held in place by tradition, precedent, and past practice. Because of this, $P_2 \leftrightarrow T_2$-type of thinking and behaving is likely to be resisted and rejected by those above, around, and below the individual level who continue to think and operate in $P_1 \leftrightarrow T_1$ terms. This important insight led to strategies of organization development which allow an entire organization membership to shift the firm from $P_1 \leftrightarrow T_1$ thinking and behavior to $P_2 \leftrightarrow T_2$ thinking and behavior.

While awareness of organization culture and how to change it without producing resistance has been emerging over the past thirty years, only recently has it become a relatively popular topic. Unfortunately, the significance of the controlling influence of organization culture is being conveyed in a (P_1) way. (T_1) behaviors are deplored; (T_2) behaviors of the 9,9-oriented sort are applauded and the leader is encouraged to prescribe (T_2) kinds of culture change from a (P_1) perspective. This is illustrated in several books including those by Peters and Waterman (1982), Deal and Kennedy (1982), Ouchi (1981), Pascale and Athos (1981), Odiorne (1981), and Kantor (1983). The promise is that benefits will accrue to the (P_1) leader who endorses (T_2) kinds of behavior or seeks to support it by altering the structural arrangements of work. All too often, disenchantment occurs when performance falls short of promise due to encountering unexpected resistance to change. Returning to Figure 3, we see that this kind of change is premised on the faulty assumptions identified by wavy lines y and z.

Is there an option for moving from $P_1 \leftrightarrow T_1$ to $P_2 \leftrightarrow T_2$? The Grid approach to organization development takes these sources of resistance to change into account and avoids reinforcing them. At the same time it facilitates movement from (P_1) to (T_2) via aiding learners to acquire (P_2) insights and values as a prior step leading to operational (T_2) changes (Blake and Mouton, 1980). The Grid Seminar provides an approach to change which involves theory-centered, self-convincing, experience-based, deception-free learning of leadership effectiveness taught according to $P_2 \leftrightarrow T_2$ theory and behavior as described in *Synergogy: A New Strategy for Education, Training, and Development* (Mouton and Blake, 1984). It affords opportunities to experiment with the kinds of (T_2) behavior that follow as a consequence of the (P_2) kinds of 9,9-oriented thinking about how to exercise leadership with and through others in small teams.

Grid Organization Development as described in Chapter 12 identifies the arrangements for stimulating enthusiasm for change in the whole organization system through double loop learning in which each learner [manager] identifies faulty (P_1) assumptions, replaces them with (P_2), recognizes distinctions between (T_1) and (T_2) behavior, and proceeds to practice the latter.

Among its more important features Grid Organization Development avoids the fallacy of (P_1) leaders authorizing or prescribing $P_2 \leftrightarrow T_2$ or 9,9-oriented behavior while retaining the values and behavior of $P_1 \leftrightarrow T_1$ as the basis for their own thinking and conduct. This is done by top leadership engaging in Grid Seminar learning (Phase 1) and then in $P_2 \leftrightarrow T_2$ or 9,9-oriented team building (Phase 2) before others participate. Since this sequence of learning cascades down through the organization, it increases the likelihood that bosses are actually exercising leadership in ways that others are being encouraged to do so.

The last three phases of Grid OD provide a basis for investigating $P_1 \leftrightarrow T_1$ assumptions and behavior that have come to be embedded within the firm's business logic and conduct and to replace them with $P_2 \leftrightarrow T_2$ kinds of business logic and conduct emerging as the soundest ways of organizing and conducting business.

Once members of a given culture have become more aware of $P_1 \leftrightarrow T_1$ and $P_2 \leftrightarrow T_2$ types of behaviors and skills at an individual level, it is essential for them, interacting as intact groups, to study and identify the $P_1 \leftrightarrow T_1$ expectations and requirements hidden within the web of silent history in which they are entangled. This aids organization members to shift the cultural practices of the organization itself in the $P_2 \leftrightarrow T_2$, 9,9-oriented direction.

Summary

We can now ask the critical question, "Where do we go from here in terms of operationalizing sound leadership?" We stand at a point in time when the old Aristotelian structures and tactics for formulating and acting no longer provide acceptable bases for operating an ordered, disciplined, and creative society. (P_1) has outlived its usefulness and acceptability.

At the same time, a model of non-Aristotelian logic is in place for $P_2 \leftrightarrow T_2$ thinking and action based on scientific analysis and evidence. Educational designs for shifting from $P_1 \leftrightarrow T_1$ to $P_2 \leftrightarrow T_2$ have been created, experimented with, revised, improved, strengthened, and are available, tailor-made for the user.

The individual and collective challenge is to apply these $P_2 \leftrightarrow T_2$ systems of leadership thought and action to the home, nursery, school, university, shop floor, executive suite, and so on. In this way it may be possible to establish a foundation for a society that is ordered, disciplined, creative, satisfying, and capable of fostering healthy, spontaneous reactions.

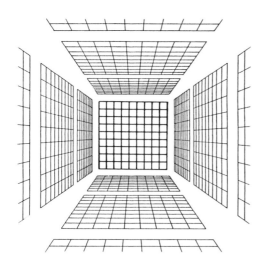

References

Argyris, Chris. *Personality and Organization*. New York, New York: Harper Brothers, 1957.

Argyris, Chris. *Increasing Leadership Effectiveness*. New York, New York: John Wiley and Sons, 1976.

Argyris, Chris, and Schön, Donald A. *Theory In Practice: Increasing Professional Effectiveness*. San Francisco, California: Jossey-Bass Inc., Publishers, 1974.

Blake, Robert R., and Mouton, Jane S. *The New Managerial Grid*. Houston, Texas: Gulf Publishing Company, 1978.

Blake, Robert R., Mouton, Jane S., Tomaino, Louis, and Gutierrez, Sharon. *The Social Worker Grid*. Springfield, Illinois: Charles C. Thomas, 1979.

Blake, Robert R., and Mouton, Jane S. *Grid Approaches To Managing Stress*. Springfield, Illinois: Charles C. Thomas, 1980.

Blake, Robert R., and Mouton, Jane S. *The Grid for Sales Excellence* (2nd Edition). New York, New York: McGraw-Hill, 1980.

Blake, Robert R., and Mouton, Jane S. *The Versatile Manager: A Grid Profile*. Homewood, Illinois: Dow Jones-Irwin, 1980.

Blake, Robert R., Mouton, Jane S., and Tapper, Mildred. *Grid Approaches for Managerial Leadership in Nursing*. St. Louis, Missouri: C. V. Mosby, 1981.

Blake, Robert R., Mouton, Jane S., and Williams, Martha S. *The Academic Administrator Grid*. San Francisco, California: Jossey-Bass Inc., Publishers, 1981.

Blake, Robert R., and Mouton, Jane S. "A Comparative Analysis of Situationalism and 9,9 Management by Principle," *Organizational Dynamics*, 10(4), Spring, 1982.

Blake, Robert R., and Mouton, Jane S. "Theory and Research for Developing a Science of Leadership," *Journal of Applied Behavioral Science*, 18(3), 1982.

Blake, Robert R., Mouton, Jane S., and Stockton, Artie. *The Secretary Grid*. New York, New York: AMACOM, 1983.

Blake, Robert R., and Mouton, Jane S. *Solving Costly Organizational Conflicts: Achieving Intergroup Trust, Cooperation, and Teamwork*. San Francisco, California: Jossey-Bass Inc., Publishers, 1984.

Blanchard, Kenneth. *The One Minute Manager.* New York, New York: William Morrow and Company, 1982.

Cooper, George E., White, Maurice D., and Lauber, John K. (eds). *Resource Management on the Flight Deck.* Moffett Field, California: National Aeronautics and Space Administration, 1980.

Deal, Terrance, and Kennedy, Allen. *Corporate Cultures: The Rites and Rituals of Corporate Life.* Reading, Massachusetts: Addison-Wesley, 1982.

Feaver, Douglas B. "Pilots Learn to Handle Crisis—And Themselves," *Washington Post,* September 12, 1982.

Fiedler, Fred E. "A Contingency Model of Leadership Effectiveness," in Leonard Berkowitz (ed.), *Advances in Experimental and Social Psychology.* New York, New York: Academic Press, 1964.

Fleishman, Edwin A. "Leadership Opinion Questionnaire," Chicago, Illinois: Science Research Associates, Inc., 1960.

Fleishman, Edwin A. "Twenty Years of Consideration and Structure" in Edwin A. Fleishman and James G. Hunt's (eds.), *Current Developments in the Study of Leadership.* Carbondale, Illinois: Southern Illinois University Press, 1973.

Hersey, Paul G. and Blanchard, Kenneth H. *Management of Organizational Behavior: Utilizing Human Resources* (4th Edition). Englewood Cliffs, New Jersey: Prentice-Hall, 1982.

House, Robert J. "A Path-Goal Theory of Leadership Effectiveness," *Administrative Science Quarterly,* September, 1971.

Jackson, Dave. "United Airlines' Cockpit Resource Management Training," *Proceedings Second Symposium on Aviation Psychology.* Columbus, Ohio: Ohio State University, April 25–28, 1983.

Kantor, Rosabeth Moss. *The Change Masters.* New York, New York: Simon and Schuster, 1983.

Kipnis, D., Schmidt, S. M., Swaffin-Smith, C., and Wilkinson, I. "Patterns of Managerial Influence: Shotgun Managers, Tacticians and Bystanders," *Organizational Dynamics,* Winter, 1984.

Korman, Abraham K. "Consideration, 'Initiating Structure' and Organizational Criteria—A Review," *Personal Psychology,* Winter, 1966.

Korzybski, A. *Science and Sanity, An Introduction to Non-Aristotelian Systems and General Semantics,* 1933. Lakeville, Connecticut: International Non-Aristotelian Library Publishing Company, 4th Edition, 1958.

Korzybski, A., and Kendig, M. "Foreword" to General Semantics Monograph III, *A Theory of Meaning Analyzed.* Lakeville, Connecticut: The International Non-Artistotelian Library Publishing Company, 1942.

Larson, Lars L., Hunt, James G., and Osborn, Richard N. "The Great Hi-Hi Leader Behavior Myth: A Lesson from Occam's Razor," *Academy of Management Journal,* December, 1976.

Lefton, R. E., Buzzotta, V. R., and Sherberg, M. *Improving Productivity Through People Skills.* Cambridge, Massachusetts: Ballinger Publishing Company, 1980.

Levinson, Harry. *The Exceptional Executive.* Cambridge, Massachusetts: Harvard University Press, 1968.

Likert, Rensis G. *New Patterns of Management.* New York, New York: McGraw-Hill, 1961.

Likert, Rensis G. *The Human Organization: Its Management and Value.* New York, New York: McGraw-Hill, 1967.

Likert, Rensis G., and Likert J. G. *New Ways of Managing Conflict.* New York, New York: McGraw-Hill, 1976.

Maccoby, Michael. *The Gamesman.* New York, New York: Simon and Schuster, 1976.

Maccoby, Michael, *The Leader.* New York, New York: Simon and Schuster, 1981.

McGregor, Douglas. *The Human Side of Enterprise.* New York, New York: McGraw-Hill, 1960.

McGregor, Douglas. *The Professional Manager.* New York, New York: McGraw-Hill, 1967.

Mouton, Jane S., and Blake, Robert R. *Synergogy: A New Strategy for Education, Training, and Development.* San Francisco, California: Jossey-Bass Inc., Publishers, 1984.

Nystrom, Paul C. "Managers and the Hi-Hi Leader Myth," *Academy of Management Journal,* June, 1978.

Odiorne, George. *The Change Resisters.* Englewood Cliffs, New Jersey: Prentice-Hall, Inc., 1981.

Ouchi, W. G. *Theory Z.* Reading, Massachusetts: Addison-Wesley, 1981.

Pascale, R. T., and Athos, A. *The Art of Japanese Management.* New York, New York: Simon and Schuster, 1981.

Peters, Thomas J., and Waterman, Robert H., Jr. *In Search of Excellence,* New York, New York: Harper and Row, 1982.

Reddin, William J. *Managerial Effectiveness.* New York, New York: McGraw-Hill, 1970.

Schutz, Will. *The Schutz Measures: An Integrated System for Assessing Elements of Awareness.* San Diego, California: University Associates, Inc., 1984.

Service, E. R. *Origins of the State and Civilization.* New York, New York: W. W. Norton, 1975.

Vroom, V. H., and Yetton, P. W. *Leadership and Decision-Making.* Pittsburgh, Pennsylvania: University of Pittsburgh Press, 1973.

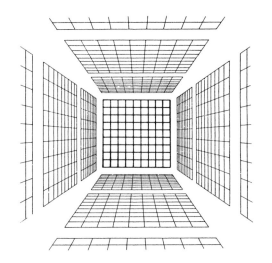

Index

To avoid confusion with page numbers, Grid numbers are italicized.